I Cannot Write My Life

ISLAMIC CIVILIZATION AND MUSLIM NETWORKS
Carl W. Ernst and Bruce B. Lawrence, editors

Highlighting themes with historical as well as contemporary significance, Islamic Civilization and Muslim Networks features works that explore Islamic societies and Muslim peoples from a fresh perspective, drawing on new interpretive frameworks or theoretical strategies in a variety of disciplines. Special emphasis is given to systems of exchange that have promoted the creation and development of Islamic identities — cultural, religious, or geopolitical. The series spans all periods and regions of Islamic civilization.

A complete list of books published in Islamic Civilization and Muslim Networks is available at https://uncpress.org/series /islamic-civilization-and-muslim-networks.

I CANNOT WRITE MY LIFE

Islam, Arabic, and Slavery in

OMAR IBN SAID's

AMERICA

Mbaye Lo and Carl W. Ernst

The University of North Carolina Press
CHAPEL HILL

This book was published with the
assistance of the William R. Kenan Jr. Fund
of the University of North Carolina Press.

Designed and typeset by Lindsay Starr
Set in MeropeBasic

COVER ART
Omar ibn Said, 1850s. Courtesy of the Yale Collection
of American Literature, Beinecke Rare Book and
Manuscript Library, Yale University.

LIBRARY OF CONGRESS CATALOGING-IN-PUBLICATION DATA

Names: Lo, Mbaye, author. | Ernst, Carl W., 1950– author. |
    Said, Omar ibn, 1770?–1863.
Title: I cannot write my life : Islam, Arabic, and slavery in
    Omar ibn Said's America / Mbaye Lo and Carl W. Ernst.
Other titles: Islamic civilization & Muslim networks.
Description: Chapel Hill : The University of North Carolina
    Press, [2023] | Series: Islamic civilization and Muslim
    networks | Includes bibliographical references and index.
Identifiers: LCCN 2023004206 | ISBN 9781469674667 (cloth) |
    ISBN 9781469674674 (paperback) | ISBN 9781469674681 (ebook)
Subjects: LCSH: Said, Omar ibn, 1770?–1863. | Muslim scholars—
    Africa, West—Biography. | Enslaved Muslims—North Carolina—
    Biography. | LCGFT: Biographies.
Classification: LCC E444.S25 L66 2023 | DDC 306.3/62092 [B]—
    dc23/eng/20230221
LC record available at https://lccn.loc.gov/2023004206

CONTENTS

TRANSLATED DOCUMENTS
OF OMAR IBN SAID

ILLUSTRATIONS

PREFACE AND ACKNOWLEDGMENTS

We were drawn into this project by a shared fascination with the story of Omar ibn Said. It has proved to be a journey of discovery into the very different world of early nineteenth-century America to investigate how Islam and the Arabic language became part of American history through institutional slavery. The conclusions we have reached about the long history of racial and religious intolerance underline the importance of recovering the stories of people like Omar.

The research required to write this book could never have been carried out without the assistance of many dedicated librarians who made their collections and their time available to us and without individuals who commented on the project. We are particularly grateful to the staff responsible for Special Collections at the University of North Carolina at Chapel Hill, Duke University, Yale University, Harvard University, the American Philosophical Society, the Smithsonian Institution, the New Hanover Public Library, the Providence Public Library, the Spartanburg County Historical Society, the North Carolina State Archives, the New-York Historical Society, the Georgia Historical Society, the Dialectical Society at UNC, the University of Leeds, the Library of Congress, and the Walters Art Museum. Each of these institutions has generously made available the rare documents that are the basis of this book. The coauthors would also like to acknowledge the support of this project by the American Council of Learned Societies, the National Humanities Center, the William R. Kenan Charitable Trust, the Duke Provost's Office for Faculty Advancement, and the North Carolina Consortium for Middle East Studies.

We would like to take the opportunity to thank the colleagues who have generously offered their insights, suggestions, and encouragement as we shared our findings. Thanks go particularly to Ariela Marcus-Sells, Ellen McLarney, Juliane Hammer, Youssef Carter, Oludamini Ogunnaike, Brandon Bayne, David

Cecelski, Emma Harver, Julie Maxwell, Jaki Shelton-Green, and four anonymous reviewers. Special appreciation goes to the bold students from UNC and Duke who joined the 2019 seminar on Omar taught by the coauthors, including Karlee Bergendorff, Emi Foss, Ethan Gilbreath, Aisha Jitan, Maryam Asenuga, Alycia Parker, Azza Ben Youssef, Hinasahar Muneeruddin, Yasmine Flodin-Ali, and Bryan Rusch; Hinasahar, Yasmine, and Bryan, as well as Samah Choudhury and John Miller, also acted as graduate research assistants. We would like to thank both Jennifer Hawes at the *Post and Courier* in Charleston, South Carolina, and Abdoulaye Gueye at the Institut Islamique in Dakar, Senegal. Gueye was tireless in helping with our outreach and research efforts in Futa Toro, Senegal. Likewise, we are thankful to Matt Miller, John Mullan, and Maxim Romanov at the Open Islamicate Texts Initiative, who guided us through the process of online digital publication of the Arabic texts of Omar ibn Said. Lastly, many thanks to the senior editors at UNC Press, Elaine Maisner and Mark Simpson-Vos, and all of the highly professional staff at the Press, for seeing this project through to publication.

Mbaye Lo and Carl W. Ernst
Durham and Chapel Hill, North Carolina

NOTE ON TRANSLITERATION

Transliteration of Arabic follows the system of the *International Journal of Middle East Studies*. The letter ʿ*ayn* is represented by (ʿ) and the vowel markers called hamza are shown by (ʾ) but omitted at the beginning of a word. Words like *ibn* ("son of") and the definite article (*al-*) are capitalized only at the beginning of a sentence, book title, or (in the case of *ibn*) as the first element of a name; *al-* is ignored in alphabetization. For West African names and places, we use simplified and accepted spelling conventions.

I Cannot Write My Life

Introduction

THIS BOOK IS ABOUT OMAR IBN SAID, a West African scholar, who was enslaved in the Carolinas for over half a century. Upon his death in 1863 in Bladen County, North Carolina, Omar, as we will call him, left behind a small body of Arabic writings, including his 1831 "Autobiography," that became a source of both wonder and incomprehension. Even his name proved to be a challenge; the varying forms that were used to refer to him—Meroh, Omeroh, Moro, Moreau, Monroe, and so on—seem to confirm the enigma that he posed. We write his name as "Omar ibn Said" following the most common spelling, even though it is incorrect. We refer to him by his personal name, Omar (Arabic 'Umar), since the paternal name used for him is both incorrect (it is properly written as ibn Sayyid, "son of Sayyid") and not equivalent to a last name in the English style. Omar has also become the symbol of enslaved Muslim scholars' presence in the antebellum United States. The Library of Congress has created an Omar ibn Said Collection of documents in English and Arabic to serve as a resource for research on slavery and Islam in America. North Carolina governor Roy Cooper declared May 23,

2019, to be Omar ibn Said Day.[1] Musician Rhiannon Giddens has written an opera based on Omar's story that had its debut at the 2022 Spoleto Festival.

Outwardly, the events of Omar's life can be summed up briefly as follows. Born around 1770 in West Africa (what is now Senegal), Omar grew up as a Muslim and studied in an Islamic seminary for twenty-five years, learning Arabic and reading the Qur'an and a range of Arabic religious and literary texts. When war broke out in 1807, he was captured and sold in slavery to Europeans. He ended up being sold in the slave market of Charleston, South Carolina, toward the end of 1807, and eventually fled harsh treatment and was jailed in Fayetteville, North Carolina in 1810. There he attracted attention by writing on the walls of his cell in strange characters that were subsequently recognized to be Arabic, and he was purchased by a prominent planter named James Owen. He lived the remainder of his life with the Owen family, moving to Wilmington in 1837. He was treated with comparatively favorable conditions within the slavery system and was spared from manual labor. He died in 1863, still enslaved, just months after the Emancipation Proclamation. Widely believed to be a convert to Christianity, he became well known in missionary circles and among supporters of the Liberia colonization project. Omar was regarded as clear evidence of the benevolence of slavery, since it had apparently rescued him from a religion that virtually all Americans despised. As for his inner life, the only evidence is the small body of Arabic writings that he left behind, which hint strongly at continuous Islamic practice regardless of his regular church attendance.

Despite the growing recent interest in Omar, however, it would not be an exaggeration to say that Omar's writings have remained unreadable. For two centuries, they have either been mistranslated, distorted, or unavailable. A variety of factors and agents colluded to render Omar's archives illegible, or as we have argued in another setting, to make them "impossible documents." Omar was right in stating, "I cannot write my life," in response to an interlocutor who demanded that he write about himself. Not only did his enslavement prevent genuine self-expression, but also racist forces during his lifetime and afterward continued to obscure his writings and manipulate parts of his story to tell it as they wished. These forces included early amateur scholars, missionaries, and Arabists who mistranslated his writings, in addition to zealous proslavery clergymen who romanticized him as a "prince." In the aftermath of the Reconstruction Era, supporters of the Confederacy's "Lost Cause," such as Alfred Moore Waddell, John Foard, and Louis Toomer Moore, crafted a new body of legend out of his legacy that appallingly converted him into proof of the benevolent influence of slavery.[2]

Lies and Unfounded Truth about Omar

From the time when Omar ibn Said reached America in 1807, as an enslaved African Muslim scholar, virtually everything written about him was a lie. He was a confounding phenomenon who could not fit the conventional expectations of the day. Accordingly, from the very first published mention of Omar in 1825, a false narrative was constructed, which persisted for the rest of his life (to 1863), portraying him in a way that legitimized and justified the religious and racial prejudices of his enslavers. They succeeded in perpetuating this distortion, although their claims would have been undermined by Omar's writing, had they accurately translated it—but no one was able to read these documents.

The most important of the self-serving lies about Omar robbed him of his own volition by making him seem to embrace his enslavement. We are repeatedly told that Omar refused the opportunity to be freed from slavery and return to Africa. His master supposedly offered to send him to his native land, his home, and his friends, but he says, "No, this is my home, and here are my friends, and here is my Bible. I enjoy all I want in this world." The story goes on to claim that, "indeed, the General [James Owen], many years since, proffered him his freedom, and offered to send him back to his native land. But Monroe [Omar] declined the offer, saying that his friends were probably either destroyed or dispersed, and that his condition was much better where he was, than it could be in his own country."[3] Rev. Mathew Grier, who served as a minister in Wilmington in the late 1850s, claimed that "Monroe [Omar] has never expressed any wish to return to Africa."[4]

To the contrary, in his 1819 letter to the Owen brothers, Omar firmly stated, "I want to be seen in our land called Africa, in the place of the river called Kaba." This letter remained untranslated until the 1980s. But the distortion did not stop there. Every source also pretends that Omar viewed his enslavement as a blessing. As noted by a zealous minister, "[Omar] blesses Him who causes good to come out of evil by making him a slave."[5] "His coming to this country," he is said to have remarked, "was all for the good."[6] This is directly contradicted by the closing of Omar's "Autobiography," where he says, "Indeed, I reside in our country by reason of great harm."

This complete distortion of the characterization of slavery was compounded by the claim that Omar became a Christian and renounced Islam. A typical account claims, "His master being a pious man, he was instructed in the principles of the Christian religion, which he received with great pleasure; he seemed to see new beauties in the plan of the gospel, which had never appeared to him in the Koran."[7] Similar was the belief that Omar had "thrown aside the blood-stained Koran and now worships at the feet of the Prince of Peace. The Bible, of which he has an Arabic copy, is his guide, his comforter, or as he expresses it, 'his Life.'"[8] Further, he was said to gradually lose interest in the Koran and show more interest in the sacred Scriptures, until finally he gave up his faith in Muhammad, and became a believer in Jesus Christ.[9]

None of the sources reflects on the irony of claiming that an enslaved person voluntarily converted to his enslavers' religion. In seven different documents, dated as late as 1855, twenty-six years after his supposed conversion, Omar begins by reciting a Qur'anic blessing and the formula, "God bless our master Muhammad"; in his documents he quotes over twenty passages from the Qur'an and only six from the Bible. Moreover, willful ignorance of Africa's Arabic literature was enhanced by anti-Islamic sentiment, with the claim that Omar's knowledge of Arabic was limited to the Qur'an: "It was found that the scraps of writing from his pen, were mostly passages from the Koran."[10] And further, "For ten years he taught the youth of his tribe all that they were wont to be taught, which was for the most part, lessons from the Koran." False again—deeper analysis reveals that Omar quotes not only Arabic grammarians but also three Muslim theologians and two Sufi mystics, not to mention the sayings of the Prophet Muhammad.

Then the claim is made that Omar closely studied the Arabic Bible, but that is also false. "A gentleman who felt a strong interest for the good Prince Moro, as he is called, sent to the British Bible Society, and procured for him an Arabic Bible; so that he now reads the scriptures in his native language."[11] There is another unsubstantiated claim that "his time is chiefly occupied in reading the Scriptures in Arabic."[12] For all the display that Omar may have made of his Arabic Bible, evidence indicates that he only ever quoted a few short passages from the Bible when called upon to perform. The few notes that he made in the margins of the Bible were a half-hearted effort to learn the English titles of some of the books in the Bible by writing them in Arabic script. Moreover, when he described how his enslavers, the Owens, had him read the Gospel, he quoted a classical text on Islamic theology to explain it. But in the absence of a clear understanding of what he wrote in Arabic, even those who sensed that there was something wrong with the rosy picture of the happy slave were unable to refute this portrayal. There is also the claim in the *Wilmington Chronicle* of 1847 that "he is an Arab by birth, of royal blood, and was captured during a war between his own and a neighboring tribe, conveyed to the coast, and sold as a slave." Such fantasy, attempting to remove him from his African origin, replaced his writings.

How We Approach Understanding Omar

This book is an attempt to correct the narrative about Omar's life and restore his original voice. Correction and restoration are the fundamentals of our revision of Omar based upon his own statements in the Arabic documents. In so doing, we are obliged to confront the falsehoods that have dominated discussions of this remarkable individual, casting doubt on his person, and rendering his documents illegible. Although a growing body of scholarship on Omar since the 1980s challenges these lies, the persistence of inadequate readings of his Arabic texts and reliance on old translations of his writings leave far too much to speculation and wishful thinking.

Nearly a dozen scholarly articles related to Omar have been published in the last two decades. Ironically, only two books have contributed to the study of Omar: Allan Austin's *African Muslims in Antebellum America* (1984; abridged 2nd ed., 1997) and Ala Alryyes's *A Muslim American Slave: The Life of Omar ibn Said* (2011). The first is a sourcebook on seven enslaved American Muslims, devoting just one chapter to Omar. The second book has both content and context limitations; it is primarily preoccupied with Omar's 1831 "Autobiography" and does not consider the sources that Omar quotes.

Our approach is based on a systematic analysis of all of Omar's surviving writings, using our own critical edition of his Arabic texts, which we have translated afresh for inclusion in this book. We have numbered the Arabic documents from 1 to 18 for clarity of reference, and their English translations are numbered according to where they appear in the chapter sequence in this book (e.g., Arabic Document 1 is the basis for Translation 3.1, as indicated in this book's "List of Translated Documents of Omar ibn Said"). The translations have also been supplied with titles related to their contents. All translations from Arabic, including the Qur'an, the Arabic Bible, and Omar's documents, are translated by us unless otherwise noted. Our corrected editions of the Arabic documents, accompanied by detailed descriptions of the manuscripts and our translations, may be consulted in the Carolina Digital Repository Collection, "Enslaved Scholars: A Website Repository for Editions of Arabic Texts and English Translations of Writings by Enslaved Muslims in the Americas" (https://doi.org/10.17615/htn5-9162). Additional information on the diplomatic editions of the manuscripts along with the corrected editions may be consulted at the website of the Open Islamicate Texts Initiative (https://openiti.org/pubs/1280CumarIbnSayyid/).

We argue, in this book, that Omar's writings were systematically distorted, ignored, and denied by the defenders of racism, slavery, and white supremacy.

The illegibility of Omar's documents was a product of not only the unsuspected range of his literary references but also the self-justifying fantasies projected on him by enslavers, missionaries, and amateur scholars. Omar's first literary attempt at communication, the letter of 1819 to the Owen brothers, was beyond the comprehension of the only Arabic scholar at Yale University, Professor Moses Stuart, and remained untranslated until Allan Austin persuaded a Saudi graduate student to provide a summary in the 1980s; a proper scholarly translation was not produced until John Hunwick's 2003 study.[13]

Furthermore, we draw on a comparative and interdisciplinary approach to bring new perspectives to Omar's writings, his life, and his legacy. We call upon literary interpretation and Islamic scholarship to explain sources and citations in Omar's text. Indeed, much will be gained by applying a system of verification and harkening back to primary sources to establish the meanings of his writings. We emphasize closely tracking and tracing his Arabic writings, using outlines to establish the sequence and overall structure of each document. The approach involves discovering his wide range of Arabic texts on Islamic theology and Sufism, including grammatical texts by Egyptian scholar Ibn Mālik (d. 1274) and the Baghdadian litterateur al-Ḥarīrī (d. 1122); a sermon of Abū Madyan (d. 1198), the famed North African Sufi; and Sufi poems from Algeria and Alexandria. Aside from two verses quoted from the Arabic grammatical texts, none of the half dozen new sources we have identified in this book has previously been recognized. These sources link him to centuries of intellectual tradition, with a strong oral dimension, drawing on networks extending to Iraq, Egypt, and North Africa. Yet he was considered a slave, uniquely permitted to write, not as an act of communication and knowledge production but as an act of exotic cultural performance.

How This Book Is Organized

For these reasons, we feel it is imperative to conduct a thorough analysis of all of Omar's writings, with close attention to the texts he quotes and with an eye on the writing strategies of other enslaved Muslims. The book's five chapters offer new perspectives on the systematic distortion of Omar's Arabic writings that encompass eighteen documents held in local and national repositories. Chapters 1 and 2 explore Omar's life story in Africa and America using both corroborated evidence and his "Autobiography." Chapter 1 argues that since Omar had spent more than three decades of his formative life in the Senegambian region, we need to understand his environment, to explain everything from his much discussed regal bearing to his enigmatic writings. Omar, like all enslaved Africans, was a living example of the complexity of his previous life. Although he was from the Fulbe community, he would have interacted, through marriage, immigration, and settlement, with other communities, such as the Mandinka, the Wolof, and others. In this chapter we discuss and describe the society, culture, and intellectual institutions of Omar ibn Said's West Africa.

Chapter 2 argues that Omar's "Autobiography" is an impossible text, because his attempts to talk about himself or address the American people are overwhelmed by his enslavement. None of the three audiences formally addressed in the "Autobiography"—"O Shaykh Hunter," "O my brothers," "O people of America"—can read or understand his writings. Thus, the enslaved Omar cannot speak, he cannot be heard, because no one can understand him. It further demonstrates that the "Autobiography" is characterized by a deliberate incompleteness, as each of its sections has been revised, so that the retention of different versions in the manuscript indicates Omar's recognition of the impossibility of the task of writing. His enslavement renders him incapable of using his voice freely.

In chapter 2 we also outline some of the reasons for Omar's inability to write about his life, which are detailed further in chapter 3. This chapter analyzes seven of the documents that are written in the form of sermons to argue that Omar's speech patterns and sermons reflect his worldview and background in the Islamic education system of West Africa. He often addresses the Owens and their associates as if they were Muslims or as if he were a shaykh, a Muslim preacher. His writings, though unintelligible to enslavers, replace personal narrative with carefully arranged quotations from Islamic texts as sermons of rebuke and calls for repentance, both explicitly and by allusion. At the same time, his quotations poignantly evoke his "brothers," the community with whom he shared the study of these Islamic texts in his faraway youth. The chapter also analyzes Omar's quotations from the Qur'an as blessings and his use of talismanic drawings as protective amulets for the Owens and their associates.

We advance more supportive evidence for the root causes of the unreadability of Omar's archives in chapter 4. We demonstrate how Omar's writings and his life story were systematically misrepresented by enslavers and their backers to present a benign view of slavery. His supposed conversion to Christianity, seen as a justification for slavery, is contradicted by his writings, which interpret the New Testament through Islamic texts. His meager annotations of an Arabic Bible (procured for him with the help of Francis Scott Key) indicate a superficial acquaintance with the Arabic text, consisting mostly of English titles of biblical books transliterated in Arabic script. In the handful of biblical texts that he wrote out in Arabic (Psalm 23; Psalm 50; Psalm 123; Romans 10:9; the Lord's Prayer; John 1:17), he nearly always prefaced them with Islamic formulas and blessings upon the Prophet Muhammad.

In closing the book with chapter 5, we illustrate the role of the experts, including missionary groups, amateur Arabists, academics, and professional societies in the systematic distortion of Omar's documents. Their involvement in the translation of his manuscripts has hindered their legibility due to the amateurish and compromised nature of their scholarship. Despite a nearly total incomprehension of Omar's writings, the response to Omar by prominent enslavers was also embedded in the early development of Arabic and Islamic studies in America among amateur scholars and missionary circles.

The five chapters are informed by clusters of Omar's documents in a way that helps the reader put the chapter in a context, while preserving Omar's authority in the story. Omar's composite documents are woven into the chapters as the original voice of the story, allowing the reader to interrogate our interpretation of the story. Finally, at a time when Americans are struggling to come to terms with the long legacy of slavery and racism in our country, the voice of Omar ibn Said, who was an early witness and victim of the contradictions of this system, deserves to be heard at last.

Perhaps restoring the rich and diverse meanings in Omar's texts in this way will contribute to unveiling the complex reality of American slavery. We hope it will also illuminate contemporary American debates on racism, religion, and the place of Arabic in American literary tradition. It is past time to recognize that Arabic is an American literary language, and that Africa is one of the main sources of America's encounter with Islam.

A Land Lost

OMAR IBN SAID is the rare enslaved African who wrote about his life while in bondage. Omar is the only enslaved person in North America known to have written a first-person autobiographical account in a non-European language— although as we shall see, Omar protested that he could not write his life. In 1831, he wrote his "Autobiography" in Arabic while enslaved in Bladen County, North Carolina, and when he died in 1863, he was still not liberated. This text (Document 4 in our reckoning) has been a subject of both praise and criticism: praise for its historical uniqueness and criticism for the limited amount of information that it provides. Omar's document offers relatively little detail about his background in Africa, in terms of his upbringing, family, and education. In fact, Omar writes more about his enslavers, the Owens, than about himself, the enslaved African Muslim. Here is how Omar sketchily introduces his personal life in Africa in the document:

My name is Omar ibn Said ['Umar ibn Sayyid]; my birthplace is Futa Toro, between the two rivers. I sought knowledge in Bundu and Futa. The shaykh was called Muhammad Sayyid, my brother, and Shaykh Souleymane Kumba and Shaykh Jibril Abdal. I continued seeking knowledge for twenty-five years. I came back home for six years. Then there came to our country a large army. It killed many people, and brought me to the big sea, and sold me into the hands of a Christian [white person] who bound me and sent me onboard the big ship in the big sea.

This opening paragraph in the "Autobiography" sums up Omar's story in Africa. Its swiftness reads like a curriculum vitae, providing signposts, not detailed narratives about his lost Futa, Bundu, and Senegambia. Surely, Omar left behind family, a community of scholars or "brothers" as he calls them, and memories. There are obviously glimpses of grief as a natural response to his lost land and people, but what was his loss in particular? What was left behind? And what memories does Omar avoid sharing with his audience? These are necessary questions that we seek to address in revisiting Omar's homeland.

Studies of enslaved African Muslims in America have underestimated the impact of elements of African cultures from their formative years in Africa. Back in Africa, Muslims like Omar did not live in isolation from their non-Muslim social and cultural surroundings. Islam was already an African religion, and Arabic had been a lingua franca of Muslim West Africa since the sixteenth century. Earlier Muslim preachers and armies from North Africa had advanced the faith into West Africa; and local clerics and marabouts (Sufi leaders) had followed suit, establishing educational centers and taking Islam into scholarly families and scholarly communities. Still, it is also true that many in West African society remained devoted to their local beliefs and indigenous cultures. In reality, the full popularization of Islam in the Senegambian regions, which is the primary concern of this chapter, is a product of nineteenth-century colonial rule, which dismantled traditional polities and opened society up to accept the authority of the new class of Sufi leaders. The wide spread of the Tijāniyya Sufi order in the region and the birth of the Murīdiyya in the last decade of nineteenth century are two classical cases. In this section, we will use Omar's documents as a guide to explore various aspects of Senegambian society, culture, and educational experiences, to help us understand the making of Omar, to put in context the key terms in Omar's documents.

Senegambia in the Eighteenth Century

We learn from Omar's document that he is from West Africa, a region where nearly half of the enslaved people brought to the New World originated. The key regions of the Atlantic slave trade in this region were the Senegambia (which encompasses today's Gambia, Senegal, Upper and Lower Guinea, and Mali), West Central Africa (which includes today's Angola, the Republic of the Congo, the Democratic Republic of the Congo, and Gabon), and by extension modern-day Ghana, and other coastal territories such as Ivory Coast, Togo, Benin, and Nigeria. Omar belongs to the Senegambian region. Three main landscapes for slavery in this region will help us understand the geography of Omar's lost land and how it related to his documents.

First, Gorée, a small island off the coast of Dakar, in Senegal, was captured by the French from the Dutch in 1677 and made into a holding station for France's slave trade in the region. The island's location midway between the Senegal and Gambia Rivers made it a suitable station to hold enslaved people before transporting them to the Americas. Gorée is not mentioned in Omar's documents, and there is no evidence that Omar was transported through the island.

Second, the Gambia River runs from the plateau of Futa Jallon in Guinea-Conakry through Senegal and the Gambia into the Atlantic Ocean. Due to its inviting natural harbors and proximity to James Island, a holding station, it became one of the first European trade routes into Africa. The Gambia River was a key waterway for the Atlantic slave trade. It is reported that, at the peak of the slave trade, about one out of every six enslaved West Africans came from this area. Earlier researchers believed that Omar was taken through this route because there is a Gambia River in the nation of Gambia. But it is far more likely that Omar was referring to the Senegal River where Futa is located, since in order to reach the Gambia River, Omar would have had to walk a distance of more than 228 miles.

The third landscape is the Senegal River. Its two main headstreams rise from Futa Jallon in Guinea-Conakry and follow northwest along the borders of Mali and Mauritania to the mouth of the river in the city of Saint-Louis. A small peninsula separates the Atlantic Ocean from the mouth of the river. The city was named after the French king Louis XIV, who made the island a French settlement in 1659. This landscape became the most important route of enslavers during slavery's waning decades in the eighteenth century. It is worth noting that the slave trade on this part of the Senegal River involved three types of transportation: small ships that navigated inland through the Senegal River, pirogues that transported captives from these small ships to their holding stations in Saint-Louis, and "the big ship[s] in the big sea," as Omar put it. There were no harbors on the Atlantic coast, so these big ships then transported the captives across the ocean to the New World. There is strong evidence that on Omar's journey to the Carolinas, he passed through the Senegal River and Saint-Louis. Sylviane Diouf has observed that three ships sailing from Saint-Louis landed in Charleston between October and December 1807, so Omar, who reported his arrival in Charleston in 1807, must have been transported in one of these ships.[1]

Futa Toro and Bundu

Indeed, I reside in our country by reason of great harm. The unbelievers seized me unjustly, and sold me to the Christians, who bought me, and we sailed a month and a half on the big sea to the place called Charleston in the Christian language.

[Document 4]

Omar reports that his place of origin was Futa Toro, making him a person of Fulbe background. A diverse yet interconnected group of people lived in the Senegambia.[2] Some were Muslims, while others Omar calls in this document "unbelievers."

European traders and slavers were mostly referred to among Muslims as "the Christians." By "Christian," Omar obviously means white people. Earlier Senegambian writers already used the word in this sense, since Christianity was introduced to the region by European missionaries and explorers. They thus use the Qur'anic term *Naṣrānī* (plural *Naṣārā*) for the Europeans who happened to be Christian. Later writers during the French expansion in the second half of the nineteenth century started using "French" and the Wolof term *Toubaab* for Europeans.

Boubacar Barry gives us an illustrative list of the different groups inhabiting the Senegambian region. They include speakers of Wolof, Mandinka, Séeréer, Soninke, Susu, Joola, Nalu, Baga, Beafad, Bainuk, Basari, and Fulbe (the latter also comprising Peul, Tukulóor, Haalpulaar, etc.).[3] These groups have coexisted since the beginning of recorded history. The largest groups, from the region where most of the enslaved Muslims in the Americas came from, are the Mande with their offshoots—Bambara, Jula (including Mande-speaking groups such as Soninke), the Wolof, and the Fulbe. There is a long history of intermarriage, trade, and settlement between these groups. Both the advent of Islam from the

North (the Sahara belt) and the rise of the trans-Atlantic slave trade from the South (the Atlantic) have impacted this group's fragmentation and recombination. The Wolof came in contact with Islam through both the Fulbe and the Mandinka-Soninke coalition, as well as through their northern Mauritanian neighbors, whom they call Naar (Moor and Arab). But Futa is the historical homeland of the Fulbe, and it was from here that they migrated to Bundu and Futa Jallon.

Futa Toro is the region around the Senegal River along the border of Senegal and Mauritania. It is one of the main centers of what is mostly known in Arabic sources as "the realm of Tukulóor" (*bilād Tukulóor*, also Takrur or Tukrur) in West Africa. Local sources written in non-Arabic (*'ajamī*) languages tell different stories of the slow development of Islam in the region. But there are indications that Islam arrived in the region in the eleventh century. Some of the earlier references to Fulbe speakers' conversion to Islam were made by the Andalusian historian and jurist ibn Ḥazm (d. 1064), who wrote, "I was informed in the year 431 [1039 CE] that the people of Sala [in Morocco] and the people of Tukrur have accepted Islam. These are two great nations of the land of Sudan [the Blacks]; their kings and commoners converted to Islam. Much praise belongs to God."[4] There are suggestions that Takrur/Tukrur was established through the influx of Haalpulaar speakers who settled in the Senegal valley. John Donnelly Fage considers Takrur to have originated with intermarriage between Berbers from the Sahara and indigenous people of Séeréer background, currently in Senegal.[5] The French ethnographer Maurice Delafosse (d. 1926), an authoritative scholar in the studies of Fulbe people (also called Fulani), recounts that they took their language from the ancient Tukrur.[6] This claim is strongly supported by the fact that in modern-day Senegambian popular culture the word *Tukulóor/Tukrur* is used to describe the Fulbe community. Inhabitants of Futa are known as the Fulbe people, but several other terms such as *Peul*, *Fulani*, *Tukulóor*, and *Haalpulaar* are used interchangeably. One reason for this variation has to do with the fact that the Fulbe are semi-nomadic people who are dispersed across the Sahel; farmers and autochthonous groups tend to name them differently. Among the Fulbe are also the Peul, the region's predominant pastoral nomads. They overlap with the Sarakhule and the Jula (two branches of Mande speakers) in many parts of the region. Djibril Niane cites a saying of the local people of Gabu in the Gambian region that, "where a Mandinka settles in the morning, he is joined in the evening by a Peul."[7]

The Fula people were the most militant supporters of Islam's spread in West Africa. They have been scholars, settlers, leaders, and armed jihadists. Five main centers of Islamic politics in West Africa are linked to the Fulbe: the Islamic imamate of Futa Jallon in Guinea in 1720; the Islamic imamate of Futa Toro in Senegal in 1760s; the Islamic theocracy of Bundu on the Senegambia border in the early eighteenth century; Macina or Masina in south-central Mali, between Ségou and Tombouctou, in the early nineteenth century; and the Sokoto Caliphate in northern Nigeria, Niger, and Cameroon, led by ʿUthmān ɗan Fodio from 1804. In all these polities, there were significant non-Fulbe groups. In some polities, such as Futa Jallon, Sokoto, and Bundu, groups such as the Hausa, Malinké, and Sarakhule represented the majority of the inhabitants, but the Fulbe remained the dominant Muslim elite. As a scholar of Fulbe background who had witnessed Futa Toro under the rule of Almaami Abdul Kader Kane (Kan) (r. 1776–1807), Omar must have had memories of visiting different towns and schools of learning between Futa Toro, Futa Jallon, and Bundu. He must have spent some time in Kajoor among the Wolof, where Almaami Kane was highly respected and supported.[8]

Bundu is the only place mentioned by Omar as a place where he spent time as a student. "I continued seeking knowledge for twenty-five years. I came back home for six years." Bundu was located between the Senegal and Gambia Rivers. By the middle of the eighteenth century, it was a multicultural center of learning, a refuge for fugitive Muslims and persecuted scholars. Bundu was established late in the seventeenth century by Malik Sy, a pacifist Fulbe scholar who completed his study in Pir, one of the earlier Islamic centers of knowledge in Kajoor, a Wolof kingdom in the region. Through teaching and providing local medicine, Sy's school flourished among the local Bundunke and beyond, attracting students, like Omar, from Muslim places such as Futa Toro and Futa Jallon. It is reported that the Islamic school of Bundu was hosting around 500 students at any given time.[9]

In the following decades, Bundu developed into a major transitional commercial zone connecting the transatlantic trade routes of the Gambia River with the trans-Saharan trade routes of the Senegal River. Michael Gomez describes Bundu's climate of tolerance toward non-Muslims, which avoided a rigid implementation of Islamic law in governance, as symbolizing "pragmatism in the age of jihad."[10] Collecting taxes and levying tariffs from traders and passing caravans made Bundu one of the most peaceful and prosperous territories in the region. Mungo Park, who visited Bundu in 1790s, noted that "religious persecution is not known among them, nor is it necessary; for the system of Mahomet [Islam] is made to extend itself by means abundantly more efficacious. By establishing small schools in the different towns, where many of the Pagan as well as Mahometan [Muslim] children are taught to read the Koran, and instructed in the tenets of the Prophet, the Mahomedan priests fix a bias on the minds, and form the character of their young disciples, which no accidents of life can ever afterwards remove or alter."[11] The main point to highlight from Park's eyewitness account is the prevalence of schools across Bundu. Obviously, his comments on the nature of these schools or the background of the students are incorrect. As we will discuss later in this study, the curriculum in these schools contained more than the Qur'an, and although most inhabitants of Bundu were not Fulbe, most of them were Muslims, and it is incorrect to describe them as pagans.

Omar's Social and Family Background

My name is Omar ibn Said ibn Adam, but from my mother's side, [she is]
Umm Hānī Yarmak. O God! May God refresh her grave.

[Document 11]

A technically correct spelling of Omar's name is ʿUmar ibn Sayyid, where "ibn" is an Arabic word for "son." We use the commonly accepted spelling, "Omar," to avoid confusion. Moreover, Sayyid or "Said" is not often used as a family name in Futa or in the Senegambia. The local equivalent to Sayyid is Seydou or Saidou. Sayyid can be a first name as well, but it does not function like an English last name. So Omar is either not providing his family name or he is Arabicizing it, which was a common practice among scholars when writing for an Arabic-speaking audience. Perhaps Omar was aware that his potential audience in America was not really interested in knowing about his background, after the disappearance of the earlier version of his "Autobiography" (discussed in chapter 2), so that he became reticent or indifferent in providing details on his origins or his family in Africa. We must therefore carefully consider Senegambian name records to make sense of Omar's background.

Originally each group has family names, called *sant* or *santa* in Wolof and *yettode* in Fula, which distinguish members from other groups. Fula speakers are associated with names like Si, Jallo (or Diallo), and Ba. Mandinka last names include Darame, Tuure, and Siise. Common Wolof names are Jóob, Faal, and Njaay. Every *sant* in each of these groups has a "praise form" used in formal greetings and honorifics. The praise form for Jóob is Jamba-Jóob, for Njaay, Njaay-Jaataa (Njaay, the lion). For Tuure (Touré) and Cissé the Mandinka praise name is Tuure-Moori and Siise-Moori (the learned men, the scholars). For Fulbe speakers there is Mabo, associated with royal advising and counseling, for

15

instance. In Gabu and Bundu, non-Muslim people often use Mooro as a praise name for Muslims of Mande background.[12] Omar ibn Said was often referred to in the American press as "Moro"; this nickname may be African rather than a mispronunciation of the Arabic name ʿUmar. For example, a January 8, 1863, article in the *New York Observer*, titled "Meroh, a Native African," noted that "his name is Meroh. It was originally Umeroh. Some write it Moro; and some put it in the French form Moreau. It is commonly pronounced as if spelled Moro."

This praise name, Moro, may have been given to Omar by enslaved Africans from the Senegambian region who recognized his Muslim background. One of the signs of intermarriage and connectivity between these groups is that many Wolof family names are also names of Fulbe, Mande, and Séeréer, or vice versa. The reason may be borrowing, assimilation, or conversion to Islam. The famed Muslim scholar Musa Kamara noted the frequency of name changes among the people of the region:

> Last names among the Peul are numerous for many reasons. One who immigrated to a country where his family name was not widespread became a foreigner in that country, and that foreignness is one of the bases of dispute. For this reason, the foreign person changes his name in accordance with the inhabitants of the host country. Another reason is when one joins a trade community among the traders of Sudan [West Africa] and his last name is not established among those trading people, it happens that this person would change his last name according to the names of those of the members of the trading community. For example, many of them have changed from Thiam to Jallo, and others from Ndongou to Sow, and from Merne to Jah. I have seen that we change from Mbaye to Sow and I have seen some who have changed from Anne to Sow, because [these were Peul names], and their profession was breeding animals and tending cattle. Many others among them changed their names again from Joop to Ba and also from Joop to Dioh. Among those who changed from Dieng to Wang, there were some who changed their name from Jallo to Kane when they became Toorobe after they were nomadic Peul pastors.[13]

A main lesson from Kamara's observation is that last names among many Senegambian groups have lost their traditional function as a marker of group membership. Thus the Wolof saying, "Last names have no home [or tribe]" (*sant dëkkul fenn*). This is because many people were switching their last names due to new assumed identities, professions, or adopted homeland.

Two inquiries about Omar's background are relevant here: the identity of the unbelievers (*kuffār*) he described as capturing him from his village, and the location of this village itself in modern-day Senegambia.

On the first point, Omar notes in his "Autobiography," "Indeed, I reside in our country by reason of great harm. The unbelievers seized me unjustly, and sold me to the Christians, who bought me."[14] In the literature of the Fulbe Islamists, the word *kāfir* (plural *kuffār*) was largely used to describe local non-Muslims with indigenous beliefs, such as the Bassari and the Bambara, who were in conflict with the local Islamic theocracies of Futa Toro, Futa Jallon, and Bundu. In his book *Most of the Pseudo-jihādists*, Musa Kamara remembers returning to Futa Toro from Futa Jallon with his nephew Sale Samba Djoume, who referred to a small village inhabited by Malinké or Bambara unbelievers.[15] There is also evidence that the Bambara identify themselves in opposition to Islam. Chérif Keita, an expert on Mande culture, explains this etymologically as a derivation from the word *Bamana*: "Bamana [means] *bam* (refuser), *ma* (God, of Islam implied), *na* (preposition). In that sense, the Bamana (Bambara) are considered those who say NO to the Islamic God and insist on retaining their traditional spirits and beliefs. In fact, there is a mystique of Bamanaya (identity of the Bamana), which centers around certain practices as drinking brewed drinks like *tchapalo* (millet beer), mead, etc., and refusing to pray as Muslims do."[16] In other words, the Bambara insisted that their identity had an anti-Islamic component. Due to Futa Toro's location near the heartland of the Bambara in Mali, it is not unreasonable to suppose that Omar was referring to the Bambara when he mentioned unbelievers. There is also evidence to suggest that Omar might have been captured by the Bambara army that was battling Almaami Abdul Kader Kane in 1807, the year in which Omar was taken into slavery.[17]

On the second point, the location of Omar's village, in his 1819 letter to John Owen (the brother of his enslaver, and a prominent North Carolina politician), Omar stated, "I want to be seen in our land called Africa, in the place of the river called Kaba."[18] There is a village in Futa called Koppé, which has attracted some attention, since the letter *p* does not exist in Arabic, so Omar might have been aiming at this spelling. But this claim remains unsupported, since Omar was a graduate of the local schooling system, where students learned the Maghribi script and how to utilize local language (*ʿajami*) equivalents to represent foreign sounds in Arabic script. Our interviews in Futa as well as modern interest in Omar have revealed a proliferation of claims about Omar's family that could not be substantiated on the basis of Omar's documents.[19] The sixty-year-old Omar, at the time he wrote the second version of his "Autobiography," uses his age and memory lapses as excuses for not writing about his life or his home village in Africa. Perhaps his reluctance can be attributed to his unwillingness to recall traumatic memories of being captured by an army "that killed many people" in his village. So, unfortunately, the evidence does not permit us to identify Omar's home village with any certainty.

But it is also tempting to speculate about Omar's failing memory of Africa as a defense mechanism, responding to his enslavers' lack of genuine interest in his experiences. The first African American poet, Phillis Wheatley (d. 1784), was seven years old when she was captured from Senegal and sold into slavery in Boston, but she remembered her mother and her daily rituals. The literate Omar was thirty-seven when he was captured. It is improbable that the seven-year-old Phillis remembered her African background, while the thirty-seven-year-old Omar did not.

The Making of Omar: Orality and Literacy

Praise be to God, who created humanity to worship him, so
he might test their actions, their words.

[Omar's Testing formula]

Omar's "Autobiography" begins on a cautionary note, with an apologia for his writing ability: "From Omar to Shaykh Hunter: you have asked me to write my life. I cannot write my life; I forget too much about my language along with the Arabic language. I read now little grammar and little language. O my brothers, I beg you in the name of God, do not blame me, for my eyes are weak and so is my body" (Translation 2.1, Document 4). Although he goes on to demonstrate his mastery of theological texts, this nod toward the importance of formal writing is evidence of its being one of several sources of knowledge in West Africa.

In contrast, one major outcome of the European Renaissance in the eighteenth century was an obsession with writing as the only mode of proper knowledge and modern science as the touchstone of truth. In this European "literacy gospel," all other modes of knowing or modes of thought were dismissed. As a result, there were literate and illiterate traditions, and primacy was given to people with a writing system. Those with no writing system were relegated to the category of people without history.[20] The colonial motto maintains that "where there is no writing, there is no culture."[21] In the spirit of this framework,

Georg Wilhelm Friedrich Hegel observed that "Africa is no historical part of the world; it has no movement or development to exhibit."[22] Savagery was the primary concept used in describing these illiterate African societies.

America's investment in slavery was part of the grand scheme of a civilizing mission and America's manifest destiny. John Atkins, a British slaver on the west coast of Africa, wrote in 1721, "When the nakedness, Poverty and Ignorance of these Species of men are considered; it would incline one to think it a bettering their Condition, to transport them to the worst of Christian Slavery; but as we find them little mended in those respects at the West-Indies, their Patrons respecting them only as Beasts of Burden; there is rather Inhumanity in removing them from their Countries and Families."[23] Atkins was echoing the centrality of the question of Black African intelligence and intellectual ability to the debate on Christian slavery.

Advocates of slavery used claims to literacy, intellectualism, and humanity to justify the virtues of their civilizing mission. The writings of the first generation of enslaved Black writers were cited by both proslavery and antislavery advocates to support their views. While both Phillis Wheatley and Ignatius Sancho (d. 1780), the first enslaved Black writer in the British territories, were celebrated in antislavery and abolitionist milieus, Thomas Jefferson disagreed. His assessment of the two first modern Black authors was motivated by the realization that praising their work would imply accepting their intellectual abilities and, therefore, accepting the merits of Black liberty:

> Misery is often the parent of the most affecting touches in poetry.—Among the blacks is misery enough, God knows, but no poetry. . . . Their love is ardent, but it kindles the senses only, not the imagination. Religion indeed has produced a Phyllis Wheatly; but it could not produce a poet. The compositions published under her name are below the dignity of criticism. The heroes of the Dunciad are to her, as Hercules to the author of that poem. Ignatius Sancho has approached nearer to merit in composition; yet his letters do more honour to the heart than the head.[24]

For Jefferson, these writers had emotion, but they lacked the intellect and the artistic ability to be true poets.

Understandably, in this framing of slavery, among both enslavers and enslaved, Africa was associated with barbaric backwardness, ignorance, and savagery. Here is an example of the concept of savage slavery from the pen of

Wheatley, who spent the rest of her life in America after a brief stint in Britain. In "On Being Brought from Africa to America," she reflected upon her religious heritage based on what she was told by the slavers:

> 'Twas mercy brought me from my *Pagan* land,
> Taught my benighted soul to understand
> That there's a God, that there's a *Saviour* too:
> Once I redemption neither sought nor knew.
> Some view our sable race with scornful eye,
> "Their colour is a diabolic die."
> Remember, *Christians*, *Negros*, black as *Cain*,
> May be refin'd, and join th' angelic train.[25]

In these lines, Wheatley expresses gratitude for Christian salvation, rationalizing slavery as redemptive, and she pushes back only hesitantly against the racial prejudice she had encountered.

This habit of denying to enslaved Africans any skill or educational accomplishment was the source of the antebellum obsession with the literate Omar. In theory, an intellectual, educated, enslaved negro from Africa could refute racist white supremacy. This pressure might also help us understand Omar's silences, his claims of forgetfulness, and his statement that he could not write about his life. But many forms of learning and knowledge transmissions had existed in the Senegambian region for centuries. The interplay between these modes of knowledge is complex, and as we will show, the Islamicate system was one of them, and had remained a key component in their transmission. By "Islamicate," a term introduced by Marshall Hodgson, we mean the large cultural complexes in societies where Islamic religion plays a significant but not determinative role, which means that non-Muslim traditions and actors must be reckoned with in ways that are not reducible to textual forms of religion.[26]

ORAL WISDOM TRADITION

Writing was only one of many methods of knowledge transmission in the region. Omar's countryman Hampaté Bâ (1901–91), considered a leading scholar of Fulbe oral tradition, remembers a lesson from his shaykh and teacher, Thierno Bokar, demanding that he pay attention to the difference between knowledge and writing:

Writing is one thing and knowledge is another.

Writing is the photographing of knowledge, but it is not knowledge itself.

Knowledge is a light which is within man.

It is the heritage of all the ancestors knew and have transmitted to us as seed, just as the mature baobab is contained in its seed.[27]

Two forms of learning coexisted and continued to exist in this region: an oral wisdom transmission and the literate Islamicate Arabic tradition. We will discuss each of these forms in turn.

Oral teaching reflects traditional ways of knowing, practicing, and transmitting knowledge. It envisions traditional wisdom as enacted in real-life situations and historic settings. Age in this culture assumes wisdom by increased experiences and shrewdness in addressing or recording newly developing life challenges. Wisdom is attributed to old age. As noted in the life lessons of the Wolof philosopher Kotch Barma (d. 1655), "An old person is necessary for the well-being of a country."[28] Various traditional religious beliefs coexisted in this region before the rise of Islam, and they became absorbed or coexisted with the spread of Islam. They have remained the backbone of the strength of Muslim Sufi orders in the region. As spiritual modes of knowing, they have shared patterns of belief in divine powers that reside among people and in nature, among the living and the dead. The spirits of the dead remain with us in rivers, the sea, the wind, and the animals. In the words of the Senegalese poet Birago Diop,

Those who are dead are never gone
They are there in the thickening shadow.
The dead are not under the earth:
They are in the tree that rustles,
They are in the wood that groans,
They are in the water that runs,
They are in the hut, they are in the crowd,
The dead are not dead.[29]

A set of ethical values was transmitted through various rituals and forms of initiation and socialization. They included rituals of manhood and seasonal initiatory events of circumcision, wrestling, and harvest. Children had access to ancestral ethical values through storytelling circles around fireplaces at night. They were socialized to acquire values of modesty (*kersa*), rigor (*fulla*), severity (*fayda*), faithfulness (*gore*), uprightness (*njub*), politeness (*yaru*), and welcoming (*yaatu*). Wisdom was introduced in animal stories and tales in which the chief characters are generally championed by the stupid hyena and the cunning hare. There are also ethical tales about the perils of hate, the punishment of wrongdoing, and problems of polygamy (jealousy among co-wives and their children). These life lessons are introduced through different animal characters such as the lion, dog, goat, monkey, and rooster.

These values were inculcated in children through socialization and shadowing the elderly. Not all age groups are equal. The older groups are expected to lead by example. Younger people can join the older group "if their hands are clean," as a Wolof proverb states, reflecting on how wisdom at an early age can elevate one in rank. Adults observe through shadowing their elders. In the words of Hampaté Bâ, this arrangement explains why "when an old man dies, a library burns down." Across the Senegambian region, there is also much focus on socializing children in the virtue of patience, which is *muñal* in Haalpulaar and *muñ* in Wolof. Oral wisdom tradition is rich in proverbs, riddles, stories, legends, and songs.

The griot class are the oral historians responsible for keeping and reciting legends. There are legends for chiefs, genealogy, and places. In times of peace or war, legends are performed with musical instruments such as the kora. In theory, there is a legend for every person; one's griot is the keeper of one's legend and genealogy, and this story is recited in public functions. This art form continued across the region and flourished under Islamicate culture. One of the most popular legends is that of Sundiata Keita, who founded the Malian empire in 1235. Here is how the griot Djeli Mamoudou Kouyaté introduces the epic:

> I am a griot. It is I, Djeli Mamoudou Kouyaté, son of Bintou Kouyaté and Djeli Kedian Kouyaté, master in the art of the eloquence. Since time immemorial the Kouyatés have been in the service of the Keita princes of Mali; we are vessels of speech, we are the repositories which harbour secrets many centuries old. The art of eloquence has no secrets for us; without us the names of kings would vanish into oblivion; we are the memory of mankind, by spoken word we bring to life the deeds and exploits of kings for a younger generation.
>
> I derive my knowledge from my father Djeli Kedian, who also got it from his father. History hold no mystery for us, we teach to the vulgar

just as much as we want to teach them, for it is we who keep the keys to the twelve doors of Mali. I know the list of all sovereigns who succeeded to the throne of Mali. I know how the black people divided into tribes, for my father bequeathed to me all his learning; I know why such and such is called Kamara, another Keita, and yet another Sibibé or Traore, every name has a meaning, a secret import.[30]

So the griot is not only the preserver of history but also the keeper of its hidden dimension.

West African society has an outstanding tradition of orality, especially storytelling. Central to this element is the communal origin of wisdom. There is a Wolof saying that "the cure of the human is the human" (*nit nitay garabam*). And as a Fulbe proverb advises, "One knows when one first knows that he does not know," a clear expression of the importance of being a humble human being. Orality is based on practical knowledge, which is what the Mande people call "culture of the spoken word." It bestows the spoken word with sanctity. In this culture, proverbs are the flowers of life, and they are used in all settings to address uncertainty and to balance between competing truths. By all evidence, this source has intrinsic value to all Africans. Among the Wolof, verbal wit and a clever tongue are the hallmark of a good speaker. Among the Mande, there is a saying that "the mouth of an elder may stink, but out of it comes wisdom." Bâ observes that in Fulbe oral tradition, "speech engages man, speech is man himself."

Furthermore, as Islamicate culture became part of the local wisdom system and tradition, old stories, glories, and proverbs were largely restructured or reinterpreted within the new norms or ethics of Islam. For example, political leaders of the Malian Empire were added to the pioneering leaders of the community of Islam. Their genealogy was associated with the East and with Bilāl al-Ḥabashī, an Ethiopian appointed by Muhammad as the first muezzin (caller to prayer) in Islam. Here is the griot Djeli Mamoudou Kouyaté talking about the founder of the Malian Empire, Sundiata:

Listen then, sons of Mali, children of the black people, listen to my word, for I am going to tell you of Sundiata, the father of the Bright Country, of the savanna land, the ancestor of those who draw the bow, the master of a hundred vanquished kings. I am going to tell you of Sundiata, he whose exploits will astonish men for a long time yet. He was great among kings, he was peerless among men, he was beloved of God because he was the last of the great conquerors. Right at the beginning then, Mali was a province of the Bambara kings, those who are today called Mandingo; they are inhabitants of Mali, they are not indigenous, they come from the East. Bilali Bounama, ancestor of the Keitas, was the faithful servant of the Prophet Muhammad [may the peace of God be upon him]. Bilali Bounama had seven sons of whom the oldest, Lawalo, left the holy City and came to settle in Mali.[31]

In this way, through the descendants of Bilal, Islam has become part of the narrative of African political legitimacy.

LITERATE ISLAMICATE EDUCATIONAL TRADITION

In the "Autobiography," Omar describes his previous life in Africa as a fulfillment of the typical duties and practices of Islam.

> Before I came to the Christian country, my religion was the religion of Muhammad, the messenger of God, may blessing and peace be upon him. I would walk to the mosque before daybreak, and would wash face, head, hands, and feet. I would pray at noon, would pray in the afternoon, would pray at sunset, would pray in the evening. I would give alms every year, gold, silver, harvest, cattle, sheep, goats, rice, wheat, and barley—all of them. I would give alms, I would go every year to jihād against the unbelievers; I would go on pilgrimage to Mecca and Medina, as is required for one who is able. My father had six boys and five girls, and my mother had three boys and one girl. The day I left my country, I was thirty-seven. I have been residing in the land of the Christians for twenty-four years, in the year one thousand with eight hundred and one with thirty, of Jesus the Messiah.

Omar's recollection of the Islamic practices of his youth echoes the orality of his Islamicate education.

Islamicate education spread in the Senegambian region with the message of Islam. Arabic was its formal vehicle of instruction, and it had become the lingua franca of the educated clergy by the sixteenth century. Using Arabic script to write local languages (ʿajami) was a common practice. ʿAjami means writing local languages with modified Arabic script; scholars also call this phenomenon aljamiado, from the Spanish adaptation of this term, to describe writing

Romance dialects with Arabic letters. "'Ajamization" is therefore connected to literacy, which is the first step in Islamic education in the region. That is why we use the term *Islamicate* rather than *Islamic*, to encompass cultural developments that go beyond central Islamic texts and norms. The Islamicate education system involves learning correct spelling through the *abjad* alphabet system, which assigns numerical values to the twenty-eight letters of the Arabic alphabet. In this way, the disciple learns how to represent local sounds using this alphabet and to pronounce them using Arabic script. Furthermore, the disciple learns the concept of counting and numbering using the abjad alphabet. This learning phase often takes years of training, as it involves both spiritual instruction and what Rudolph Ware calls "embodied knowledge."[32] Spiritual training is about learning, memorizing, and rehearsing Qur'anic verses and chapters without knowing their meaning. Physical pain and punishment are associated with this phase of the Qur'anic learning method. Since the Qur'an is divided into *Qiṣār As-Suwar* (Short Suras) and the *Ṭiwāl As-Suwar* (Long Surahs), students in these schools start with the first phase.

During the first phase, Qur'anic verses were written on wooden tablets and read repeatedly to the teacher or shaykh (known as Serigne in Wolof, Ceerno or Thierno among the Fulbe, and Mooro or Modibo among the Mande). Once the pronunciation was mastered, the student moved on to rehearsing and memorizing the verses. After these were memorized, that portion of the Qur'an was replaced with new verses, while using the same methods of rehearsal and memorization. Thierno Ka studied at the school of Pir, one of the oldest Qur'anic schools in the Senegambian region, later devoting his 1982 doctoral dissertation to the study of its history and method. We partially draw upon his work for examples of Islamicate learning in the Senegambia region. He observed three stages in the routines of instruction, all impacted by the rainy seasons and the need to work in the fields. A typical day was structured as follows: first, early morning learning sessions, then revision sessions after breakfast. This involved one-on-one rehearsal with the shaykh. The goal of the one-on-one session was to ensure that the students knew the written words on the wooden boards. This session also included time to decide whether to erase the board and move on to a new lesson or keep working on the old material. Furthermore, there was the evening or night session for rehearsal and memorization. Finally, the third stage was a review session of the day, week, and month in which the student reviewed all content associated with that specified period.[33]

The school of Pir in Kajoor (or Cayor), one of the Wolof polities, was founded by 'Umar Faal (d. ca. 1695) in the second half of the seventeenth century. One of his disciples, Malik Sy, would become the founder of the school in Bundu in 1695, which Omar credited with his education. Another earlier Islamic school around the time of Omar was that of Kokki in Nijambur. It was established by Matar Ndumbe Jóob (the first Serigne Kokki, 1701–83). Both of these schools remain centers of Qurʾanic learning and Islamic sciences.

Diversity exists within the Islamicate system and structure due to learners' ethnic background, regional location, and level. In his 1925 book, Shaykh Musa Kamara wrote that, because the political system was not hereditary among the Fulbe-speaking Muslims of Futa, their scholars were drawn to politics when their status grew in society. The adverse effect of scholars becoming politicians was that the scholars' offspring became preoccupied with worldly affairs and governance, rather than seeking knowledge. This is why scholarly families did not develop among the Fulbe speakers within their political establishment, which was not the case with their neighbors. As Kamara notes,

> One still can find the transmission of knowledge among the offspring of the scholars (ʿulama) of the Maures [Mauritanians]. As royal power and political authority among the Maures belong exclusively to certain families, they do not pass it to others. As such, a son of a scholar does not find a pathway to prestige except through learning, and then he must consecrate himself to it. Since his lust for political power is removed and he does not pursue it, he gets what he values and what is destined for him from knowledge.
>
> Similarly, we still find the transmission of knowledge among the offspring of Soninké scholars, who are known as Sarakolé. We also find it among other groups such as the Zāghawa, because royalty and political authority are reserved for particular families and no one else challenges them for it. Therefore, the offspring of their scholars would work diligently on acquiring knowledge; once they acquired the knowledge, they would often obtain political prestige, God willing.[34]

In short, scholarly families did not generally develop as much in Futa Toro because of their connections with political leadership.

In some places, there were established scholarly families known by family names such as Kunta, Tuure (Touré), Daad, Lo, Ann, Ba, and so on. These families possessed their own libraries, litany (wird), and secrets of talismanic recipes. Knowledge was transmitted mostly from shaykh to disciples through arranged marriages to bring loyal students to the esteemed family lineage. This is how the priority of ties of ink over ties of blood was established among the scholars. This contributed to the creation of metropolitan areas and centers of Islamic learning, centered around the lodge (Wolof: *daara*) and the shaykh. Graduates of these schools were revered socially and highly respected politically. Kings and chiefs sought their advice and prayers, while ordinary people come to them for medicine, talismans, and prayers.

The system of lodges was organized for highly individualized instruction. There were two types of lodge: the local lodge (*daara alxuraan*) and the regional lodge, or seminary (*daara xamxam*). The latter was for advanced learning, as found at Pir, Kokki, and Bundu. It was designed to accommodate students of diverse ethnic backgrounds into all levels of learning. At the highest level of seminary, one is supposed to have memorized the entire Qur'an before moving on to study Islamic sciences. A memorizer of the Qur'an (*ḥāfiẓ*) is supposed to write out the Qur'an from memory and should produce one handwritten copy. A student in these seminaries is called a seeker of knowledge or Taalibe (or Taalibé in the French-based spelling). The profession of Taalibe warrants suffering for the sake of learning the Qur'an. Islamic virtues of resilience such as steadfastness in the face of adversity, ethical teachings (*ādāb*), and the skill of patience (*ṣabr*)—a foundational concept in Islamic teaching—are the central elements of life in the seminary system. Some of the local lodges were nomadic, as few people were enrolled in these local centers. Still, enrollment in seminaries numbered in the hundreds. Local lodges generally met in homes and under the baobab tree. In a few cases, they were coeducational, but in most cases they were for boys only. Parents sent children to learn the Qur'an at seminaries where the teachers become de facto guardians. The lodge dwellers are considered brothers, mostly depending on farming and donations from visiting parents. Learning hours were greatly reduced during the day throughout the rainy season, as students were occupied with clearing fields, planting, or farming. There is a categorical difference between a Taalibe's service in these lodges and plantation slavery. Plantation slavery was not part of the economic system of West Africa.

Slavery, as a form of social classification, existed in Senegambian culture with a set of rights, a notion of freedom, and defined restrictions governing people who were held in bondage.[35] There is an old Wolof saying that "a slave who accepts whatever orders are given to him, deserves them [*Jaam nak, luñ ko teg mu nangu ko dagan na*]." The saying reminds people of their rights and dignity that are protected by customary practices and ethical wisdom. In popular culture, slavery, as a systematic form of cruel and inhuman economic exploitation,

was associated with both Europeans and Mauritanian Arabs (or Moors). React-
ing against these types of external slavery, one imposed by the Europeans
through the Atlantic slave trade, and the other by Mauritanian Arabs through
the trans-Saharan slave trade, contributed to the popularity of Muslim lodges
and theocratic polities in the eighteenth century. Islamic polities were motivated to resist the Atlantic slave trade and even to call for the abolition of slavery in many areas of the region. At the very least, they sought to issue decrees
that prohibited enslaving Muslims. According to Kamara, opposing slavery was
the root cause of the popularity of Almaami Abdul Kader Kane (d. 1807). He led
the Tooroodo Revolution in Futa Toro after the death of its founder, Sulayman
Baal, and, by some scholars, is associated with Omar's upbringing and potential
enslavement.[36] Kane was a learned scholar of Islam and Arabic who ended the
enslavement of Muslims by Mauritanian Arabs, as well as by European traders.
Kane's 1789 letter to the French commandant in Saint-Louis welcomed commerce with Europeans but opposed the enslavement of Muslims. He noted, by
citing Qur'an 49:12, the conclusion that enslaving our brothers is a sin, because
it is like eating the flesh of the dead. "We don't want you under any circumstances to buy Muslims," he wrote, "neither from near here nor from afar. And
we repeat: If your goals are always to trade in Muslims, then you should stay in
your country, and do not return to our country. Let all who come to our country
for this purpose know that they will lose their lives."[37] It is clear that the effects
of the international slave trade were arousing serious objections in West Africa.[38]

In the indigenous Senegambian culture, the role of slavery differed from its
later development in the Atlantic slave trade. In the old days, most griots came
from the slave class; yet they wielded much influence on society, on both layper-
sons and chiefs. The griots were feared by rulers and given license by people for
their social functions. There is much evidence that they were to be spared even
in times of war and conflict. It is no wonder that, due to these privileges, they
were very resistant to Islam. For Islamic interpretations brought new notions of
slavery with regulations and rights for enslavers, which had adverse effects on
traditional society.

In addition to the griot class, the enslaved were also divided into two groups:
those born in the household of slavery and those captured in war. Only the
second category was sold in the slave trade. The slave population was larger in
Muslim polities of West Africa, where the slave trade was religiously regulated.[39]
Most local slaves were household slaves, and by custom, they could only be sold
if they committed a major crime such as witchcraft, murder, or treason. But the
development of the transatlantic slave trade imposed a new form of economic

slavery around the Senegal River. James Searing has claimed that the growth of the Atlantic trade, around the Senegal River and in lower Senegal, stimulated the development of slavery in these regions.[40] This form of "plantation" slavery was implanted in these regions within the European settler society, but it was never incorporated into the socioeconomic fabric of the local economy. In the cases of both Gorée Island and Saint-Louis, slave societies were small, a creation of European settlers and former slavers. Therefore, it is a methodological error to use colonial examples to study the evolution of the local slavery system. It was this latter form of slavery, the Atlantic slave trade, that was affected by the French decree of 1848, in which the French government abolished slavery in its colonies. But the ancient traditional notion of slavery was phased out as the norms of griots and social dependency disappeared in the twenty-first century.

Omar's statement at the beginning of this section echoes the oral nature of the seminary experience. Omar is obviously talking in general terms about what a Muslim does, rather than what he himself used to do. Omar's verb "to walk" is conjugated in the third person and in the present tense (he walks). Since in many parts of his "Autobiography," he uses the third person for himself, we keep that pattern of speech as first-person singular in the translation. Nevertheless, the present tense also alludes to a continuous past tense, which leads to our conclusion that this is a generalization. There is no evidence so far of Omar going to Mecca or conducting warfare under the banner of jihād. His speech reflects his learning experience, which was based on recitation, memorization, and the copying of the Qur'an and other Islamic texts. In the seminary, students learned the normative teachings of Islam, the five pillars of Islam, traditional Sufi chanting (*dhikr*), the meaning of talismanic amulets, and shadowing the shaykh or the lead instructor. Students were trained as Islamic scholars, marabouts, and healers. Both maraboutism and healing involved trade. This is why Omar is reported in different documents as having been engaged in trade. Niane, in his classic study of Gabu and Bundu, notes that "the marabouts are almost always traders; they sell goods, or else they sell amulets, talismans, especially prized by animists."[41] It is against this background of the local West African adaptation of Islamic literacy that we interpret the writings of Omar.

THE SCHOOLING OF OMAR:
CONTENT AND CURRICULUM

"Praise be to God, with much praise.
He bestows bounties that overflow" with the good.

[Omar quoting the *Summary* of Khalīl]

Like the oral culture of the Senegambian region, Islamicate education depends mostly on oral transmission. Books contain knowledge, but knowledge belongs in "the chest," according to a local saying. There is strong evidence that scholars at Pir and Kokki (two Wolof territories) used local language for instruction and learning, although their books were written in Arabic. In Bundu, Arabic was the lingua franca. Francis Moore, an eighteenth-century British writer, noted in his travel narratives that Pulaar-speaking communities were "generally more learned in the Arabic, than the people of Europe are in Latin, for they can most of them speak it."[42]

There is a rich discussion in the literature about the academic contents of Islamicate education in the Sudanic region. What types of subjects were covered and what books were used to educate scholars like Omar? There was no disagreement on what should be learned. In all learning centers of Islamic knowledge, there was a focus on four main subjects: the exegesis of the Qur'an (*tafsīr*), Mālikī jurisprudence (*fiqh*), theology (*tawḥīd*), and Arabic language and grammar (*naḥw*). For these teachers and scholars, the best sciences are those that help one understand the Qur'an as a means of worshiping the Most High.

In the beginning of this section, Omar notes, "Praise be to God, with much praise. He bestows bounties that overflow," adding his own clarification, "with the good." This is a quotation from the *Summary* (*Mukhtaṣar*) of Khalīl, a popular legal work quoted twice in Omar's "Autobiography" and once in his Bible. There is a complement to this legal work, called *The Epistle* (*Kitāb al-risāla*) by Ibn Abī Zayd al-Qayrawānī (d. 996), which Omar quotes in Document 6. A popular phrase in this book sums up the hierarchy of the sciences. The students in Omar's Islamicate schools were often introduced to Muslim jurisprudence through this segment. It reads, "The first and best of sciences, and the closest of them to God, is knowledge of his religion and the laws of what he commands and forbids, and what he calls for and what he exhorts against in his book, and through the saying of his prophet; this entails understanding his jurisprudence, and safeguarding it and then acting upon it."[43] In the application of this vision, the four subjects listed above were established. Arabic grammar was historically prized, for without it, learning or developing proficiency in the other three subjects was considered impossible.

Recent literature on the academic content of Islamic education has opened up a dramatic picture of a widespread living tradition. Bruce Hall and Charles Stewart have tried to map out a body of hundreds of Islamic manuscripts from West African libraries, produced over a period of three centuries from 1625 to 1925, to offer a methodological approach to describing an Islamic curriculum.[44] Their study identifies six main areas of study: the Qur'an, the Prophet Muhammad, jurisprudence, Arabic language, theology, and Sufism. Ousmane Kane has also provided synopses of authors and texts that were of greatest interest to Sudanic Africans.[45] More recently, Robert Launay's *Islamic Education in Africa: Writing Boards and Blackboards* surveys a plethora of Islamic educational content and context from colonial times to the present day.[46] Fallou Ngom has recently provided case studies of Qur'anic and Islamic schooling from the Senegambian region.[47]

For the sake of specificity in the context of Omar's background, we will limit our examples to the school of Pir. In one of the most comprehensive studies, supplemented with field studies and interviews, Ka provided the following curriculum as well as specified text books for the school of Pir. It seems from his presentation that the subjects of study were divided in two main parts: (1) religious sciences (*'ulūm islāmiyya*) consisting of exegesis of the Qur'an (*tafsīr*), hadīth sayings, Prophetic biography (*sīra*), Mālikī jurisprudence (*al-fiqh al-Mālikī*), and Arabic language sciences. Supplementary nonreligious subjects were grouped under (2) ancient sciences, comprised of logic (*manṭiq*), astrology (*'ilm al-nujūm*), and talismanic sciences.

Standard textbooks were commonly associated with these sciences. For example, the books related to Mālikī jurisprudence were the famous Mālikī textbooks used by scholars and students. They were, for the beginner, *The Epistle* (*al-Risāla*) by the Tunisian Ibn Abī Zayd al-Qayrawānī (d. 996); for the intermediate, the book known as *al-Akhḍarī*, after its author, the North African 'Abd al-Raḥmān ibn Muḥammad al-Akhḍarī (d. 1575); and for the advanced, the *Compendium of Legal Opinions* (*Kitāb al-mudawwana*) of Saḥnūn (d. 855); to which was added a major compendium of Prophetic sayings, *The Paved Way* (*al-Muwaṭṭa'*) by the founder of the Mālikī school, Imām Mālik ibn Anas (d. 795). Other books on this list for Islamic studies include *The Distinguished Jurist's Primer* (*Bidāyat al-mujtahid*) by Ibn Rushd (aka Averroes, d. 1198); the *Summary* (*Mukhtaṣar*) by the Egyptian scholar Khalīl ibn Isḥāq al-Jundī (d. 1365); and *Gifts for the Judges* (*Tuḥfat al-ḥukkām*) by Muḥammad ibn 'Āṣim of Granada (d. 1426).

A variety of collections in theology and mysticism was also available in these schools. They used *The Book of Legal Opinions* (*Kitab fatāwā* or *Uṣūl al-Subkī*) by the Egyptian Taqī al-Dīn al-Subkī (d. 1355); *The Sublime Revelation* (*al-Fatḥ al-rab-bānī*), a collection of speeches and lessons by the Persian Sufi saint Mawlānā ʿAbd al-Qādir al-Jīlānī (d. 1166); and *The Revival of the Religious Sciences* (*Iḥyāʾ ʿulūm al-dīn*) by Abū Ḥamid Muḥammad al-Ghazālī (d. 1111). The mystical poems of Abū Madyan Shuʿayb al-Ghawth (al-Andalusī) (d. 1198) were circulated among Sufi disciples. His poem on the conduct of a disciple, often referred to as the "Way of God's Friends," is still a popular chant memorized by advanced students in the seminary system. Omar cited Abū Madyan in his writings, and he must have been familiar with one of his most popular poems:

> There is no pleasure in living except accompanying the friends
>   of God,
>   for they are the [true] sultans and the masters and the leaders.
> So accompany them and show proper manners in their lodges,
>   and leave your fortunes in their hands, no matter if they seem
>   to forget you.
> And take advantage of the time and always attend on them,
>   and know that pleasure and contentment are the reward of
>   their companions.
> And abide by the rule of silence, except if you are asked, then say,
>   I have no knowledge, and mask yourself in ignorance.
> Please, find flaws only in yourself; and know that
>   your flaws have been apparent, even if they are concealed.
> And always lower yourself and ask for forgiveness for no reason,
>   and stand up with honesty when apologizing.
> If a flaw appears from you, apologize, and own up, with
>   your apology for your failures and shortcomings.
> And say: your servant is more deserving of your pardon;
>   please, show pardon and be lenient and clement, O friends
>   of God.[48]

The ethos of repentance displayed in this poem sets the stage for the formal apology that Omar directs to his absent "brothers" in the "Autobiography," emphasizing the Sufi component of his community, for which Abū Madyan was such a powerful spokesperson.

ARABIC SCHOLARSHIP AND LITERATURE

Arabic scholarship and literature developed widely in the Senegambia region, but from the wealth of existing manuscripts hardly any texts have been published, let alone translated. For the seventeenth century, the main reference book that chronicled political developments in the region is the *History of Fattash* (*Tā'rīkh al-Fattāsh*), an Arabic book associated with the Tombouctou scholar al-Ḥājj Maḥmūd Katī (d. 1593). It chronicles the history of the Songhay Empire, starting with Sonni Ali's reign (1464–92) and going to the end of the sixteenth century. For the seventeenth century, the *History of Sudan* (*Tā'rīkh al-Sūdān*) by ʿAbd al-Raḥmān ibn ʿAbd Allāh al-Saʿdī (d. 1656) provides context for political development in the region up to 1613, while covering other contemporary documents.[49]

These historical works also provide evidence for a flourishing scholarly tradition, citing many of the key works of Islamic scholarship mentioned above. This note from al-Saʿdi describes the accomplishments of a scholar by the name of Qāḍī Maḥmūd:

> [Maḥmūd] devoted himself to teaching. Jurisprudence from his mouth had a sweetness and elegance, his easy turn of phrase making the subject wonderfully clear without affectation. Many people benefited from him. He revived scholarship in his land, and the number of students of jurisprudence increased, some of them showing brilliance and becoming scholars. The books he most frequently taught were the *Mudawwana*, the *Risāla*, the *Summary* of Khalīl, the *Alfiyya*, and the *Salālijiyya*. Through his efforts teaching of [the *Summary* of] Khalīl spread in those parts, and one of his students put together a commentary in two volumes, based on notes taken from his teaching.[50]

The role of Islamic scholars was pervasive and widely appreciated.

The eighteenth century was tumultuous. The Atlantic slave trade intensified, wreaking havoc on people and their villages. In response, religious scholars proposed alternative solutions to ordinary people in Futa Jallon, Bundu, and around the Senegal River. The rise of militant Islam impacted the literary world of scholars. The most erudite treatise of Islamic jurisprudence in the Pulaar language of Futa Jallon was written in this era. The long poem *Eternal Happiness* by Thierno Samba Mombeya (1765–1850) consists of 552 verses organized around the themes of faith, law, and the path. It is one of the oldest collected 'ajamī texts in Pulaar. A variety of rich and diverse literature was written during this time. Omar al-Futī Taal came from the same Fulbe background as Omar bin Said and was among the last Fulbe leaders who attempted to revitalize the fading order of the Imamate Islamic systems in the Sudanic region. His 1845 book, *The Spears (Al-Rimāḥ)*, was a masterful summary of his teachings and philosophy. This Arabic book offers lessons on mysticism and Sufi doctrinal beliefs, as well as a collection of sermons.

The reach of Islam in West Africa was deepened not only by literature in local languages but also by the engagement of some Muslim women scholars in politics, education reform, and writing in different languages. Nana Asma'u (1793–1864), the daughter of Usman dan Fodio, the founder of the Sokoto Caliphate in northern Nigeria, and literate in Arabic, Hausa, and Fulfulde (Fulani), is considered a scholar and a historical source in her own right.[51] "Sufi Women" is one of her many popular poems that are still memorized and widely distributed among Sufi disciples across northern Nigeria. It was written in her native languages of Hausa and Fulfulde in 1831. Here are some translated lines from the poem:

> My aim is to tell you about Sufis —
>> To the great ones I bow in reverence.
> I am mindful of them while I am still alive,
>> So that they will remember me on the Day of Resurrection.
> The ascetic women are all sanctified;
>> For their piety they have been exalted.[52]

The poem reflects Asma'u's wide range scholarship and engagement with literature, history, and women's standing in Islam. Her edited and published works make her one of the most prolific advocates of the Sokoto Caliphate.

As we indicated earlier, by the third decade of the nineteenth century, the French governor of Senegal, Baron Roger, wrote that there were in Senegal "more negroes who could read and write in Arabic in 1828 than French peasants who could read and write French."[53] A major shift happened in the second half of the nineteenth century with the French expansion and the rise of its colonial order. Several learning centers developed across the Senegambian region, and most adopted new literary schools that accommodate both Arabic and 'ajamī writings. Amir Samb's 1978 book on the Arabic literature of Senegal discussed the eleven major Arabic and Islamic centers that developed in the region during the second half of the nineteenth century.[54] They were continuations of the old seminary centers in Kajoor, Bundu, and other places. For example, there was the school of Aynumaan, led by the judge and translator Khaali Majaxate Kala;[55] the school of Ndar (Saint-Louis), led by El-Hajj Major Cissé; and the school of Ganguel Souleé, led by Shaykh Musa Kamara. Most of these schools were reformist, nationalistic, and generally accommodating of French modernity. Two of these schools—those established by Shaykh Amadou Bamba (1853–1927) in Touba and Musa Kamara (1864–1945) in Futa Toro—merit a separate discussion.

Bamba was a prolific scholar, a poet, and a Sufi saint. He introduced himself as "the Servant of the Messenger [*Khādim al-Rasūl*]," and was locally known among his followers as the Shaykh of Tuubaa (or "Touba" in the French-based spelling). Tuubaa was a school and city that he founded to reach and educate the masses about his newly established Sufi order, known as the Murīdiyya. The French colonial administration's suspicion of Bamba's growing popularity and influence across the region led to his exile from Senegal to the equatorial forest in Gabon in 1895 and then again to Mauritania in 1903. Bamba's writing is about Islamic mysticism and devotional poetry praising the Prophet. As he often notes, "My religion is the love of God." This love of God was the center of his focus on peace as the only theological manifestation of Islam. His books and poems, read and chanted by his followers, include such popular works as *Paths to Paradise* (*Masālik al-jinān*), *The Imperative of Crying for the Saints* (*Ḥuqqa al-bukā*), and *Gifts of the Holy Lord* (*Mawāhib al-quddūs*).

Bamba initiated what Cheikh Anta Babou terms the "Greater jihād,"[56] which framed jihad as a withdrawal from the colonial state rather than a military confrontation with it, as was the popular trend at his time. His withdrawal from the colonial space was projected through various forms of intellectual engagement that aimed at achieving both cooperation with and independence from the French authorities. For example, Bamba contested the French interpretation of jihād as exclusively promoting violence. For Shaykh Amadou Bamba, the question of jihād was not how French authorities understood or interpreted it but what it truly means in Islam. "I do jihad," he wrote, "but with the sciences [knowledge] and with piety and faith."[57] For Bamba, this is the true meaning of jihad in Islam, and it was integral to his conception of his Murīd community. This perspective allowed Bamba to demarcate the boundaries of jihād anew, removing it from the violence that, for much of the second half of the nineteenth century, devastated the Senegambian region. In redefining jihād as a "service, an educational act" that is central to a Murīd's education and upbringing, Bamba relied on old traditional values of hard work, independence, and community to recast Islam.[58]

Musa Kamara came from Futa, like Omar ibn Said. Kamara, arguably the most prolific social historian of the Senegambian region, wrote mostly in Arabic, with a few poems and treatises in his native Pulaar (Haalpular). Kamara's scholarship spanned many disciplines, including human civilizations, the ethnography of Sudanic Africa, theology, and poetry. His contribution places him beyond what Louis Brenner sets as "the parameters of Islamic knowledge in West Africa," the mostly didactic traditional method of learning Islam.[59] Amar Samb, a Senegalese scholar, considers Kamara to be "the writer, who topped his equals . . . with a great erudition and intensity of immersion in literary and scientific arts."[60] Jean Schmitz, a French specialist on Kamara, characterizes him as "ahead of his time," a saint "who believed in disconnecting Islam from politics."[61] During the 1935 inauguration of Dakar's Cathedral of African Memory, Kamara was designated the representative of the marabout class of French West Africa. At this gathering, he called for the unity of Christians and Muslims, characterizing them as "People of the Book." His "People of the Book" thesis was then expanded into a major corpus on religious dialogue, *They Are Almost One* (*Kāda al-ittifāq*).

Before his passing in 1945, Kamara deposited his work at what is now the Institut Fondamental d'Afrique Noire (IFAN) at CAD University in Senegal, an act that has saved his work from loss and larceny. Samb counts twenty-four books by Kamara on history, theology, and literature at IFAN,[62] while David Robinson identifies twenty-eight works written by Kamara.[63] In a chapter in his autobiography titled "My Reading and Authorship," Kamara discusses twenty works that he has written and shared with other scholars, including their commentaries on and praise of some of the works.[64]

Kamara's magnum opus is *The Flowers of Gardens in the History of Black Peoples* (*Zuhūr al-basātīn*). It is one of the most original works on the history of West Africa. It situates the history of Futa Toro within a broader regional history of Sudanic Africa. More than 1,000 pages long, this book offers a rich context necessary for understanding political events during Omar's time in Senegambia. *The Precious Collection* (*Al-Majmūʿ al-nafīs*) is comparable to *Zuhūr al-basātīn* in importance, as both address issues of history and ethnology based on collected oral and written source material. Issues examined in this manuscript include a geographical description of Futa Toro, a historical treatise on Futa Jallon in Guinea-Conakry, and a discussion of the various clans in Mauritania. The manuscript is uniquely valuable in its treatment of the construction, composition, and rise of the Islamic clerics, or *tooroobe*, of the Middle Valley region of the Senegal River.[65]

Conclusion

This chapter has discussed Omar's West African background, with is multiple ethnicities, rich and diverse intellectual milieus, orality, and marvelous Islamicate scholarship. Omar was separated from these environments forever when he was captured in the village of Kaba and walked through waterways of Futa Toro to his holding station at the mouth of the Senegal River in Saint-Louis.

Based on what we have learned from Senegambian oral history and read in slave narratives, we can imagine what happened to Omar in his forced journey from Saint-Louis to Charleston, South Carolina, in 1807. There, Omar the Fulbe scholar was reduced to a negro slave. Omar the Muslim believer was relegated to a property, attached to a number, which he could not understand when it was read in what he calls "Christian language." He would be overwhelmed by the cruelty of his guards as they led him to the "big ship in the big sea." He must have thought of telling them about himself. He was a Muslim who had memorized the Qur'an, and the law of the land was clear that no Muslim should be enslaved. But how could he speak with them? As a marabout, he was not trained to implore anyone but God; as a scholar, he was not expected to ask others but to answer their questions. He must have been preoccupied by what the future held in the land of the white people (*Tubaab*). The learned Omar had surely heard, during his stints in the school of Pir in Kajoor among the Wolof, the saying that "Tubaab baaxul" ("The white man is up to no good"). At that moment, he must have felt paralyzed by fear and anxiety.

As he lay in the dungeon of the "big ship," surrounded by women, children, and wounded clansmen, he would close his eyes and pray. From his days at the seminary, he remembered an Islamic adage that "prayer is the travel companion of the believer." A Muslim must invoke God in times of distress, but from which books could he read, from the *Hadith* of *Sahih Bukhari*, the words that the Prophet used to repeat in times of stress and calamity? He could not now remember the source, but he knew the Arabic words, and thus kept repeating them: "There is none worthy of worship but God, the Mighty, the Forbearing. There is none worthy of worship but God, Lord of the Magnificent Throne. There is none worthy of worship but God, Lord of the heavens and Lord of the earth, and Lord of the Noble Throne."[66]

His prayer must have been interrupted by a someone yelling his name, Moro, and telling him in what seemed to him like Mandinka or Soninke, "Pray for me, Moro." He must have heard that plea many times before in Bundu. Moro, meaning Muslim healer, marabout, or cleric, is how non-Muslims addressed any

Muslim scholar. As a marabout he ought to have maintained his composure, because the beauty of the scholars is their calm attitude in times of upheavals, so that he could read a few prayers in a measured voice, and then murmur some intelligible words. The person seeking a prayer ought to have gained some solace, smiling back to the marabout in appreciation. One is tempted to assume that two years later these fellow Africans would help Omar escape from the plantation of Johnson, whom he later identified in his "Autobiography" as his first cruel enslaver in Charleston, South Carolina.[67] Omar must have drawn strength from the Qur'anic verses (2:214) that warned sincere believers they would be "visited by [difficult] circumstances," as was the case with God's people who "passed away before." He must have felt relief: this was his time and turn, these were afflictions and trials from God to test his state of belief. He did not have his books to consult the exact text, nor did he have his "brothers" to refresh his memory. His teachers were right: "Believing in the Divine decree and destiny is one of the pillars of Islam." Then Omar must have repeated one of his favorite formulas (quoted in the "Autobiography," D.1, D.2) to confirm his belief in God's just decree, "by grace, and not under constraint," thus echoing a long-standing philosophical discourse about God's absolute justice in whatever his decree is, good or bad, satisfactory to the creation or not.[68] Then Omar must have realized that only what he could recall would be able help him in this trial. As a Muslim, he should not despair of the mercy of God. He should pray and ask for his guidance. Perhaps he should write his life as soon as possible. He must ask these "Toubaabs" to return him to Futa, his wife, his children, and his disciples.

In essence, the old Omar of the Senegambia was gone without return, and a new Omar emerged on the plantations of the Carolinas. Deprived of all belongings, he would cling to his memory to fulfill his craving to write his life. A fading memory that was like a dream, ornamented with verses from the holy Qur'an, Prophetic sayings, the wisdom of the ancestors, and canonical texts of Islam. He remembered the old saying, "Knowledge is what is kept close to the chest [memorized], and certainly not what is left written in books." Moving forward, he would be quoting all Islamic and Arabic sources from memory; this included works in verse (and prose), different commentaries on classical books such as the *Summary* of Khalīl, al-Ḥawḍī's *Wāsiṭat al-sulūk*, Ibn Mālik's *Alfiyya*, and so on. As Omar struggled to write his life, some of his writings were distorted and destroyed by the guardians of the racist system of slavery, but a few documents survived for us to reconsider. We hope these chapters will help the reader remove the obstacles that have prevented us from hearing Omar's voice.

A Life Unread

THE "AUTOBIOGRAPHY" of Omar ibn Said, crucial to the understanding of his story, is a document with characteristics that distinguish it from other surviving writings of enslaved Africans. Written in 1831, it apparently replaces a previous Arabic autobiography that he completed in 1825, and which was lost in Philadelphia. At a time when John Owen, as governor of North Carolina, approved legislation increasing the penalties for teaching slaves to read and write, his brother James Owen (Omar's enslaver) urged Omar to write his "Autobiography." While other narratives of slavery were mainly designed to highlight its horrors and advance the cause of abolition, fictional accounts of Omar's life widely circulated in newspapers were used to justify slavery because of his supposed conversion to Christianity (a conversion he did not mention in the "Autobiography").

This contradiction between what Omar wrote and what his enslavers reported about him, and the lack of any audience, rendered Omar's "Autobiography" illegible. At the beginning of the text, Omar acknowledges that he has been asked to write his life, but he then announces that he is unable to do so. Each section of the "Autobiography" is presented twice, the revision seeming to reflect his protest that he cannot write his life. His enslavers continued to claim that he had converted to Christianity, but Omar's terse description of Christian practices is framed by quotations of Islamic texts. His revisions of the "Autobiography" shift its emphasis away from conversion to enslavement, which he calls "great harm." He addresses the American public by praising his enslavers, but the text contains language addressed to his companions in an Islamic seminary; evidently no one in his circle could understand what he wrote. The text was repeatedly translated by people who did not recognize his quotations of Islamic texts, adding to the ambiguity surrounding Omar's life.

The nearly 100 writings by formerly enslaved Africans that were published before 1860 can be labeled as "freedom narratives," or "liberation narratives," insofar as their main thrust is to represent slavery from the perspective of one who is freed from it. Omar's narrative, in contrast, is dominated by his unrelenting enslavement. In short, Omar's "Autobiography" is different. The first section of this chapter will explore these distinctive aspects of his text.

It is also important to consider the social context that is not explicitly mentioned in Omar's writings, namely, the slavery economy of North Carolina and the place of the Owens—and Omar—within it. Accordingly, the second section of this chapter focuses on the Owens, their role in North Carolina as enslavers, and the relationship that they claimed with Omar.

Omar's "Autobiography": A Text without an Audience

TRANSLATIONS WITHOUT RECEPTION

The "Autobiography," fundamental for understanding the life of Omar ibn Said, poses problems that have challenged translators. The manuscript of Omar's Arabic "Autobiography" contains the following description in English: "'Autobiography' of Omar ibn Said, slave in North Carolina, 1831. Arabic. The life of Omar ben Saeed, called Morro, a Fullah Slave in Fayetteville, N.C. Owned by Governor Owen. Written by himself in 1831 & sent to Old Paul, or Lahmen Kebby in New York, in 1836. Presented to Theodore Dwight by Paul in 1836. Translated by Alex. Cotheal, Esq., 1848 (the beginning at the other end)." As a description, this is inadequate. Although it is called an autobiography, which suggests that it is the primary source of information about his life story, it was systematically ignored and replaced with fictions. Dozens of articles written about Omar in the nineteenth century confidently depict him in ways contradicted by his own writings. The "Autobiography" remained a life unread. Omar knew this and effectively disowned the text he produced, proclaiming twice at the beginning of the manuscript, "I cannot write my life."

The 1831 manuscript was not Omar's first attempt at autobiography. Evidence indicates that he had written about his life some six years previously, but this document was lost. One of the editors of the *Philadelphia Recorder*, which reprinted the very first article published on Omar in August 1825, added this postscript:

> We can vouch for the truth of this article, as we were well acquainted with Prince Moro, & have had several conversations with him on the state of Africa. He speaks English more imperfectly than any African we have ever seen, but still can make himself intelligible. He represents himself as having been educated at Tombuctoo, and he certainly writes Arabic in a most beautiful manner. He composed a history of his own life and it was sent to some of our literary institutions but what has become of it we do not at present know. He belongs to the Foulah tribe.[1]

There is no trace of this earlier document in any of the learned societies of Philadelphia. The careless treatment of the manuscript was typical of the reception Omar's writings received. His 1819 letter to John Owen (discussed in chapter 3) has been preserved but was not translated until the 1980s.

The "Autobiography" was first translated in 1848, and then a second time in 1860, during the final years of Omar's life. Then the document went missing for most of the twentieth century. Its first translations were selective, flawed, and dismissive of the author. If the purpose of an autobiography is to narrate the author's life from a particular moment in time addressing "the endless complexity of life, selection of facts, distribution of emphases, choice of expression,"[2] Omar's "Autobiography" did not fit that definition. His enslavement overwhelmed his entire outlook on his own life, constraining the freedom that would have been required to narrate it. As a result, Omar compensated for his inability to talk about himself by praising his enslavers and addressing faraway audiences unable to heed his plea or understand his message. It is, therefore, correct to describe Omar's life as unread and his story as untold.

There are four published translations of the "Autobiography," produced by Alexander I. Cotheal (1848), Isaac Bird (1860), John Franklin Jameson (1925), and Ala Alryyes (2011). We will discuss each of these in turn, outlining their limited scope and their deepening of the original document's illegibility. The first stage was marked by Cotheal's rendering of the document into English. Cotheal could be described as an amateur scholar whose previous qualification was a translation of a US treaty with Oman from Arabic to English. Cotheal also acted as the treasurer of the American Ethnological Society for many years. He was a friend of Sir Richard Burton, who translated the *Thousand and One Nights*, a book that had influenced the American popular imagination about Arabia since the late eighteenth century.[3] This connection is a reminder of the way orientalist stereotypes of the Qur'an and fantasies about Arabian princes found their way into Omar's public persona.

Cotheal's manuscript translation, dated 1848, was first published in a missionary periodical in 1850.[4] His version is the shortest of the existing translations, and the most restrictive reading of the document. He leaves out portions that were either unclear to him or which he deemed unworthy of translation.[5] Another obstacle to understanding the document is Cotheal's contemptuous comments in the introduction, ungrounded in any solid evidence. The first sentence of his preface to the translation declares, "The narrative is very obscure in language, the writer, as he himself declares, being ignorant of the grammatical forms, confounding together gender, number, person, time."[6] This is an unfortunate example of the translator blaming the text for his own deficiencies. Although succeeding translations were more adequate, Cotheal's negative remarks about Omar's command of Arabic have lingered. He is the translator who first called him Omar ibn Said, although Omar's name in the documents is spelled Sayyid, not Said. Cotheal's version also features avoidable errors, such as failing to decipher Omar's distinctive Arabic spelling of English words like "general" (*dhinal*), which Cotheal thought was the name Daniel, or "governor," which Omar wrote as *kamuna*.[7]

Rev. Isaac Bird of Hartford completed another unpublished translation in 1860, "Translation of the Life of Omar ibn Said."[8] Bird (1793–1876), a Congregational minister, was sent overseas by the American Board of Commissioners for Foreign Missions in 1822, and he lived a missionary life among Muslim populations in Syria, Palestine, Istanbul, and Egypt. His translation draws on Cotheal's version but provided a complete translation of Omar's manuscript. His work is legible and captures the gist of Omar's document, but it fails to correct Cotheal's major errors. Bird's correspondence with Theodore Dwight reveals a surprisingly casual attitude toward preserving the manuscript. "You may have seen a notice of that slave Moro, in the *Observer* some weeks since, written by Dr. Plumer of Philadelphia (or Baltimore). I wrote to Mr. E. D. G. Prime to ask the loan of the manuscript which Dr. P. said he had in his possession written by Moro, to be sent to me or to yourself. Dr. P. replied that the paper was packed away, but as soon as he could come at it he would send it. But it has not come to me, and probably not to you as yet."[9] The carelessness with which these scholars handled the manuscript suggests their disdain for the text.

Since both Cotheal's and Bird's translations took a long time to be published (nearly twenty years in the case of Cotheal and nearly thirty years in the case of Bird), they added no meaningful audience to Omar's "Autobiography." Omar was already more than eighty years old at the publication of the first translation and more than ninety when the second translation appeared. There is no indication that he was ever made aware of them. Those who wrote about Omar during the antebellum era seemed no more aware of the translations, much less the original. We have examined over a dozen articles about Omar published during this period, and none refer to his "Autobiography." Both it and his 1819 request to be returned to Africa were ignored by publications during his lifetime.

The tension between the desire to construct a narrative around Omar and the lack of interest in his writings led to the creation of fictions. Some writers, like George Post, noticed his unease when asked about his previous life: "One peculiarity, however, marked him from the time of his acquaintance with Scripture. It was his dislike to be questioned as to his early history. Mr. Hathaway frequently asked him to give him some account of this matter, whereat he was accustomed at once to take his hat and wish him good morning." Such observations became the basis for the claim that Omar had been enslaved as punishment for an unspecified crime. They could not imagine that he still missed his home and family, unaware that he continued to sign his name with his mother's name attached to it for decades after arriving in exile in America. Omar himself regarded his capture and enslavement as the real crime, a seizure committed "unjustly."

Antebellum newspapers were particularly obsessed with the story of his conversion from Islam to Christianity, which they attributed to the generosity of his enslavers. These reports about Omar were secondhand stories and hearsay collected from acquaintances of the Owens and missionaries who claimed to have met him.

The third English version, "Autobiography of Omar ibn Said, Slave in North Carolina, 1831," was put together by John Franklin Jameson (1859–1937) with the help of Dr. F. M. Moussa, secretary of the Egyptian Legation in Washington.[10] It was published in the *American Historical Review* in 1925. Jameson's account brings in outside sources, adding two novel deficiencies to the interpretation of Omar's seminal document. First, Jameson did not know Arabic, and he admits that his version is based on Isaac Bird's translation and Theodore Dwight's writings on Omar. In other words, it is more an edited version than a new translation. Second, Jameson presents richly fantasized stories about Omar without critically commenting on their merits, thus promoting the fiction of Omar in the new century. Among his sources are fabrications by amateur writers like Louis T. Moore, whose "Legend of Omar" disassociates Omar from both blackness and Africanness, and ludicrously describes him as being "responsible for the introduction of Christianity in the country of Arabia." Jameson's introduction favors these uncorroborated stories and introduces unsubstantiated commentaries on Omar's life into the reading of his text.

More recent developments have done little to improve the readability of Omar's "impossible document." The Arabic text of the "Autobiography" was lost between 1925 and 1996, when it was rediscovered in an attic trunk by descendants of Howland Wood, a noted numismatist who once owned the "Autobiography." Other attempts were made to study the text. The most prominent examples are Allan Austin's *African Muslims in Antebellum America: A Sourcebook*, and Ala Alryyes's edition of *A Muslim American Slave: The Life of Omar ibn Said*. These new readings of Omar seek to place the original texts in the larger context of enslaved African Muslims in America. Austin's book, a significant contribution, documents the lives of seven enslaved American Muslims, including Omar. But as a repository of writings by and about Omar, the chapter devoted to him is marred by unsystematic translations by random speakers of Arabic, with limited to no analytical context provided for their choices. The limitations of Alryyes's translation include recycling previous translations into his text, and postulating personal speculations about Omar without evidence; Omar's quotations of Arabic texts go mostly unrecognized.

The limitations of these new readings of Omar fostered the rebirth of his legend in modern scholarship in ways that reimagined him according to current standards, while erasing the man from his writings. Omar became a legendary personality who meant different things to different writers. He has been depicted by some as arguing a binary opposition between Africa and the West, "a differing image of the 'West' and the 'Christian.' The image is not as that to which the African must aspire and with which he must necessarily affiliate, but rather as 'Other' in the realm of this enslaved Muslim African's world."[11] In contrast, Jonathan Curiel draws on contemporary interreligious dialogue when he sees Omar's manuscript as "the first plea for religious coexistence written by a Muslim in America."[12] This manufacturing of new images of Omar was based not on nineteenth-century racist and orientalist tropes but on a body of scholarship that draws largely on current identity politics to inform its reading of Omar's writings. The unintended consequences of this rebirth are that it again both alienates Omar's "Autobiography" from its intended audience and renders the document unreadable and impossible. Omar's account has remained unread and his life mysterious.

THE LITERARY FORM OF THE TEXT: A NEW INTERPRETATION

Given the reserve and restraint that characterizes Omar's writings, how can one avoid projecting speculations onto them? The methodological discussion that follows is based on the assumption that Omar's writings need to be accurately described and coherently analyzed. We also assume that the composition of these texts is not random, and that their structure is deliberate. That does not mean that we can divine Omar's intention or state of mind from what he wrote. But we can use the basic categories of literary classification to clarify what his writings imply.[13]

This literary analysis was necessary to meet a basic requirement of textual scholarship: establishing a critical edition of the original text. Previous interpreters of Omar's writings have been satisfied with referring to the manuscripts as if their contents were obvious, treating the "Autobiography" as a straightforward account of facts rather than as anything more complicated. But experienced scholars know that handwritten documents often bring ambiguities and problems of decipherment. Our edition of the Arabic texts, published online, employs two levels of description: first, the diplomatic edition, which reproduces the contents of the manuscript as precisely as possible, including apparent errors and idiosyncratic expressions; and second, the standardized edition, which presents the corrected text in accordance with scholarly norms. In the online publication, the diplomatic version is presented in footnotes to the standardized version. This makes clear just how we have read the text and restored it for optimum readability.

One must acknowledge the technical challenges faced by readers of Omar's Arabic documents, especially their nonstandard legibility, which at times is enhanced by the Maghribi style of writing Arabic. Omar admits in the opening statements of his "Autobiography" his difficulty in retaining his Arabic literacy. His apology, directed at his "brothers" from his years in a theological academy, should not be taken literally, however. Some commentators have concluded that his Arabic is so bad as to be unreadable, rejecting his writings as not worth studying. This is a mistake. Omar was not a scholar of the first rank, in the sense of being able to compose literary Arabic at a high level, but his quotations from a wide range of theological and mystical texts reveal that he had achieved a high level of competence through learning and memorization of important Islamic writings. In this respect, his inexact reproduction of Arabic is a testimony to the efficacy of the Islamicate educational system. He demonstrates this mastery of Arabic texts immediately after apologizing for forgetting his Arabic, making clear that his apology was a formal gesture of humility. In practice, the reading problems include several issues. Omar frequently refers to himself in the third person, but this does not mean that he has forgotten basic grammar (he uses first-person constructions roughly 20 percent of the time). There are parallels in the writings of other enslaved Muslims, like Shaykh Sana See in Panama, who also refers to himself in the third person, suggesting both the resonance of Senegambian wisdom traditions that are often presented in a third-person format and a Sufi rhetoric of self-deprecation. In our translation, we have put Omar's self-description into the first person for clarity. Other inconsistencies in his writing include phonetic shifts, where he switches from the "intensive" Arabic consonants to sounds more familiar in his native language. This kind of imprecise spelling, and the inexact quotation of literary texts, is characteristic of cultures with a high degree of orality. That is not a good reason to dismiss them as unreadable. "A literate culture," as Walter J. Ong points out, "tends to overrate verbatim repetition or record."[14]

In editing the texts, which are all fully translated in this book (see the List of Translated Documents in the Table of Contents), we began by transcribing all eighteen surviving documents, making systematic comparisons in order to determine patterns and structures. The most obvious of these patterns is repetition of significant phrases, which can be classified as regular formulas.[15] Some of the formulas used by Omar are widely used in Arabic texts as markers of Islamic religious content. "In the name of God, the Merciful, the Compassionate," which we call the Qur'anic Invocation, appears ten times in Omar's writings (Documents 3, 4 [twice], 6 [twice], 7, 12, 13, 14, 18). An expression found at the beginning of almost every chapter of the Qur'an, it also serves as a ritual phrase used by Muslims at the beginning of any significant activity. It is regularly accompanied by the Prophetic Blessing, "May God bless our Master Muhammad," which occurs nine times in Omar's texts (Documents 3, 4, 6, 7, 12, 13, 14, 16, 18).

Invocation or calling upon God also occurs in Omar's writings in the form of quotations of poetry with theological content. Quotations from the Qur'an are frequent, and there are also some sayings of the Prophet Muhammad. Separation markers used to indicate verses of poetry alerted us to the need to track down the sources of quotations.

Two other formulas are frequently used by Omar, which may be his own expressions. One is the Testing formula, found six times (Documents 1, 2, 4, 5, 6, 14): "God created humanity in order to worship him, so that he could test their words and their deeds." The other is the Good formula, occurring in ten places (Documents 1 [three times], 5, 6, 11 [three times], 13, 16): "The good is with God, and belongs to no other." These formulas evidently illustrate Omar's fundamental religious orientation, the belief that God controls all things and is essentially good.

Another important formal gesture is the salutation or direct address to the intended recipient of the document. Sometimes this is done by name, as in several writings addressed to the Owen brothers or others in their circle. Less directly, it is possible to extrapolate an intended audience by clarifying the vocabulary and form of a particular text, and the background that would be needed to understand it. The counterpoint to the salutation is the signature, whether included briefly or more fully. A simple "From Omar" serves as a beginning twice (Documents 4, 18) and once as an ending (Document 6). One text (Document 8) likewise declares, "My name is Omar," while six others add his father's name: "My name is Omar son of Said [*sayyid*]" (Documents 3, 4, 7, 11, 12, 18). In five places (Documents 3, 7, 11, 12, 18), Omar includes the phrase, "but from my mother's side, [she is] Umm Hani Yarmak—may God refresh her grave," an uncommon public tribute to a female family member in formal Arabic. And in three places (Documents 11 [twice], 17), Omar expands his genealogy by a generation: "My name is Omar son of Said son of Adam."

Beyond these basic elements easily recognized as part of a letter, other literary forms or genres can be clearly discerned in Omar's writings, as we shall demonstrate in chapter 3. An unusually prominent feature in these texts is the sermon, presented in terms of both the threat of punishment for those who fail to repent and the promise of reward and salvation for those who obey God. Consolation, addressed to figures like the Prophet Muhammad, is also to be found (Document 15). It should be added that Omar left clear markings of the beginning and end of many documents. Invocations signal the beginning of many documents, while the end is twice indicated by the Arabic phrase meaning "it has ended" (Documents 8, 18), once enhanced by the English word "end" written in Arabic script (Document 18).

The special properties of certain Qur'anic verses for protection and healing mean that they are frequently included as blessings rather than for argumentative content. The use of protective talismans in Omar's writings is an extension of the blessing function of the sacred text (Documents 1, 2, 5, 6, 9, 12, discussed in chapter 3). The preface of the "Autobiography" belongs to this category of blessings: it is Qur'an 67:1–30, the Chapter of Sovereignty or Dominion (the Surat al-Mulk). Placing such a prominent and extensive quotation at the beginning of an enslaved person's autobiography, without an explicit commentary justifying its relevance, has struck some readers as both powerful and alarming. Some have wondered about the reason for its elusive presence: Is Omar trying to deliver a secret message to his audience? Or is this just another manifestation of indifference to the task of writing?

What we know for sure from Muslim traditional practices is that this chapter is associated with healing powers as well as benefits and virtues, and that the literate Omar must have memorized it, as do many learned people of Islam. This chapter is also called the defender of God-fearing people on the Day of Judgment; it also delivers God-fearing people from hellfire. In a hadith report, Ibn ʿAbbās, a nephew and companion of the Prophet of Islam, reports that

> one of the companions of the Prophet pitched a tent on a grave without knowing that it was a grave. Suddenly he heard a person from the grave reciting Surat al-Mulk till he completed it. So, he went to the Prophet and said: "O Messenger of God, I pitched my tent on a grave without realizing that it was a grave. Then suddenly I heard a person from the grave reciting Surat al-Mulk till he completed it." The Messenger of God said: "It is the defender; it is the deliverer—it delivers from the punishment of the grave" (al-Tirmidhī, Book 45, Hadith 3133).

It is narrated that the Prophet of Islam read it every night before going to bed. Islamic tradition includes many descriptions of its benefits.

While some scholars have seen Omar's quotation of sura 67 as an implicit argument against the institution of slavery, we find it more persuasive that it was included as a blessing, a gesture for which there is significant evidence in Muslim tradition.[16] We have not seen any examples of sura 67 being used as a blanket argument against slavery. In Islamic legal doctrine, the enslavement of Muslims was considered repugnant, though it did occur in practice, but no such bar was agreed to the enslavement of unbelievers. Ironically, knowledge of the Qur'an and Islamic texts could have been instrumental in liberating Omar from slavery, had he remained in Africa.[17] Other literate Muslims who were enslaved in Africa wrote letters appealing to Islamic principles to improve their circumstances, but they did not seem to suggest that slavery could be abolished.[18] No evidence suggests that this Qur'anic text inspired Omar to become an abolitionist, while there is a widespread precedent for his use of it as a blessing.

The last formal element that claims our attention is an unusual one, Omar's transcription of English words and names in Arabic script; this may be considered an 'ajamized version of English. This is not to be confused with transliteration, for all accounts concur that Omar could not read English at all. So instead of converting words from Roman script into Arabic script, he did his best to write down what he heard, in some cases giving a definite impression that he was hearing a southern accent. This phenomenon of using Arabic letters to record English was observed by William Brown Hodgson in a transcription of parts of the English New Testament into Arabic characters. Hodgson regarded that "Negro patois" as a unique occurrence, not realizing that Omar was doing something similar, despite the fact that they exchanged correspondence in Arabic. We have compiled a list of all the recognizable 'ajamized English words and names used by Omar in a separate appendix, which is supplemented by the list of his transcriptions of the titles of biblical books, discussed in chapter 4. While some of his transcriptions of English may be surprising, they evidently reflect the phonetic environment of the languages that he grew up speaking.

CONFLICTING NARRATIVES

Returning to the "Autobiography," several fundamental questions still need to be asked regarding its form and structure. First of all, can this be regarded as an autobiography in the ordinary sense of the word? It is certainly true to say that it contains narrative material in the first person, in which the author describes events that took place during his lifetime. Yet Omar more frequently uses the third person to describe himself and his actions.

Why does Omar repeat in his opening sections, "I cannot write my life"? There are at least two possible explanations. The first is the lack of an audience for his Arabic writings. In that sense, the attempt to write his life would be fruitless, since no one was able to understand what he said. The second is his writing from slavery, as one commanded to write by others, which is not authorship in the ordinary sense of the term. The result of these conditions is that the reports about Omar in English-language newspapers had taken over the telling of Omar's story, in a fictional mode that owed nothing to his Arabic autobiography. He had lost control over his life, and agency in telling his life story. This is how we understand this peculiar feature of the "Autobiography," each of whose sections has been revised. By presenting two different accounts of each of these parts of his life, Omar is saying in effect that neither of them can be adequate, and the task he has been set to do is impossible.

Altogether, the main text is complex, containing five sections, each of which is presented once, then presented a second time in revised form (and a third time in the case of section C). We have accordingly grouped the text into sections as follows: (A) Salutation and apology; (B) Narrative of enslavement; (C) Address to the Americans; (D) Reading the Gospel and Qur'an; and (E) "Conversion." Adding the numbers 1, 2, or 3 with different indentations to designate the different versions produces the following outline:

Outline of Document 4

[PREFACE. QUR'AN 67:1–30]

A.1. Salutation and apology

   A.2. Salutation and apology, revised

B.1. Narrative of enslavement

C.1. Address to the Americans

D.1. Reading the Gospel

E.1. "Conversion"

   C.2. Address to the Americans, revised

   C.3. Address to the Americans, second revision

   D.2. Reading the Qur'an and the Gospel, revised

   E.2. "Conversion," revised

   B.2. Narrative of enslavement, revised

The sequence of the different sections appears at first glance inconsistent. The first version of section A (A.1) is immediately followed by its revision (A.2), and then come the four other first drafts (B.1, C.1, D.1, E.1). At that point the revisions of the last three sections (C.2, C.3, D.2, E.2) are introduced, with the revised B.2 conspicuously out of sequence as the concluding section.

The shift of B.2, the enslavement narrative, to the final position suggests that the enslavement narrative has replaced conversion to Christianity as the dominant theme of the "Autobiography." Omar knew that as far as white enslavers were concerned, the culmination of his story was his conversion to Christianity, a fantasy, as we argue in greater detail in chapter 3, but to them a proof of the benevolence of slavery. Omar's subtle rearrangement of his text was a quiet defiance of the tale told about him. We will defer our full consideration of the debate over Omar's conversion to chapter 4, but for the moment let us observe that the structure of the "Autobiography" displaces the conversion narrative from his life story by emphasizing his enslavement as the defining feature of his life in America.

AUDIENCES ADDRESSED AND IMPLIED

The two sections on salutation and apology at the beginning of the text offer a mesmerizing rhetorical sleight of hand, first offering an apology for bad Arabic and fading memory, and then undercutting the apology with an effortless quotation of a classical text on Islamic theology. This gesture is worth exploring because previous commentators failed to recognize the quotation; they took literally Omar's apology as a sign that he had forgotten his Arabic learning. They did not realize that for decades he continued to quote from memory the theological and mystical writings he studied in Futa and Bundu.

One must remember that where Omar came from, apologizing is a moral virtue and an expected part of the pedagogy of effective speech. As we noted in chapter 1, Omar would have been familiar with the advice that the early Sufi Abū Madyan al-Andalusī (d. 1198) gave to his disciples:

> Please, find flaws only in yourself; and know that
> your flaws have been apparent, even if they are concealed,
> And always lower yourself and ask for forgiveness for no reason,
> and stand up with honesty when apologizing.

Omar's apology was not a factual admission but a performance of ethical ideals aimed at a distant audience of his "brothers" from the academy. Three audiences are directly addressed in the "Autobiography" with a formal gesture, using the Arabic equivalent of "O" to signal the message's addressee. The first two of these apostrophes occur in Omar's mea culpa, where he faults himself and apologizes to someone he calls Shaykh Hunter. Omar writes, "O Shaykh Hunter: I cannot

write my life, I forget too much about my language and the Arabic language."
He then continues, "O my brothers, do not blame me." The irony is that Omar
is trying to simultaneously address two different audiences: Shaykh Hunter and
his "brothers." All we know of Mr. Hunter is that Omar respected him enough
to bestow him with the title of shaykh, a sign of respect and veneration. It can
also be assumed that this was a white associate of the Owens, possibly a Christian minister such as Rev. James Hunter (d. 1831), a Methodist who was active
in North Carolina, or Rev. Eli Hunter, who was associated with the American
Colonization Society (ACS).

But that opening address quickly turned into an apology directed to his
"brothers," his colleagues in Bundu and Futa with whom he learned and studied
the Qur'an and Islamic sciences. Only those fellow students could have recognized the quotations from Islamic texts that Omar inserted into the "Autobiography." "Brothers" is a title given to seminary colleagues to indicate their status as
an intellectual class of spiritual equals. Omar elaborates further in his address
to the two audiences in the revised salutation and apology (A.2), where he com-
plains, "From Omar to Shaykh Hunter: you have asked me to write my life. I
cannot write my life, I forget too much about my language along with the Arabic
language. I read now little grammar and little language. O my brothers, I beg
you in the name of God, do not blame me, for my eyes are weak and so is my
body." Again, Omar is reverting to Abū Madyan al-Andalusī's summary of Sufi
ethics for the disciple: "Please, find flaws only in yourself." He thus blames his
inability to write on his declining health.

This apology for bad Arabic is canceled out by Omar's deployment of statements on Islamic theology at key points of the "Autobiography." Immediately
after his initial apology (A.1), Omar quotes a masterwork of Islamic law, the
Summary of Khalīl, the influential Egyptian jurist. This text is a popular work
of Mālikī law, so fundamental in North and West Africa that the French government published the first printed edition of the text in Paris in 1855. From
the opening doctrinal section Omar quotes a line on God's beneficence: "Praise
God with much praise. He bestows bounties that overflow" (to which he adds
a clause, "with the good").[19] Then, in the two sections (D.1, D.2) where he
describes how the Owens would have him read the Gospel, Omar introduces a
theological quotation to describe what he read about in the Gospel: "Our Creator, and our master, the corrector of our conditions, both now and at the end,
as a gift rather than as a constraint to his power." While the author of this phrase
has not been identified, its vocabulary is commonly found in Islamic theological texts.[20] Omar then quotes the saying of Khalīl a second time, in the revised

version of Reading the Gospel (D.2), as an additional confirmation of Islamic theology. He also inscribed this saying as a marginal note in the endpapers of his Arabic Bible. From these previously undetected quotations, we may draw two conclusions: first, Omar was signaling to his "brothers" that he was still in command of his repertoire of Islamic texts, which he continued to include in his writings for years; and second, his understanding of Christian texts was articulated in terms of the Islamic theology that he studied for twenty-five years—in other words, the notion that he had become a Christian and rejected Islam was simply wrong.

At this point a question may arise, since upon examination it now appears that, immediately after the quotation from Khalīl, Omar has quoted a verse from the New Testament (John 1:17), using exactly the same words as in the 1811 Arabic Bible owned by Omar, containing the testimony of John the Baptist recognizing Jesus as Messiah. Could this be a sign of a Christian conviction? Omar's quotation of this biblical verse is at first sight surprising, and it has not been noticed in previous scholarship. It seems to be the only case in his writings where he uses a biblical verse as part of an argument, rather than as a performance designed to reassure a Christian audience with a familiar text. It is not obvious, however, that Omar is interpreting this verse with the customary Christian claim that the law of Moses—and by implication the law of Muhammad—is superseded by the grace of Christ. (Although there is no conjunction between the two clauses in the Greek text, the King James Version presents them in opposition by inserting the word "but": "For the law was given by Moses, *but* grace and truth came by Jesus Christ.") How might Omar have interpreted this verse from an Islamic perspective?

The presence in the Arabic Bible of key words also found in Islamic texts would furnish a Muslim scholar with an obvious approach. One of these key terms is "bounty" or "benefaction" (*niʿma*, plural *niʿam*, also translated as "blessing, boon, favor"). It provides a verbal connection between this New Testament verse and the immediately preceding quotation from the *Summary* of Khalīl, which speaks of the "bounties" or (*niʿam*) that God distributes to creation. As mentioned above, Omar has twice used this teaching from Islamic theology in his "Autobiography" as a way of interpreting the New Testament, and it may be added that he wrote out the first words of Khalīl's dictum in the endpapers of his Arabic Bible, literally inscribing it upon the Christian scripture. Now, in the Arabic version of John 1:17, the singular term *niʿma* renders the Greek word *charis*, usually translated into English as "grace." It is unlikely that Omar would have understood this term in its Christian sense as a power uniquely delegated by God to Jesus, since he deploys Khalīl's reference to God's "bounties" as an unrestricted aspect of divine benevolence. Therefore we interpret John 1:17 in Omar's text not as an assertion of the superiority of Jesus to Moses but as praise of both prophets.

Another key term connecting the Arabic Bible to Islamic texts is "law" (Arabic *sharʿ*, the root form of *sharīʿa*). For a scholar trained in an Islamic academy, this is a term of great importance. It has none of the negative associations of "law" in Christian polemics against Judaism, so the two clauses would not be opposed. Moreover, for Muslims, the law is in harmony with the "truth" that the biblical verse links to Jesus. Indeed, the term "truth" (*al-ḥaqq*) has specific associations with the Qurʾanic doctrine that Jesus is not divine. Omar may have been thinking of Qurʾan 4:171, "Do not speak anything but truth to God; Jesus son of Mary is only the messenger of God."

For these reasons, we translate the Arabic term *niʿma* as "bounty," reflecting the assumptions of Islamic theology, since there is no evidence to support the idea that Omar ever adopted the Christian teaching that grace was exclusively available through Jesus. His invocation of blessings on the Prophet Muhammad in his quotation of Romans 10:9 in Document 14 confirms that point. In other words, Omar was happy to praise Jesus (and other prophets), but this did not alter his reverence for the Prophet Muhammad. Nevertheless, this quotation provides an interesting example of Omar's reflection on a biblical text from an Islamic perspective.

Omar's lack of a real audience is further evidenced in his Address to the Americans (C.1), where the third audience category—the people of North Carolina, South Carolina, and the United States—has been added. The invocation of the American people creates a moment of suspense each time, as the reader prepares for an important announcement. But as Omar contemplates his enslavement, he hesitates, following this address with praise of the Owens family: "O people of North Carolina, O people of South Carolina, O people of America, all of you! Have you among you any two good men such as Jim Owen and John Owen? These are good men. Whatever they eat they give to me to eat; and whatever they wear they give me to wear." The only subject that he has in common with the people of America is the institution of slavery, so to them he can only speak of his enslavers with the praise expected of a grateful slave, paying particular attention to their children. Compare this address with the last revision of this passage (C.3), featuring the extraordinary four repetitions of a key phrase: "Is there not among you, is there not among you, is there not among you, is there not among you a lineage like this, who fears God so much?"

In both cases hesitancy is followed with praise of the Owens. But in Arabic literature, the expression "is there not among you," is normally followed by blame, not praise. It echoes similar Qur'anic expressions in form and meaning, such as Qur'an 11:78, which reads, "Now fear God, and cover me not with shame about my guests! Is there not among you a single right-minded man?" Omar's remark, considered in this light, takes on an ironic tone that makes it faint praise indeed.

Omar was fully aware of how his enslavement limited his speech. This awareness is most evident in the way he searches for and addresses his audience. None of the three audiences formally addressed in the "Autobiography"—"O Shaykh Hunter," "O my brothers," "O people of America"—can read or understand his writings. Shaykh Hunter cannot understand him, his brothers are not there to heed his call, and the people of America are not there to listen to him or to understand his speech. Thus the enslaved Omar cannot speak, he cannot be heard, because no one can understand him. Speaking to an absent audience is no speech at all.

Slavery, the Unspoken Context

SLAVERY IN NORTH CAROLINA

A vast amount of scholarship is devoted to the history of slavery in the United States, far more than we can address in this study. But it is essential to bring up a few relevant aspects of slavery in North Carolina in order to understand the situation of Omar ibn Said. North Carolina slave society has often been traced back to two groups of white European settlers of the colony, euphemistically known as the "yeoman farmers" and the "gentry," who represented two competing sectors.[21] White yeoman farmers were portrayed as seeking independence from hierarchy, opportunity based on mobility, and democratic institutions. The gentry were the slave-owning large landholders; they believed in a hierarchical form of representative government and sought to use key institutions of society to promote their commercial interests. Despite this claimed distinction, both groups benefited from land grants from the British Crown, which were designed to recruit settlers to farm the land, and they colluded to eliminate the indigenous population physically from areas of European settlement. Slavery actually encouraged "the creation of a new white smallholding class" by reducing tensions between large landholders and white farmers.[22] It was in parallel with those developments that Blacks came to form a third social category in the colony; they consisted of both free people and slaves. While North Carolina had fewer large plantations and more small farmers than the adjoining states of South Carolina and Virginia, slavery had been central to its economic structure since the earliest phase of colonial rule.

Following the war of independence from Britain, the ranks of the gentry expanded to include ambitious middle-class families. In North Carolina, the new gentry were wealthy planters who assessed a family's prestige in terms of the number of slaves and acres owned. Many members of the new gentry profited from their military or political roles in the Revolutionary War to get land in the newly independent colonies, for farms that required intensive slave labor, which was increasingly required for North Carolina's crops of cotton, tobacco, and rice.[23] From 1790 to 1860, the enslaved increased from one-quarter to one-third of the state's total population. The significant presence of Blacks was a natural development of the interstate slave trades that had persisted since Omar's landing in Charleston in 1807, the last year of the legal international slave trade.

Slaves were concentrated in northern and southern counties bordering Virginia and South Carolina. Many were isolated on remote plantations, or on small farms with fewer slaves. Harsh working conditions existed across the state, including in the Roanoke River Valley and near the Virginia border, where wealthy tobacco and cotton plantations were concentrated. There were also significant enslaved populations in the central eastern counties as well as on cotton and turpentine plantations along the Cape Fear River. This latter district had much in common with South Carolina rice plantations or sugar plantations in Jamaica. It was marked mostly by absentee owners, brutal discipline, and a society in which the vast majority of the population was Black.[24] A portion of the free Blacks were drivers, house servants, cooks, and seamstresses.

JAMES AND JOHN OWEN AS ENSLAVERS

The Owens were among the new gentry who began accumulating land in the colonial era, later expanding their holdings after supporting the Revolutionary War (see fig. 1.1). They became one of the leading families of planter aristocrats in antebellum North Carolina. Their family documents include a 1774 land grant for 640 acres from King George III to Thomas Owen, just before the end of British rule in the United States.[25] During the Revolution and afterward, Thomas Owen (1735–1806) acquired over 3,000 acres in Bladen County.[26] Thomas Owen died in 1806, leaving his wealth to his wife and their three children: James, John, and Mary. This enabled his children to join the exclusive small group of the genteel class, who controlled the plantation economy and the state's politics.

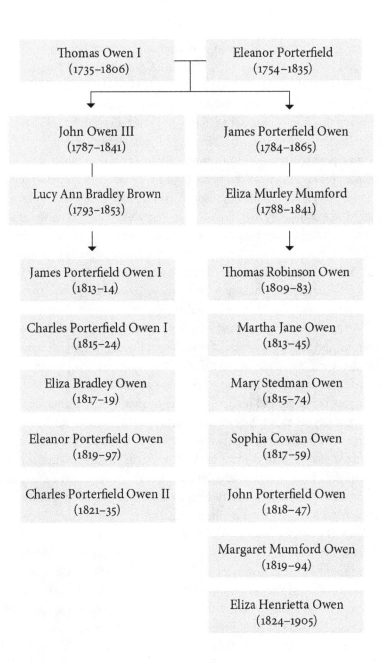

FIGURE 1.1.
The families of John and James Owen.

James ("Jim") Owen (1784–1865) took charge of Milton Plantation in Bladen County, and he had an active political career. A member of the House of Commons (1808–11) and later a US congressman (1817–18), he also was an adjutant general in the state militia during the War of 1812, retaining the title of general for the rest of his life. He was active in the Presbyterian churches of Fayetteville and Wilmington, and was an officer in the American Bible Society.[27]

Jim was praised in antebellum newspapers as "a gentleman well known throughout this commonwealth for his public services, and always known as a man of generous and humane impulses."[28] Nevertheless, he was a planter, and acquiring and expanding plantations and slaveholding was central to his activities. The Owen family, accompanied by Omar, attended the First Presbyterian Church of Fayetteville every week. Southern newspapers often mentioned a devoted Omar who only missed the house of God a few Sabbaths of the year.[29]

Jim and his household, including Omar, moved to Wilmington in 1837, where they transferred their church membership to the Presbyterian Church of Wilmington. Jim became a leading investor in the industries of the region, the port of Wilmington, and the development of what was at the time one of the longest railroads in the world, from Weldon to Wilmington.[30] The changing nature of North Carolina politics and the increasing polarization over slavery in the state thwarted Jim's business ventures, and his attempt to expand with new plantations in Alabama did not pay off either. Moving his plantations to Alabama might have been part of the exodus of white farmers and planters to Georgia, Alabama, and Mississippi in the 1830s due to the fear of slave revolts in North Carolina, the recent forced removal of the Native population, and the richer soils of the Deep South. During the Civil War, the Owens returned with Omar to Bladen County, where they settled on the plantation of Jim's deceased younger brother John. When Omar died at the age of ninety-three, he was buried in the family's graveyard.

John Owen (1787–1841) was a cornerstone of the family's relationship to Omar. He spent a year as a student at the University of North Carolina in 1804 and was a member of the university's oldest student organization, the Dialectic Society. John's university education was cut short when students rebelled against a rigid behavior code imposed by university administrators after a number of incidents of misbehavior. In what came to be known as "the secession of 1805," John Owen was one of forty-five students (a majority of the student body at that time) who left the university rather than submit to an oath of obedience and collaboration with informers.[31] This incident did not end his connection with the university, however, since he later served on the board of trustees from 1820 until his death in 1841. His political career included serving in the North

Carolina House of Commons (1812–13) and state senate (1819, 1827); he was also elected governor (1828–30). He died in 1841 and was buried in Pittsboro, leaving his estate, Owen Hill, to his older brother Jim.[32]

Despite his interest in Omar, John Owen did not sympathize with abolitionists. During his term as a governor, new laws were passed curtailing the well-being of both slaves and free Blacks in North Carolina. Louis Sheridan (d. 1844), a free Black, was considered once the richest person in Bladen County, and one of the richest people in North Carolina. The Owen administration benefited from this nationally respected "merchant entitled to unlimited credit," as Governor Owen once described Sheridan, even as he summoned his financial dealing to support the state.[33] Sheridan was then run out of the state under these new anti-Black laws and forced to emigrate to Liberia under the tutelage of the American Colonization Society. John's paternalistic relationship with Omar mirrors his general tendency to paternalize Black intellectuals as long as they served his political interest, but there is no evidence that he ever came close to undercutting the interests of the slaveholding class.

By all accounts, Jim was a typical enslaver with no recorded sympathy for manumission or abolition; he even acquired a second plantation in Alabama. Although he did not attend the University of North Carolina, the family association with UNC would continue in the next generation; like their uncle John, both Jim's sons, Thomas Robinson Owen and John Porterfield Owen, were students there and, like John, members (in 1828 and 1836) of the Dialectic Society.[34] Jim and John were both among the top 5 percent of slaveholders in North Carolina in the 1830s. At this time, almost 95 percent of North Carolina slaveholding families owned fewer than twenty slaves and 85 percent of them owned fewer than ten slaves.[35] Later on in North Carolina, "a little more than 2 per cent owned more than fifty slaves in 1860 and 70.8 per cent owned less than ten."[36] North Carolina had fewer slaves per family than other states, since "there were 52 slaves in North Carolina to every 100 whites, 53 in Virginia, 140 in South Carolina, 91 in Georgia, 105 in Mississippi."[37] As demonstrated in table 1.1, based on antebellum census data, the Owens were in the top echelon of the slaveholder class throughout that period.

It is noteworthy that the initial count of the enslaved was limited to Bladen County, hitting a peak when John Owen was in Raleigh as governor (and identified as "His Excellency" in the census). John's widow Lucy assumed ownership in Wilmington after his death in 1841, as did James's daughter Eleanor before 1860.

TABLE 1.1. Total number of people enslaved by the Owen family

NAME OF ENSLAVER	1810	1820	1830	1840	1850	1860
James Owen	49	28	16	9		
John Owen		43	78	58		
Lucy Ann Owen					54	
Mrs. [Lucy Ann] Owen, Wilmington					7	
Eleanor Porterfield Owen						43

Source: US Census.

BLACK VOICES FOR FREEDOM

The Owens were not in the least interested in supporting efforts to free the enslaved. John's patronizing attitude toward enslaved Africans was on display in the case of George Moses Horton. In 1829, while John was governor, Horton became North Carolina's first published Black poet with the printing of his collection *The Hope of Liberty*. Horton inspired his readers to think about freedom for people like him who were in bondage. His poem "On Liberty and Slavery" declared,

> Alas! and am I born for this,
> To wear this slavish chain?
> Deprived of all created bliss,
> Through hardship, toil and pain!
>
> How long have I in bondage lain,
> And languished to be free!
> Alas! and must I still complain—
> Deprived of liberty.
>
> Oh, Heaven! and is there no relief
> This side the silent grave—
> To soothe the pain—to quell the grief
> And anguish of a slave?[38]

Horton hoped that money from the sale of his book might be sufficient to purchase his freedom. He was disappointed when his enslaver dismissed the prospect. Prior to publication, Horton's poems appeared in proabolitionist journals in New York, and in a Massachusetts newspaper, the *Lancaster Gazette*, as well as in North Carolina's *Raleigh Register*. His supporters raised funds to buy his liberty. Governor Owen joined the petition and fundraising drive, promising to add 100 dollars to the originally proposed money if the poet's enslaver was willing to accept the offer. In an address in 1828, Horton thanked Governor Owen among other dignitaries for supporting the campaign to bring about his emancipation. Many enslavers and white southerners were sympathetic to the idea of freeing enslaved Blacks, like Horton, as long as they would be sent to Liberia. This was a popular move, since it would rid the state of free Blacks. However, when the poet's enslaver refused to bargain on his freedom, Governor Owen gave up and moved on. John seems to have been only interested in associations that were useful in advancing his political ambitions, and advocating for the freedom of bondspeople was not one of them.

It is ironic that both John Owen and George Moses Horton were at the same time connected to the University of North Carolina at Chapel Hill, the first public university in the United States. While John had attended the university without completing his degree and later served as a trustee, Horton, around 1817, started commuting every Saturday afternoon and all day Sunday from his plantation in Chatham County to Chapel Hill, where "he sold fruits and poems."[39] At UNC, Horton worked as "a jack-of-all-trades for the white male students and faculty of the university, selling fruit, running errands, giving speeches on demand, and composing love poems made-to-order for students."[40] Following the failed attempt to purchase his liberty, Horton used the money he earned from his activities at UNC to hire his time from his enslaver, rather than working on his plantation. Horton's liberty would not be secured until the Civil War. When the Union army reached the Tar Heel State in 1865, the sixty-eight-year-old Horton attached himself to one of the Union army's volunteer cavalry units to reach freedom.

Perhaps John's reaction to the rising abolitionist tide during his governorship, by supporting increasingly restrictive slave laws, sheds light on how we should assess his paternalizing relationship with Omar. If John truly sympathized with Omar's plight, as many antebellum publications claimed, there were many occasions during John's political journey when he could have used his influence to address the concerns of the state's enslaved people. He witnessed the rise of the Black intellectual and abolitionist movement in the 1830s. The completion of

Omar's "Autobiography" in 1831 came not long after the publication of George Moses Horton's *Hope of Liberty*. The same year also witnessed the uprising of enslaved Blacks seeking freedom in Southampton County, Virginia, which borders North Carolina. They were led by the preacher Nat Turner. During this time, and under the tenure of Governor Owen, another Black intellectual, David Walker, was projecting his antislavery activism into Wilmington, North Carolina. Governor Owen, then nearing the end of his second term, reacted by pushing for more violent and restrictive laws against the Black community.

David Walker (d. 1830) was born in Wilmington, North Carolina, but later moved to Boston as a businessman. In 1829, he published a pamphlet, *Walker's Appeal in Four Articles, to the Coloured Citizens of the World*, that particularly addressed Blacks in American slave society.[41] Walker advances well-articulated abolitionist ideas grounded in religion and logic, noting,

> My beloved brethren: — The Indians of North and of South America — the Greeks — the Irish, subjected under the king of Great Britain — the Jews, that ancient people of the Lord — the inhabitants of the islands of the sea — in fine, all the inhabitants of the earth, (except however, the sons of Africa) are called men, and of course are, and ought to be free. But we, (coloured people) and our children are brutes!! and of course are, and ought to be SLAVES to the American people and their children forever!! to dig their mines and work their farms; and thus go on enriching them, from one generation to another with our blood and our tears!!!![42]

Walker appealed to "the American people themselves," and especially to the white Christians of America and to enslaved Blacks to dismantle the institution of slavery. To the latter group he said, "At the close of the first Revolution . . . there were but thirteen States in the Union, now there are twenty-four, most of which are slave-holding States." Walker's comparison between Great Britain's occupation of the colonies, which justified the American Revolution, and the institution of slavery underscored the duty to revolt among enslaved Blacks. He rejected the American Colonization Society's promotion of repatriating Blacks to Africa, noting that Blacks belong more to America than do whites, because Blacks have enriched this country "with our blood and tears." He thus asked the enslaved Blacks, "Had you rather not be killed . . . than to be a slave to a tyrant, who takes the life of your mother, wife, and dear little babies?"

As copies of the *Appeal* were smuggled into Wilmington and then spread to other cities of the state, alarm, rumors, and panic spread among the slaveholders, who in 1830 petitioned Governor Owen for protection. Owen swiftly responded by enabling the North Carolina legislature's meeting in November 1830 to enact the "most repressive measures ever passed in North Carolina to control slaves and free blacks."[43] Draconian penalties were adopted to punish anyone who taught slaves to read or write; laws were enacted and enforced to punish the sharing of abolitionist publications. By 1835, new laws that prevented free Blacks from preaching in public, attending school, or voting were adopted in the state.

Perhaps, in a more analytical reading, John Owen embodies the contradictions of the "peculiar" institution of slavery. His actions as Omar's patron clearly contradicted his actions as a leader of the state. He reminds us of Louis Rubin's remark on the life of South Carolina's notorious enslaver James Henry Hammond, in which "almost every cliché and generalization about the nineteenth-century South received implicit contradiction."[44] John wanted Omar to write about his life so he could parade the slave's cultural artifacts proudly among his associates; at the same time, as governor, he pushed for laws criminalizing teaching enslaved people how to read or write. John's circle forced Omar to convert to Christianity in outward appearance while also urging North Carolina legislators to prohibit free Blacks from preaching the Gospel in public. John's relatively short life, a towering babel of misdeeds and contradictions, reveals a greedy and reckless persona, unconcerned with the suffering of the enslaved.

THE OWENS AS ENSLAVERS

A hidden pillar of paternalism in slavery was the enforcement of a regime of only acknowledging Black mothers, denying them fathers. This established an environment of fear, upholding the slaveholder as a father figure among the enslaved. In his autobiography as a North Carolinian, and a former slave affiliated with UNC, Sam Morphis described the difference between slavery and freedom in just these terms: "Another difference forced itself upon me. The white boys had a father and a mother; I had a mother only. This seemed to me a very strange fact—and observing it made stronger the feeling that I was not like others. My life seemed limited in whatever direction I looked."[45] Slaveholders were adamant on retaining their power over their enslaved Blacks by discouraging marriage and dismissing the existence of fatherhood within the slave system.

An extensive literature describes how many slaveholders were vested in maximizing profit-making opportunities presented by enslaved mothers through encouraging reproduction and childbearing.[46] In the decades following the banning of the international slave trade in 1808, the domestic trade in enslaved people gained ground. North Carolina depended mostly on slaves imported from Virginia and South Carolina as well as on systematically forcing enslaved women to bear more children. This was done in many ways, ranging from violence and the threat to separate an enslaved family unit, to favoring women who produced a large number of children.[47] Addressing the fact that enslaved Blacks managed to preserve marriage among themselves despite all the difficulties in North Carolina, John Chapman notes that some enslavers may have discouraged marriage of their female slaves, probably to increase their own wealth; this was a strategy of discouraging family ties that might have interfered with women breeding.[48] Examples of extensive sexual exploitation of enslaved women by powerful landowners have been fully documented in recent reports prepared in petitions to remove those men's names from buildings at the University of North Carolina at Chapel Hill.[49]

John's personal papers illustrate his paternalism in dealing with people in bondage. An anonymous document found in his papers lists the first names of female slaves and their children and dates of birth, focusing on fourteen women who bore a total of thirty-eight children from 1826 to 1837. Seven women each had only one child during that time: Betsy, Charlotte, Clarissa, Mary, Nancy (M), and Nancy (T). Seven others bore multiple children: Chloe (six children), Pender (six), Nancy (four), Celia (four), Maria (two), Betty (six), and Sabina (two). The document also names four children born from 1806 to 1816, and ten other children presumably born after 1837; the names of these children's mothers are not recorded. In a half-dozen cases, the name of a mother, her child, and the birthdate are crossed out, with no explanation—perhaps to mark a sale. The last page adds the names of four more women who bore five children between 1854 and 1856.[50] The document is silent on the question of paternity. We do not know how many children had Black fathers and how many were fathered by a white slaveholder, through rape or coercion.

Although John is often presented as a politician, and his brother as a planter, the evidence shows that John kept many enslaved Blacks in bondage. The Owen folders at UNC contain documents about John's purchases of "Negroes," with some recurring names of family friends. A bill of sale from Bladen County records one transaction thus: "I, Hinton James, for and in consideration of the sum of four hundred dollars to me in hand paid by John Owen, have here by deed to him the said John a certain Negro man slave named Jin." The document was signed on 19 April 1814 by Hinton James and witnessed by Thomas Davis. Hinton James seems to be a close associate of John; he served three terms in the state legislature. He also served as mayor of the town of Wilmington. James is considered the first student to join the University of North Carolina at Chapel Hill in 1795. He is memorialized in historic buildings and landmarks of UNC and Chapel Hill. A historical landmark sign in his honor reads as follows: "In 1795 when UNC–Chapel Hill opened its doors, Hinton James was the first student to enroll. James had walked all the way from his hometown of Wilmington, North Carolina some 90 miles away. It is said that his feet were so sore that he had to stay in bed for a while to recuperate before he could start classes. He turned out to be an enterprising student whose name often appeared on the honor roll."[51]

As in stories of Omar's life, some exaggeration and fantasy appears in this presentation of Hinton James. Slave labor was crucial in the foundation of the university as well as in supporting the well-being of its first generation of students. Chapman observed that, "in Chapel Hill, large numbers of slaves serviced the needs of the young men from wealthy families who attended the university, freeing them to pursue their studies or their leisure." Five years before James's arrival on the new UNC campus, "slaves began clearing land to build the first public university in the new nation. Black workers labored through the summer heat to clear a main street for the village of Chapel Hill and to construct the foundations of Old East, the first building at the University of North Carolina."[52]

OMAR AND THE OWENS

The last question to investigate here is the relationship between Omar's "Autobiography" and the stories written about him in newspapers. In cases of contradiction between these sources, we give the weight of credibility to his documents. One consequence of the illegibility of his writings was that Omar was not under pressure to self-censor what he wrote, so we treat them as reliable in contrast to the published narratives about him that justified slavery.

One aspect of the "Autobiography" that corroborates published accounts, to a certain extent, is Omar's repeated declaration that the Owens treated him well, with good food and clothing. There is no reason to doubt this account, unless it becomes exaggerated to a point that becomes unbelievable. And it is striking to see how frequently Omar refers to the Owens in a complimentary fashion in the "Autobiography," labeling both Jim and John Owen (and John's wife, Lucy) as "good" half a dozen times. The Arabic term that Omar uses (ṣāliḥ) can also mean "upright, virtuous, righteous," and he uses this term to describe John Taylor, a prominent merchant in Wilmington. Omar frequently paired this word with the notion of "fearing God." He was clearly relieved to escape from the clutches of an abusive enslaver whom Omar describes as "a small, weak, and wicked little man called Johnson, a complete infidel, who had no fear of God in anything" ("Autobiography," B.1). The relative comfort and good treatment that Omar received from the Owens was evidently something that he appreciated, given the situation. He seems to have had an affectionate relationship with the Owen children (and the Taylor children), for whom he wrote several protective talismanic documents.

Omar's encounter with Jim is first mentioned in the enslavement narrative of the "Autobiography" (B.1). Omar was introduced to Jim through his brother-in-law, Bob Mumford, who was the sheriff of Cumberland County in Fayette-ville, where Omar was arrested and jailed as a runaway slave in 1810. After Omar had spent two weeks in jail, Mumford took him home as county property. This might have to do with the practice that an unclaimed fugitive slave would have to be auctioned at the Fayetteville Market House to cover the jail's costs. It was the slave's "luck" that Mumford happened to be the brother-in-law of Gen. Jim Owen, who paid his bond and offered to take him in while the process of finding his owner ran its course.

What motivated Jim to show interest in this particular fugitive enslaved person remains a mystery. Local accounts of Omar's jail stories corroborate Omar's quick glance over the event in this section. It has been said that during his time in the jail, Omar became the talk of the town and the amusement of the children when he used the coal from his jail cell's fireplace to write in Arabic on the cell's walls. This mysterious writing by a Black man, an unknown text that no one in the surrounding towns could read, attracted local and regional attention. It is highly probable that the Owens, through Bob Mumford, foresaw the occasion as a transactional opportunity in a rapidly changing society, where new members of the gentry were scrambling for public attention and name recognition. This was the beginning of Omar's relationship with the Owens. Omar refused to leave them or go back to his notorious former owner in Charleston. Jim's shadow remains present in Omar's life. His name is mentioned twelve times in the "Auto-biography," more than anyone else's.

The hyperbole of later accounts, however, takes this friendly relationship and transforms it into something it was not. An article published in Wilmington in 1847 claims that the relationship was practically family: "He has been extremely fortunate as respects a master. He fell into the hands of Gen. Owen, of Wilm-ington, who, naturally of a generous and humane disposition, has treated him with extreme lenity, and indeed more like a relative than a servant."[53] Diplomat

William Brown Hodgson also described the relationship as voluntary and benevolent: "Betwixt himself and his indulgent master, Governor Owen, there has not existed other than the relation of patron and client."[54] Another report, from 1884, of a "romantic experience . . . [and] a strange story" offered detailed psychological observations about their connection: "In the meantime Governor Owen had become so much interested in Omeroh—and the interest seemed to be mutual, for the poor captive was instinctively drawn towards the courtly gentleman who treated him so kindly. . . . Willingly he went with Governor Owen to Owen Hill. He was allowed to wander at will, and a neat cabin was furnished for him."[55] The same source added touching details about Omar's death: "When he died, as was the case during his life, his remains were treated with as much respect as if he had been a member of the family. He sleeps in the family graveyard at Owen Hill and his photograph is valued by all the surviving descendants of Governor and General Owen as that of a cherished member of their household and friend."[56] These stories have clearly entered the realm of fantasy. For all the kind words that the Owens may have said about Omar, he was not a member of the family, and as for the assertion that he was not really a slave—that was just a lie.

Omar's manuscript is contained in a notebook with the first four numbered pages containing the complete text of sura 67, carefully copied in small handwriting, with twelve to thirteen lines per page. The "Autobiography" proper begins on page 5 in a very different hand, with only seven lines per page, in large letters that must have been written with a different pen from the one used in the preceding text. Eight blank pages follow, and then the text begins again formally on page 14, with an opening invocation ("in the name of God"), in a smaller hand, in what is clearly a revision of the opening section on page 5. It is debatable whether sura 67 forms a part of the "Autobiography," but it is included here as a preface, since it was written in the same notebook.

One feature of this manuscript that calls out for additional comment is the hesitation implicit in the two opening sections. Omar begins on page 5 by declaring, "I cannot write my life," and then stops. He starts over on page 14 by repeating this statement, which we have chosen as the title of this book. The eight blank pages that separate these two beginnings stand in mute protest against the demand of white enslavers that he should write an account of his personal history that they were unable to read, and did not want to understand. Although we call this Omar's "Autobiography," it is clearly not an autobiography in the usual sense of the term.

Translation 2.1.

DOCUMENT 4: AUTOBIOGRAPHY

"In the name of God, Most Gracious, Most Merciful. May God bless our Master Muhammad" [Qur'anic Invocation and Prophetic Blessing formulas].

Blessed be he in whose hand is the kingdom, for he has power over all, / who created death and life, to test which of you is best in deed, for he is the glorious, the forgiving. / He is the one who created the seven heavens in layers. You have not seen any defect in the creation of the merciful one, so raise up your glance—do you see any gaps? / Turn your gaze back twice more as your heart will turn back to you, exhausted as it is confined. / We have adorned the world's heaven with lamps, slinging them like stones at the devils; we have established for them a fiery doom. / And for those who disbelieve in their Lord, there is the punishment of hell and a road to nowhere. / When they are cast into it, they hear it shrieking, [page 2] as it bubbles, / it nearly comes apart from rage. / Everyone cast into it is asked by the troops guarding it, didn't a warner come to you? / They say, yes, a warner came to us, but we called him a liar and said, God has not revealed anything, so you are in a big mistake. / They say, if we had only listened and understood, we would not be among the people of the fire. / So, they recognize their sins? Away with the people of the fire! / Those who fear their Lord in the hidden world will have forgiveness and a great reward. / Whether they conceal their thought or display it, he knows what is in their hearts. / Does he not know, when he created it? / He is the one who brought the earth low for you; so walk upon its highlands and eat what he provides, for toward him is the resurrection. / Are you sure that he who is in heaven will not make the earth engulf you while it is quaking? / [Page 3] Are you sure that he who is in heaven will not send a windstorm upon you? So, you will know how my warning is! / Those who were before them had called it a lie; but then how was my reproach! / Have they not seen the birds above them, stretching and closing their wings? No one restrains them except the Merciful one, who has insight into all things. / Who is this army who can help you, except the Merciful one? The unbelievers are only deluded. / Who is this who will sustain you if he restrains his sustenance? But they are stubborn in their arrogance and disdain. / Is he who goes prostrate on his face better guided, or he who walks erect on a straight path? / Say,

"He is the one who created you, and made for you hearing, sight, and hearts, little though you thank him." / Say, "He is the one who sowed you in the earth, and to him you will be gathered." / [Page 4] They say, "When will this promise be fulfilled, if you are truthful?" / Say, "Its knowledge is only with God; I am only a clear warner." / When they see it approach, the faces of the unbelievers will be terrified, and it will be said, "This is what you asked for!" / Say, "Tell me, whether God destroys me and those with me, or he has mercy on us, who will shield the unbelievers from a painful punishment?" / Say, "He is the Merciful; we have faith in him, and we trust in him. So, you shall know who is in clear error." / Say, "Have you seen that if your water goes to the depths, who will bring you fresh water?" [Qur'an 67:1–30].

[A.1. SALUTATION AND APOLOGY] [PAGE 5]

O Shaykh Hunter: I cannot write my life, I forget too much about my language and the Arabic language. O my brothers, do not blame me. "Praise be to God, with much praise. He bestows bounties that overflow" with the good.[57]

[A.2. SALUTATION AND APOLOGY, REVISED] [PAGE 14][58]

In the Name of God, the Merciful, the Compassionate [Qur'anic invocation]. Praise be to God for his glorious kindness, his generosity and grace, who is worthy of all honor. "Praise be to God, who created humanity to worship him, so he might test their actions, their words" [Testing formula].

From Omar to Shaykh Hunter: you have asked me to write my life. I cannot write my life, I forget too much about my language along with the Arabic language. I read now little grammar and little language. O my brothers, I beg you in the name of God, do not blame me, for my eyes are weak and so is my body.

[B.1. NARRATIVE OF ENSLAVEMENT]

My name is Omar ibn Said ['Umar ibn Sayyid]; my birthplace is Futa Toro, between the two rivers. I sought knowledge in Bundu and Futa. The shaykh was called Muhammad Sayyid, my brother, and Shaykh Sulaymaan Kumba and Shaykh Jibril Abdal. I continued seeking knowledge for twenty-five years. I came back home for six years. Then there came to our country a large army. It killed many people, and brought me to the big sea, and sold me into the hands of a Christian [white person] who bound me and sent me onboard the big ship in the big sea [page 15]. We sailed upon the big sea a month and a half, until we arrived at a place called Charleston in a Christian language. There they sold me. A small, weak, and wicked little man called Johnson, a complete infidel, who had no fear of God in anything, bought me. I am a small man, unable to do hard work, so I ran away from the hands of Johnson to the church[59] and then I walked to a place called Fayetteville. I saw some church buildings,[60] and I entered them to pray. A young fellow who was riding a horse saw me, then his father came to the place. He informed his father that he had seen a black man in the church building.[61] A man named Handah came with another man, one of them on horseback, attended by many dogs. They took me and made me go with them twelve miles to a place called Fayetteville, to big houses from which I could not go out. I remained in the big house, called jail in the Christian language, for sixteen days and nights.

[Page 16] One Friday someone came and opened the door of the big house. I saw many men, all Christians [whites]. They called out to me: Where [what] is your name, Omar?[62] Where [what] is Sayyid? I did not understand the Christian language.[63] I saw a man called Bob Mumford,[64] he talked to me, and asked me to get out of the big house [jail]. I agreed very much to go with them to their place. I stayed in Mumford's place for four days and nights. Then a man called Jim Owen, the husband of Mumford's daughter, Betsy Mumford, asked me if I agreed to go to a place called Bladen. I said, "Yes," I agreed to go with them.[65] So, I have remained in the place of Jim Owen until now.

Before I came into the hands of General Owen, a man by the name of Mitchell bought me. He asked me if I were willing to go to a place called Charleston.[66] I was saying "No, *no, no, no, no, no, no,* I am not going to the Charleston place. I stay in the hand of Jim Owen."[67]

[C.1. ADDRESS TO THE AMERICANS] [PAGE 17]

O people of North Carolina, O people of South Carolina, O people of America, all of you! Have you among you any two good men such as Jim Owen and John Owen? These are good men. Whatever they eat they give to me to eat; and whatever they wear they give to me to wear.

[D.1. READING THE GOSPEL]

Jim, with his brother, has me read the Gospel.[68] God is "our Lord, our Creator, and our master, the corrector of our conditions, both now and at the end, as a gift rather than as a constraint to his power."[69] This opened my heart to the way of guidance, to the way of Jesus the Messiah, to a great light.[70]

[E.1. "CONVERSION"]

Before I came to the Christian country, my religion was the religion of Muhammad, the messenger of God, may blessing and peace be upon him. I would walk to the mosque before daybreak, and would wash face, head, hands, and feet. [Page 18] I would pray at noon, would pray in the afternoon, would pray at sunset, would pray in the evening. I would give alms every year, gold, silver, harvest, cattle, sheep, goats, rice, wheat, and barley—all of them. I would give alms, I would go every year to jihād against the unbelievers; I would go on pilgrimage to Mecca and Medina, as is required for one who is able. My father had six boys and five girls, and my mother had three boys and one girl. The day I left my country, I was thirty-seven. I have been residing in the land of the Christians for twenty-four years, in the year one thousand with eight hundred and one with thirty, of Jesus the Messiah.[71]

[C.2. ADDRESS TO THE AMERICANS, REVISED]

O people of North Carolina, O people of South Carolina, O all people of America, all of them! The first son of Jim Owen is called Thomas and his sister is called Martha Jane.[72] [Page 19] This is a good lineage. Tom Owen and Nell Owen had two sons and a daughter. The first boy was called Jim and the other one is John. The girl was named Melissa. My master Jim Owen and his wife Betsy have two boys and five girls. The first is Tom, then John, and Martha, Mary, Sophia, Margaret, and Liza [Eliza]. This is a good lineage. The wife of John Owen is called Lucy. A fine wife, she gave birth to three children and then two. Three of them died and two remained.

[C.3. ADDRESS TO THE AMERICANS, REVISED AGAIN]

O people of America, people of North Carolina—Is there not among you, is there not among you, is there not among you, is there not among you[73] a lineage like this, who fears God so much?

[D.2. READING THE QUR'AN AND THE GOSPEL, REVISED] [PAGE 20]

I am Omar, who previously loved to read the book of the Great Qur'an.[74] General Jim Owen with his wife reads the Gospel; He has me read the

Gospel very much. God is "Our Lord, our Creator, and our master, the corrector of our conditions, both now and at the end, as a gift rather than as a constraint to his power."[75] This opened my heart to the Gospel, to the way of guidance. "Praise be to God, with much praise. He bestows bounties that overflow" with the good.[76]

[E.2. "CONVERSION," REVISED] [PAGE 21]

"For the law was given through Moses, and bounty and truth through Jesus" [John 1:17]

Previously I would pray what Muhammad said:[77] "In the name of God the Merciful, the Compassionate. / Praise be to God, the Lord of creation, / the Merciful, the Compassionate, / the Master of the day of judgment. / It is you whom we worship, and you whose aid we seek. / Guide us on the straight path, / the path of those who receive your grace, not those who have angered you, nor those who go astray" [Qur'an 1:1–7].

But now I pray the word: "Our father who is in the heavens, your name is sanctified. Your kingdom will come, your wish will be on the earth as it is in heaven. Our bread that is for tomorrow, give us today. And forgive us what we owe, as we forgive one who owes us. Do not put us into tests, but save us from evil, for the kingdom, and the power, and the glory are yours forever. Amen" [Lord's Prayer, Mt. 6:9–13].

[B.2. NARRATIVE OF ENSLAVEMENT, REVISED] [PAGE 22]

Indeed, I reside in our country by reason of great harm.[78] The unbelievers seized me unjustly, and sold me to the Christians, who bought me, and we sailed a month and a half on the big sea to the place called Charleston in the Christian language. I suffered in the hands of a small, weak, and wicked little man who feared no God at all, nor did he recite or pray at all.

I was afraid to remain with a little wicked man, who committed so many evil deeds. So, I escaped into God's church.[79] Our lord led me into the hands of a good man, who fears God, who loves to do good deeds, who is called General Jim Owen, and whose brother is called Governor John Owen. These are two righteous men. I am in a place called Bladen County. [Page 23] I remain in the hands of Jim Owen, who never beats me, or curses at me. There is no hunger or nakedness or hard work to do. I am a small and feeble man who stayed twenty years, without any harm, in the hands of Jim Owen.

Sermons Unheard

Calls to Repent: The Art of Quotation

What categories do Omar's writings fall into? What is the literary function of the quotations in his writing? At what audience is his writing aimed? Answering these literary questions has been hampered from the beginning by inadequate knowledge of Arabic literary traditions in Africa and by enslavers' low expectations about the intellectual abilities of Africans. The mere fact of an enslaved African's literacy was a cause for amazement, and in the case of a Muslim it was assumed to be limited to the Qur'an—a scripture whose text remained unknown to most and viewed with suspicion by nearly all. But a close reading of the documents using modern resources for the study of Arabic texts, combined with literary and rhetorical analysis of their structure, yields different conclusions. Omar's writings, often characterized as written in bad Arabic to the point of being unintelligible, turn out to contain quotations from a wide range of texts illustrating Omar's engagement with Islamic theology. Based in a culture of oral memorization, these brief quotations evoke the complete texts in which they occur, and their strategic arrangement creates an argument that defines Omar's role as that of a preacher of Islamic theology and moralizing Sufi themes. His writing is not all discursive argument, however. Like other Muslim scholars in Africa and elsewhere, Omar called upon the divinely authorized powers of blessing that could protect others in the form of talismanic devices. The question of his audience remains a challenge, however, and we defer it to the end of chapter 4, when the survey of documents is complete.

DOCUMENT 1: LETTER TO JOHN OWEN

Much of his earliest surviving text, the letter of 1819, can be interpreted as sermon rhetoric (warning against damnation for sin, exhorting to do good), but some Qur'anic passages also have a performative function of blessing that must be considered alongside the textual argument. As we saw in chapter 2, irregular features in these writings (alternative spellings, unconventional grammar, inexact quotations) reflect an education with a strong oral element, the anomalies of being enslaved in a foreign country, and the absence of any audience trained to understand these writings. Such inconsistency should not be considered a defect. Omar was a shaykh without disciples; his sermons went unheard. But the clues hidden in Omar's brief and allusive quotations lead us to appreciate his well-crafted argument, which circles around his request to be returned to Africa. It was his misfortune that no one could or would read this request.

How does Omar demonstrate his connection to Islamic traditions? In a pioneering article on Omar's 1819 letter to John Owen, John Hunwick perceptively remarks that Omar's brief quotations effectively invoke the full texts where they occur, since they were probably memorized; in addition, he must have known more than he quoted. Unfortunately, as one can see in the case of the "Autobiography," most interpreters of Omar's writings have taken a narrower approach, construing too literally his opening apology. Evidently addressing his long-ago companions in Futa Toro ("O my brothers!"), in this declaration he repeatedly asks them for forgiveness, as he has forgotten much of the Arabic language. Yet immediately after this confession, in a gesture that has remained unnoticed until now, he recites a phrase adapted from the opening of a masterwork of Islamic law and theology, the *Summary* of Khalīl: "Praise God with much praise; he bestows bounties that overflow with the good." In other words, this apology is an obligatory performance of humility, a formality that is instantly undercut by his effortless demonstration of his mastery over a text that he and his companions had memorized decades previously.

The 1819 letter, a sermon addressed to John and James Owen (Document 1), is the second-longest of Omar's writings. It has a complex structure, since over 90 percent of the text consists of quotations from Arabic religious works. We will first briefly outline the letter's contents, then discuss the texts it quotes, and finally offer a full translation. This analysis is based on formal gestures of salutation, invocation, sermon, and blessing. We will follow the same procedure for other, shorter writings (Documents 5, 6, 8, 15, 16) that are largely composed of quotations of Arabic Islamic texts.

Outline of Document 1

A. Salutation

    A.1. Testing formula

    A.2. Greetings to John Owen

B. Invocations

    B.1. Divine names (al-Ḥawdī)

    B.2. Opening with God (al-Ḥarīrī)

    B.3. Substance and action (ibn Mālik)

    B.4. "Hey you!" (al-Ḥarīrī)

    B.5. Good formula

C. Salutation in English

    C.1. Talisman diagram

    C.2. "I write this"

    C.3. Address to James Owen

    C.4. Date in English

D. Sermon

    D.1. Vanity of polytheism [Qurʾan]

    D.2. Good formula

D.3. Doom of the arrogant rich [Qur'an]

D.4. Call to repent (Abū Madyan)

E. Invocations for page 2

E.1. New opening with God (al-Ḥarīrī)

E.2. Good formula

F. Sermon and blessings

F.1. Verses for blessing (Qur'an)

F.2. Do good and be saved (Qur'an)

F.3. Do good and be saved (hadith)

F.4. Judgment warning (Qur'an)

F.5. Do good and be saved (hadith)

F.6. Judgment warning (Qur'an)

F.7. Judgment warning (Qur'an)

G. Appeal to return to Africa

H. Blessing

H.1. Blessing verses (Qur'an)

Structure and Meaning of Document 1

The overall structure of the letter builds up to the main appeal, in which Omar asks the Owen brothers to let him return to Africa. It is noteworthy that the form of this document addresses the Owens with sermons of repentance and exhortation, treating them almost as if they were Muslims. In addition to the quotations of recognized sources, Omar repeatedly draws upon a pair of formulas (perhaps his own compositions), addressing God's control over both good and bad. The first is the Testing formula, "Praise be to God, who created humanity to worship him, so he might test their actions, their words, and their condition in this world" (Document 1, A.1). The second is the Good formula, "The good is with God, and belongs to no other" (Document 1, B.5, D.2, E.2). Both formulas are threaded through the other documents, adding a layer of serenity and confidence to the accompanying quotations.

The first verse of poetry quoted in this letter contains several of the Arabic names of God, which are often recited in Sufi chanting ritual (*dhikr*) and are frequently invoked in theological writings. It is an exact quotation from the second line of a theological ode, "The Pearl Necklace of the Path" (*Wāsiṭat al-sulūk*), by a North African scholar, al-Ḥawḍī al-Tilimsānī (d. 1505). Al-Ḥawḍī was well known as a poet who focused on theological topics, such as his versification of one of the Arabic treatises of his famous townsman Abū Madyan. It begins with what is often called the proof of God's existence by contingency (the need for an eternal cause to sustain the ephemeral world):

> Praise be to God, who is demonstrated
>> by our creation, then by our need of him,
> The First, the Only, without beginning,
>> the Last, the Eternal, without end.

Calling on the names of God provides a suitable invocation to begin the letter. The poem is a creed summarizing the doctrines of the Ashʿarī school of theology, a widely accepted philosophical framework of Sunni Islam that was endorsed in the Mālikī school of law, which is dominant among Muslims in North and West Africa. The text, written in verse to facilitate memorization, is based on the popular *Shorter Creed* of al-Ḥawḍī's teacher al-Sanūsī (d. 1490), a leading scholar whose theological writings formed a basic part of the "core curriculum" of West African Islamic education.[1] He was so pleased by al-Ḥawḍī's "Pearl Necklace of the Path" that he wrote an extensive commentary on it.[2] The poem, consisting of 144 verses, was highly esteemed by the sultans of North Africa, several of whom kept copies, written in gold ink, in their libraries. Manuscripts of this text are also found in major West African libraries in Ségou and Tombouctou.[3] It is striking that al-Ḥawḍī's treatise is included in half a dozen manuscript anthologies of West African origin that are preserved in the Bibliothèque Nationale de France; one of these anthologies (Arabe 5671) also contains the poem by Abū Madyan described below.[4] So it is not surprising to find quotations from both works in this letter.

The next three lines are verses from poetic works on Arabic grammar that have been used as instruction manuals for centuries. The first of these lines comes from the famous Baghdad author Al-Ḥarīrī al-Baṣrī (d. 1122), in *The Tale of Grammar* (*Mulḥat al-iʿrāb*). Omar twice quotes the opening line (B.2 and E.1

in the translation), showing how to begin a text properly by invoking God; the second occurrence is at the top of page 2, a second beginning. Another verse from the same text (B.4) mentions five Arabic particles that introduce the vocative case, or direct address, when one announces that someone else is spoken to directly; the equivalent in English would be the archaic "O" or the more contemporary "Hey you!" Although the formal opening of the letter is only addressed to John Owen, when this verse appears in the section of the letter that mentions his brother Jim Owen, the verse in effect asserts that he too is addressed by the letter. The third grammatical verse comes from the Andalusian grammarian Ibn Mālik (d. 1274), whose *Alfiyya* (*Thousands*) was and is still a widely used textbook. One can watch numerous YouTube videos of lectures on both these texts. This verse (B.3) describes the distinctive properties of the verb and the noun; while the implication is not very specific, one may conclude that both action and substance are the subject of the letter—that is, it will be comprehensive. The invocation section closes with a repetition of the Good formula.

The text on the page is interrupted by a talismanic drawing; we discuss its protective qualities later in this chapter. In the midst of it a few words are written, which may all be read as English words spelled in the Arabic alphabet. The first phrase is "I write this" (*a rayt dis*), followed by "Shaykh General Jim Owen," combining Arabic and English titles of respect. Just below the diagram, the English date is provided in Arabic letters, another example of ʿ*ajamī* English: "November four, eighteen hundred and nineteen" (*nūwiba fuwwā ātīn ḥadad an nātīn*). One may hear the echo of a southern accent in this transliteration.

At this point, the letter shifts into sermon mode, with an assembly of quotations that build an argument framed around the two classical Qurʾanic exhortations: the threat of punishment for the unbelieving sinner, and the promise of forgiveness and reward for those who repent. Two Qurʾanic passages follow (D.1 and D.3), separated by the Good formula, each one condemning a form of idolatry. The quotation from Qurʾan 53:21–23 denounces the worship of goddesses by the pre-Islamic Arabs of Mecca, while the passage from Qurʾan 111:1–2 curses Abū Lahab, one of the Prophet Muhammad's most stubborn opponents. Notice how he is harshly criticized for both his wealth and his arrogance—a combination that appears again in other verses that Omar quotes. How directly does Omar intend these condemnations as a critique of Christian polytheism, or of the entitlement of white enslavers, or of Owen's wealth and power?

The next salvo from Omar's pen is a pair of verses from a rhyming sermon by the most revered Sufi saint of North Africa, Abū Madyan Shuʿayb (d. 1198).[5] Born near Seville, he is buried in a tomb in Tlemcen in Algeria, where he is familiarly known as Sidi Boumediène. The poem quoted here by Omar is an ode of 120 lines, "The Pearl Ode in A" (*Maqṣūrat al-jawhara*), which is primarily a sermon calling upon believers to repent their sins and to seek God's forgiveness.[6] It was a highly popular text, as one can see from the 134 digitized copies from libraries in Mali that can be viewed on the website of the Hill Manuscript Museum and Library. It is worth noting that the opening to this poem is also quoted in an Arabic manuscript belonging to enslaved Muslims in Brazil.[7] Abū Madyan was well known as a preacher, often speaking to crowds at the city mosque or even at home to invite them to repent and seek God's forgiveness.[8] In his poem "The Pearl Ode," Abū Madyan calls upon his reader to adhere to Islamic rituals, abstain from what is prohibited, perform what is legitimate, reject the vanities of this world, practice piety and asceticism, seek out the wise, avoid the ignorant, and carry out an inner jihād against one's lower self. Above all, he holds up as models to be followed the Prophet Muhammad, the Sufi mystics, the transmitters of Prophetic sayings, and the jurists of the major legal schools. Typical of the balanced Sufism of North Africa, Abū Madyan mentions ecstatic mystics like Abū Yazīd and Manṣūr (Ḥallāj) in practically the same breath as the sober founders of the Mālikī and Ḥanafī schools of law. The verses quoted by Omar (lines 64–65) speak to someone growing old, warning him that the end is coming, and that he is an idiot or a fool to ignore it. If, as we assume, this letter is addressed to the Owen brothers, this stern warning is remarkable coming from someone they had enslaved.

At this point, literally turning the page of the manuscript, the reader encounters for the second time the verse from al-Ḥarīrī (E.1) about beginning with the name of God—evidently Omar saw the second page as a new beginning. This leads to a shift of emphasis, combining warning with promised reward, a transition marked by another quotation of the Good formula. The next section assembles seven quotations to hammer this point home. The first (F.1) is Qur'an 2:285–86, two lengthy verses that function here as a blessing; the Prophet Muhammad declared that they would produce a special reward for anyone who recites even a single letter from them.[9] This is followed by Qur'an verses and Prophetic sayings (F.2, F.3, F.5) promising divine rewards for doing good, and dire warnings about the Judgment Day (F.4, F.6, F.7).

This all leads up to what is evidently the letter's central point: the request to return to Africa (G.1). This liberation is the good deed that can be accomplished by the Owen brothers, for which they should receive a reward from God. By implication, they would ignore the request at their peril. This point having been made, the letter concludes with a major blessing, by quoting the first thirteen verses of sura 67 of the Qur'an (H.1; as mentioned in chapter 2, Omar also quotes this chapter in full in the pages preceding his "Autobiography"). With these stipulations in mind, it becomes possible to read Omar's letter of 1819 as a reasoned sermon, designed to bring about his liberation and return to Africa.

Translation 3.1.

DOCUMENT 1: LETTER TO JOHN OWEN[10]

————

[A. SALUTATION]

A.1. "Praise be to God, who created humanity to worship him, so he might test their actions, their words, and their condition in this world" [Testing formula].[11]

A.2. Greetings to Major John Owen and his companions in the Christian community in the place of the town called Raleigh.

[B. INVOCATIONS]

B.1. "The First, the One, without beginning, / the Last, the Eternal, without end."[12]

B.2. "I speak, after the opening, a word / praising the Everlasting, the Mighty in power."[13]

B.3. "The genitive case is restricted to the noun, just as / the jussive mood is restricted to the verb."[14]

B.4. "The vocative is one you call with 'O' or 'Ho' / or 'Eh?' or 'Uh,' or if you wish, just 'Hey.'"[15]

B.5. "The good is with God, and belongs to no other" [Good formula].

[C. SALUTATION IN ENGLISH]

C.1 [Talisman]

C.2. I write this.

C.3. Shaykh General Jim Owen.

C.4. November four, eighteen hundred and nineteen.

[D. SERMON]

D.1. "Do you have the males, while he has the females? / This would be an unfair division! They are only names invented by you and your fathers; God revealed no proof about them" [Qur'an 53:21–23].

D.2. "The Good is with God, and belongs to no other" [Good formula].[16]

D.3. "The hands of Abu Lahab will perish, and he will perish. / His wealth is of no use to him, or what he acquired" [Qur'an 111:1–2].

D.4. "By God! You're turning gray; what are you waiting for? / My brother, haven't you considered those who preceded you?

"Are you crazy, or are you an idiot? / Your hair is white, but your heart is black."[17]

[E. INVOCATIONS] [PAGE 2]

E.1. "I speak, after the opening, a word / praising the Everlasting, the Mighty in power."[18]

E.2. "The Good is with God, and belongs to no other" [Good formula].

[F. SERMON AND BLESSINGS]

F.1. "The Messenger has faith in what was revealed to him from his Lord, and the believers too. All have faith in God, his angels, his scriptures, and his messengers. We do not distinguish between any of his messengers. They say, we have heard, and we have obeyed. Your forgiveness, our Lord! You are our destination. / God does not burden a soul except to its capacity. It gains by what it earns, but loses by what it takes. Do not punish us if we forget or make a mistake, and do not burden us as heavily as you burdened those before us, Lord. Do not burden us with what we have no power over. Excuse us and forgive us and have mercy on us. You are our Lord, so give us victory over the unbelieving people" [Qur'an 2:285–86].

F.2. I have listened to the word of God most high: "One who does good, let his soul gain, and one who does ill, his soul will be the loser" [Qur'an 41:46].

F.3. I have listened to the word of God most high:[19] "God fulfills the need of one who fulfills the need of the believer" [Sahih al-Bukhari, book 46, hadith 3].

F.4. "On the day when a man flees from his brother, / his mother, father, / wife, and children, / on that day every man will have business to occupy him" [Qur'an 80:34–37].

F.5. I have listened to the word of God most high: "God fulfills the need of one who fulfills the need of the believer" [Sahih al-Bukhari, book 46, hadith 3].

F.6. "It is a day when no soul controls anything for another, for that day the command belongs to God" [Qur'an 82:19].

F.7. "The day when a man will see what his hands have prepared; and the unbeliever shall say, I wish that I were dust!" [Qur'an 78:40].

[G. APPEAL]

G.1. I want to be seen in our land called Africa, in the place of the river called Kaba.

[H. BLESSING]

H.1. "Blessed be he in whose hand is the kingdom, for he has power over all, / who created death and life, to test which of you is best in deed, for he is the glorious, the forgiving. / He is the one who created the seven heavens in layers. You have not seen any defect in the creation of the merciful one, so raise up your glance—do you see any gaps? / Turn your gaze back twice more as your heart will turn back to you, exhausted as it is confined. / We have adorned the world's heaven with lamps, slinging them like stones at the devils; we have established for them a fiery doom. / And for those who disbelieve in their Lord, there is the punishment of hell and a road to nowhere. / When they are cast into it, they hear it shrieking, as it bubbles, / it nearly comes apart from rage. / Everyone cast into it is asked by the troops guarding it, didn't a warner come to you? / They say, yes, a warner came to us, but we called him a liar and said, God has not revealed anything, so you are in a big mistake. / They say, if we had only listened and understood, we would not be among the people of the fire. / So, they recognize their sins? Away with the people of the fire! / Those who fear their Lord in the hidden world will have forgiveness and a great reward. / Whether they conceal their thought or display it, he knows what is in their hearts" [Qur'an 67:1–13].

Impact of Document 1

How was this letter received? The main piece of evidence is a letter dated October 10, 1819, written by John Louis Taylor, who had been named the first chief justice of the North Carolina Supreme Court on January 1 of that year. The intervention of such a prominent figure indicates that the Owen family traveled in influential circles; John Owen himself was a state senator at this time. Taylor's letter was addressed to Francis Scott Key, well known as the composer of the American national anthem, "The Star-Spangled Banner" (1814). It is less well known that the lyrics are based on an earlier song composed by Key, containing anti-Islamic passages such as the following, aimed at the Barbary pirates:

> And pale beamed the crescent, its splendor obscur'd
> by the light of the star-spangled flag of our nation,
> Where each flaming star gleam'd a meteor of war,
> and the turban'd head bowed to the terrible glare.[20]

In any case, in his letter, referring to Omar as Moreau, Taylor described his Islamic education and good breeding, observing that "he is unwilling to return to his native country"—which we know to be untrue.

Moreover, Taylor believed that Omar might be "useful to the Colonization Society," an organization of which both Taylor and Key were members, a topic to which we will return. Taylor asked Key to provide an Arabic Bible to persuade Omar to convert to Christianity. Taylor indicates that this letter had aroused considerable curiosity: "Many persons were desirous of procuring a translation of the inclosed letter, which I hope to obtain by your assistance. The gentleman to whom it was addressed is wholly ignorant of its content; I have others in my possession, but the one selected is the best and neatest display of penmanship."[21] Several questions are raised by this document, however. First is the matter of dates — Taylor's letter, dated October 10, introduces a letter that ostensibly would not be written until nearly a month later. This discrepancy suggests either that Omar was still struggling to work with the American calendar in the Arabic script, or perhaps that the document that we see is one of the other manuscripts written by Omar that were in Taylor's possession, and that, unfortunately, have gone missing. Second, Taylor claims not only that Omar does not wish to return to Africa but also that Omar would be available to assist Christian missionaries to bring Africans into the Christian fold. As we will show in a later chapter, we have every reason to think both these assertions are false. This inaccuracy is perhaps not surprising, given that the person addressed by the letter — John Owen — could not read its contents. Still, it is amazing to see how confidently these elite Americans could make such false judgments without any real knowledge.

We also know that Omar's letter, plus Taylor's cover letter, were turned over to Moses Stuart (d. 1856), a professor of biblical studies at the Andover Theological Seminary who donated these documents to the seminary, now part of Yale University, in 1837. Stuart was to some degree a student of Arabic, as a supplement to his biblical scholarship, so presumably he had been asked to translate Omar's letter. Among his own papers is a file marked "Arabic grammar," which suggests his level of understanding of that language.[22] On examination, this turns out to be a notebook in which Stuart had copied out the paradigms of Arabic verbs according to the Arabic grammar of the French orientalist Sylvestre de Sacy. In other words, by today's standards, Stuart was at best on the level of a second-year student of Arabic, and he could not have understood much of this text.

So it was not until 1869, fully half a century after the composition of this letter, that anyone recorded having read the text at all. This was done by George E. Post (1838–1909), an American missionary and botanist associated since 1866 with the Syrian Protestant College, which later became the American University of Beirut. In an article, "Arabic-Speaking Negro Mohammedans in Africa," written for the *African Repository*, Post gave an account of Omar, including the text of John Louis Taylor's letter, which he saw in 1867 in New Haven. Here is his description of the text: "The Arabic letter is a bombastic collection of sentences from the Koran, and at the end of it is a drawing, rudely executed, possibly an attempt at the plan of some building which Moreau had seen in his own country, followed by some cabalistic sentences, not clearly intelligible to me during the cursory examination which I then made of them. There occurs, however, in that letter, one sentence in Arabic, from which it would appear that this slave was taken from a town called Kaba, in a province called Bewir, in Africa."[23] This passage reveals in several ways Post's inability to read the document. First is the arrogant dismissal of the quotations from the Qur'an as irrelevant. Second is the assumption that the talismanic diagram (discussed below) must have been a drawing of a house, an unlikely suggestion of an architectural use. Third is the declaration that the intervening sentences are "cabalistic," evidently meaning that they are unintelligible—to him. Finally, in true orientalist fashion he attempts to squeeze out some technical meaning from the text by noting something about the place called Kaba, where Omar was captured. This is simply based on a mistake by Post. The word he identifies by the place-name Bewir is actually the Arabic word *baḥr*, meaning river or sea. But the biggest mistake of all is his failure to recognize that the sentence where Omar mentioned this place was precisely where he asked to return to Africa. Post either could not or would not read this sentence, and so he perpetuated the lie, claiming that Omar did not wish to leave his enslavement in America or to return to his home in Africa. This systematic weakness, if we can call it that, puts everything that Post says under suspicion.

Accordingly, when Post claims to have seen a document written by Omar in the possession of a Dr. Budington of Brooklyn in 1868, calling for all to come to Jesus, this seems entirely unbelievable. The same applies to the claim that Arabic-speaking African Muslims were demanding Arabic Bibles. Considering the obviously willful ignorance displayed by Post, and the conflict between his statements and Omar's actual texts, it seems necessary to subject his accounts to the most skeptical consideration.

So when did this text ever get translated into English? Not until the 1980s, when Allan Austin was putting together his sourcebook, *African Muslims in Antebellum America*. He contacted a Saudi graduate student at the University of Massachusetts Amherst, Abdullah Basabrain, and asked him to translate the text of the letter, so it finally appeared, in a three-page footnote to his book.[24] That ad hoc provisional version was replaced in 2003 in John Hunwick's scholarly article, and now by the present translation. Still, it is remarkable that it took so long to achieve a translation of Omar's first writing. We believe that the disappointment of that failed communication contributed to Omar's realization that "I cannot write my life." There was literally no one who could read it.

DOCUMENT 5: QUR'AN VERSES, NO. 1

We do not have a clear sense of the audience for Document 5. Charles Frederick Heartman, a noted bibliophile and collector who had an interest in African American subjects, acquired it from a New Jersey newspaper editor, Harold E. Pickersgill (1872–ca. 1940), but how the latter obtained it is not known.[25] This text was part of a collection the New-York Historical Society purchased from Heartman in 1942.[26] It contains five passages from the Qur'an, framed by Omar's two favorite formulas. Written on the back of the manuscript is a notation: "the annexed is written by Old Morau Srvant of Gen. Owen Wilmington NC Jan. 8th 1845. J. L. H." Whoever signed that note with the initials J. L. H. was probably either a friend or neighbor of the Owen family in Wilmington, or perhaps a visitor curious to meet "Old Morau," one of the many variations on Omar's name.

Outline of Document 5

A. Testing formula

B. Repentance (Qur'an 66:8)

C. Threat of hellfire (Qur'an 104:1–9)

D. Salvation by God (Qur'an 106:1–4)

E. Sermon on miserly hypocrisy (Qur'an 107 title)

F. True revelation (Qur'an 4:105)

G. Good formula

H. [Talisman]

From the organization of this document, it is apparent that Omar was using the well-established structure of the sermon. He begins (Document 5, A) with the Testing formula, which depicts the condition of humanity in the world, subject to temptation and external compulsion. Then, in the most direct fashion possible, he quotes the Qur'an on the need to repent for one's sins (B). The sequel is a short Meccan sura (104:1–9, "The Crusher"), that warns against the arrogance of the rich and threatens punishment by hellfire, vividly described (C). In contrast, the next quotation (106:1–5, "Quraysh") presents an idyllic portrait of

(Muhammad's) Quraysh tribe, whose community and concord is demonstrated by their caravans; if they focus on worshipping God in his "house" (the Ka'ba in Mecca), their protection by God is assured (D). The tone of warning is evoked again by simply mentioning (E) the title of the next chapter (107, "Charity"). This unquoted text contains another criticism of the hypocrisy of the arrogant rich, who pretend to be pious but refuse to give charity to those who are suffering. This selection moves toward an ending (F) by quoting the Qur'an's self-description as the truth and the criterion by which everything is to be judged. It concludes (G) with the Good formula, affirming that everything God does, and is, must be considered the good.

The sequence of arrangement in Document 5 alternates between the threat of punishment for the unrepentant and the promise of reward for the faithful in the form of divine protection. Because of its broad coverage of these themes through brief quotations, this selection of verses could have been generically suitable for practically any recipient. Written twenty-six years after Document 1, this text presents Omar as consistently following the preaching model that he had learned in his youth.

Translation 3.2.

DOCUMENT 5: QUR'AN VERSES, NO. 1

[A. INVOCATION]

"Praise be to God, who created humanity to worship him, so he might test their actions, their words, and their condition in this world" [Testing formula].

[B. SERMON]

"Believers! Repent to God with sincere repentance!" [Qur'an 66:8].

[C. SERMON]

"Woe to every backbiter and slanderer / who gathers wealth and counts it up. / He figures that his wealth will make him immortal! / But no! Let him be thrown into the Crusher. / And how will you know what the Crusher is? / It is the fire of God, blazing, / Which will rise above their hearts. / Indeed it will close over them / In outstretched flames" [Qur'an 104:1–9].

[D. SALVATION]

"By the community of the Quraysh, / and their joining in winter and summer journeys— / Let them worship the Lord of this House, / Who has fed them from hunger, / And saved them from fear" [Qur'an 106:1–4].

[E. SERMON]

The Chapter of Charity [Title of Qur'an 107].

[F. REVELATION]

"Indeed, We have revealed to you the Book with the truth, so that you may judge between the people by what God has shown you" [Qur'an 4:105].

[G. BLESSING]

"The Good is with God, and belongs to no other" [Good formula].

[H. TALISMAN]

DOCUMENT 6: THE TAYLOR VERSES

Compared to other short writings by Omar, this document has a more detailed personal connection as well as greater complexity, combining several passages from the Qur'an with a Psalm from the Bible. Moreover, it contains three intricately composed talismanic diagrams, to which we will return at the end of the chapter, but for the moment we should acknowledge that these are designed for special protection and blessings. The text, which is dated August 1853, is connected to an individual known to Omar—John Allan Taylor (1798–1873), a prosperous businessman in Wilmington and a leading member of the Presbyterian Church to which Omar belonged. Omar in fact refers to him as "a very good man," the same high praise he gave to Jim Owen. It is a historical irony that the Greek Revival building that Taylor built as a family home in 1847 later served as the Wilmington Armory, a principal staging area for the infamous Wilmington Insurrection of 1898.

Outline of Document 6

A. Invocation

    A.1. Islamic blessings

    A.2. Good formula

    A.3. Testing formula

B. Date and salutation

C. Invocation [Qur'an 1:1–7)

D. Slavery and resentment (Psalm 123)

E. Religious difference (Qur'an 109)

F. Destiny

    F.1. God's decree (Qur'an 97)

    F.2. Belief in destiny (al-Qayrawānī)

    F.3. Divine beneficence (theological fragment)

G. Talismans

H. Addressees

I. Address label

The organization of this document is unusual, because it explicitly raises the issue of slavery and places it into the context of the theological conviction that the all-powerful decree of God controls the destiny of everything in creation. In practical terms, this means that Omar is acknowledging that his enslavement is part of that divine plan, which he stoically accepts despite all of its negative characteristics, including his forced participation in Christianity. The document begins with a formal series of invocations (Document 6, A), a dated salutation to Taylor (B), and a blessing in the form of the first chapter of the Qur'an (C).

The appearance of Psalm 123 here (D) is striking, because it is the only text quoted by Omar that explicitly mentions slavery. It might be thought that this Psalm offers a positive evaluation of slavery, through the analogy depicting the relation between humans and God in terms of a slave gazing on the "master" or "mistress." The author of a tract in support of slavery called *The Governing Race* found the opening lines of this Psalm to be clear evidence of divine approval. "David thus pictures the trust of the slave in the kindness and power of the slave-holder. . . . What a wonderful ascription of praise to the love and tenderness of the good master and mistress!"[27] But the last two verses take a harsher tone. In the ancient Near Eastern milieu where the Psalms originated, the shift from adoration to complaint in verses 3–4 probably implied an unspoken request that God demonstrate his patronage of the Israelites and confound their scornful rivals, worshipers of other gods. In the very different atmosphere of antebellum America, how would these verses sound to the enslaved? Who would the enslaved think of when hearing about "ridicule from the arrogant, [and] contempt from the proud"? It is indeed conceivable that the arrogant and the proud would be logically identified with the enslavers, a complaint that expresses the resentment of the powerless. Frederick Douglass made a similar association when he pointed out that the church was intimately tied to the authority structures of slavery. "The slave prison and the church stand near each other. The clanking of fetters and the rattling of chains in the prison, and the pious psalm and solemn prayer in the church, may be heard at the same time."[28] In this way, Psalm 123 could be read as a bitter protest against enslavement.

The next reference (E) is so brief as to be scarcely noticeable, but it is worth pausing to reflect on the title of chapter 109 of the Qur'an, "The Unbelievers." Here is the complete text, unstated but easily recalled by any reader of the Qur'an: "Say, O Unbelievers! I do not worship what you worship. / And you do not worship what I worship. / And I am not a worshiper of what you worship. / And you are not worshipers of what I worship. / You have your faith and I have mine" (Qur'an 109:1–6). In its original historical context, this chapter signaled the clear distinction between the believers who accepted Muhammad's revelation and the unbelievers of Mecca who rejected it. As a response from a trained Muslim scholar to a Christian audience, it is hard to avoid the implication that Omar is pointing out that there are divisions between religious groups, between Muslims and Christians, and that despite his attending the Christian church, he is still holding onto a Muslim identity.

The problem, then, is twofold: enslavement and forced conversion. How does Omar respond to that dilemma? The next sequence makes it plain that this is a destiny decreed by God, which must be accepted. The next text (F.1) is chapter 97 of the Qur'an, the title of which (*al-Qadr*) can be legitimately translated as either "Destiny" or "Power." It is often interpreted as a depiction of the divine decree, the heavenly tablets of destiny found in ancient Near Eastern tradition, which in an instant seals the fate of the world and everyone in it. If that message was not clear enough, it is spelled out further by a quotation (F.2) of the authoritative treatise on law and theology, *The Epistle* of Ibn Abī Zayd al-Qayrawānī (d. 996). This is a masterwork of the Mālikī school, used as a school text for over a thousand years.[29] "It is necessary 'to have faith in predestination [*al-qadr*], the good and the bad, the sweet [and the bitter], all that was decreed by God, our Lord.'" Omar continues with an additional comment (F.3), an unidentified theological fragment that is apparently a continuation of the statement of al-Qayrawānī: "our Creator, and our Master, the corrector of our conditions, both now and at the end, as a gift rather than as a constraint to his power." While we have not been able to find this exact phrase in earlier texts, it might have come from a commentary on al-Qayrawānī (over 100 commentaries have been written on it). Regardless of the source, the last clause includes vocabulary (e.g., "as a gift [*faḍlan*] rather than as a constraint [*wujūban*] to his power") commonly found in Islamic theological texts. So it is all the more remarkable that, in the "Autobiography," Omar twice quotes this unidentified theological fragment (Document 4, D.1 and D.2) as a description of how he read the Gospel at the Owens' command. This quotation indicates that Omar was reading the New Testament as a confirmation of Islamic theology.

The letter closes with a list of the names of members of the Taylor family, and then what amounts to an address label for an envelope, stating the name of the sender and the name and address of the recipient. What John Taylor made of this document we do not know. A notation in English states, "This is supposed to be 'Arabic' and was written by 'Uncle Moreau,' a slave of Gen. James Owen, and given to me by him. —H. T. Tennant." This signature can be reasonably identified as Harriette Taylor Tennent (1838–1905), daughter of John Taylor, as mentioned in the document. Having received it directly from Omar, Harriette evidently kept the manuscript as a family heirloom, taking it with her to Spartanburg, South Carolina, when she married Edward S. Tennent, then passing it on to their son Edward Smith Tennent (1862–1938), who in turn left it to his daughter, her grandmother's namesake, Harriette Taylor Tennent. When she died in 1982, her husband David W. Reid (d. 1985) donated the document to the Spartanburg County Historical Association.[30]

Translation 3.3.

DOCUMENT 6: THE TAYLOR VERSES

————

[A. INVOCATION] [PAGE 1]

A.1 "In the name of God the Merciful, the Compassionate. May God bless our master Muḥammad" [Qur'anic and Prophetic blessings].

A.2 "The Good is with God, and belongs to no other" [Good formula].

A.3 "Praise be to God, who created humanity to worship him, so he might test their actions, their words, and their condition in this world" [Testing formula].

[B. SALUTATION]

I write this letter in 1853, on the first of the month of October—August [*aksat*], called *August* ['*ūkas*]. I sent this letter with a very good man named Taylor: Kitty Taylor, John Taylor, and Harriett Taylor.[31]

[C. INVOCATION]

"In the name of God, the Merciful, the Compassionate. / Praise be to God, the Lord of creation, / the Merciful, the Compassionate, / the Master of the Day of Judgment. / It is you whom we worship, and you whose aid we seek. / Guide us on the straight path, / the path of those who receive your grace, not those who have angered you, or those who go astray" [Qur'an 1:1–7].

[D. SLAVERY]

"I lift up my eyes to you, to you who sit enthroned in heaven. / As the eyes of slaves look to the hand of their master, as the eyes of a female slave look to the hand of her mistress, so our eyes look to the Lord our God, till he shows us his mercy. / Have mercy on us, Lord, have mercy on us, for we have endured no end of contempt. / We have endured no end of ridicule from the arrogant, of contempt from the proud" [Psalm 123:1–4].

[E. RELIGIOUS DIFFERENCE]

"The Chapter of the Unbelievers" [Title of Qur'an 109].

[F. DESTINY] [PAGE 2]

F.1 "In the name of God the Merciful, the Compassionate. Truly, We revealed it in the night of Destiny. / And how will you know what the night of Destiny is? / The night of Destiny is better than a thousand months. / The angels and the spirit descend in it, with permission from their Lord, with every order. / It is peace, until the rising of the morn" [Qur'an 97:1–5].

F.2 It is necessary "to have faith in predestination, the good and the bad, the sweet [and the bitter], all that was decreed by God, our Lord."[32]

F.3 "Our Creator, and our master, the corrector of our conditions, both now and at the end, as a gift rather than as a constraint to his power."[33]

[G. TALISMANS]

[H. ADDRESSEES]

Master Taylor and his wife, Kitty Taylor, and his son John, and his daughter Harriette Taylor.[34]

[I. ADDRESS LABEL] [PAGE 3]

From Omar to Master named Johnny Taylor, Wilmington City, New Hanover, North Carolina.[35]

DOCUMENT 8: THE CHAPTER OF HELP

This document, unlike the preceding ones, is short and simple, consisting more or less of a single chapter from the Qur'an, known as the Chapter of Help (110:1–3). In fact, it splices in a verse from another chapter, "Ranks" (61:13), which serves as a kind of commentary based on overlapping vocabulary. Chapter 110 is regarded as having been delivered at the very end of the life of the Prophet Muhammad, as a recognition of the Muslim victory over the Meccan unbelievers. It therefore has triumphal overtones, and in talismanic usage these verses are invoked by those seeking victory in the name of Islam. It also concludes with a sermon's emphasis upon repentance and divine forgiveness.

It is therefore surprising to see that Omar presented this particular document to Mary Jones, the wife of a prominent Christian missionary. Her husband, Charles Colcock Jones Sr. (1804–63), was a Presbyterian minister trained at the Princeton Theological Seminary and the author of *The Religious Instruction of the Negroes in the United States*.[36] The owner of three plantations in Georgia, he was also attracted to the Liberia project of the American Colonization Society. Reverend and Mrs. Jones evidently met General Owen at a health spa in Virginia, the Rockbridge Alum Springs, a popular resort among the well-to-do. A note in English on the back of the sheet identifies it as follows: "The Lord's Prayer written in Arabic by Uncle Moreau (Omar), a native African, now owned by General Owen of Wilmington NC. He is 88 years of age & a devoted Christian. Given to Mary Jones, at the Rockbridge Alum Springs, Rockland County, Va., by General Owen on July 27, 1857." A similar situation led to the production of Document 18, which was given to its recipient at a different hot spring, this one in West Virginia. Jim Owen must have regularly brought Omar or his documents with him on jaunts to these resorts, where he could be relied on to produce another intriguing Arabic document for the curious.

It is doubly curious that this document presents a plea for victory that is not only implicitly opposed to Christianity but also labeled falsely as a text from the New Testament. One wonders whether Omar himself had provided the misleading identification of the text. This phenomenon was not unheard of in American encounters with enslaved Muslims. Such was the case when the recently liberated Prince Abdulrahman ibn Ibrahima was giving a lecture tour in the United States in 1828 after having been enslaved for forty years in Mississippi. When he wrote out a document at the request of a diplomat, he described it as the Lord's Prayer in Arabic, when in reality it was the first chapter of the Qur'an, the "Opening." This attribution was not corrected until 1837, when William Brown

Hodgson examined the text and reported its actual contents. Hodgson did not criticize this as a deception, seeming to regard it instead as a reasonably equivalent substitution. Indeed, the contents of the two prayers overlap significantly in recognizing divine authority, seeking divine aid, and praying for guidance away from error. Hodgson's explanation was nevertheless condescending: "Judging from the capacity of other Muslims, I imagine it would have been difficult for the Prince to have made a version of our Prayer, and he therefore wrote his own."[37]

Translation 3.4.

DOCUMENT 8: THE CHAPTER OF HELP

"When help shall come" [Qur'an 110:1] "from God, and victory is near, so bring good tidings to the believers" [Qur'an 61:13]. "And you shall see the people enter into the religion of God in droves: / recite the praise of your Lord, and ask his forgiveness, for he is inclined to forgive" [Qur'an 110:2–3].[38] The End.[39] My name is Omar, O A'mār.[40]

DOCUMENT 15: QUR'AN VERSES, NO. 2

This document is one of four from the Owen and Barry Collection in the New Hanover County (North Carolina) Public Library. It was evidently preserved by the Owen children, and the translation that follows is the first ever published. The document is on blue paper, of uncertain date, with discolorations that make the writing difficult to decipher. A thorough examination reveals that this is a powerful sermon, comprised of five passages from the Qur'an enhanced by two verses of Arabic poetry from different Sufi poems.

Outline of Document 15

A. Invocation of divine attributes (al-Ḥawdī)

B. Sermon on arrogant wealth (Qur'an 28:76)

C. Sermon on hellfire (Qur'an 104:1–9)

D. Mystical prayer (al-Manẓūma al-Dimyāṭiyya)

E. Consolation (Qur'an 94:1–2)

F. Repentance and forgiveness (Qur'an 66:8)

G. Election by God (Qur'an 3:42)

The opening line (Document 15, A) is a quotation of a verse of poetry that Omar has already cited once in Document 1. It is a recitation of the attributes of God, taken from a theological poem written by al-Ḥawḍī in the fifteenth century. It not only frames the document in relation to God's transcendence of creation but also emphasizes the dependence of humanity upon the divine creator. It is followed (B) by a fragmentary quotation from the beginning of a verse from the Qur'an, "Qarun was from the people of Moses," which by itself might seem inexplicable. But if we complete the verse, as most readers of the Qur'an would be able to do, we get the following: "Qarun was from the people of Moses, [but he oppressed them. And we gave him such treasures that their keys alone would burden a work gang; so his people said to him, 'Do not gloat. God does not like those who gloat']" (Qur'an 28:76). The reference here is to Qarun, known in the Bible as Korah, who led a rebellion against Moses. In the Qur'an he is a symbol of not only arrogance but also vast wealth, so his mention here is clearly a criticism of the wealthy. It is worth noting that Omar also wrote this fragmentary reference on the endpapers of his Arabic Bible, indicating that he continued to think about verses like this, which were implicitly critical of the beneficiaries of slavery. To emphasize the point, the next passage (C) is chapter 109 from the Qur'an, a warning to slanderers and backbiters who think their wealth will protect them from the punishments of hell.

The bottom line on the first page concludes it (D) with a verse from "the Damietta poem," which was widely read in Sufi circles. It takes its name from the Nile River delta, known as Damietta, which was the home of al-Dimyāṭī, an otherwise little-known author of the fourteenth century.[41] The poem was quite popular; of the thirty-two manuscript copies digitized by the Hill Manuscript Museum and Library, half are from libraries in Mali. It is an ode consisting of sixty-six verses, and most of its verses contain one or two of the ninety-nine names of God, which are commonly the subject of meditation and the means of healing through ritual chanting. In this verse, the poet addresses two of the divine names, "Forgiving one" and "Wrathful one": "Forgiving one, I've asked you for pardon and repentance; / Wrathful one, remove deceptions with your wrath!" In Sufi practice, not only does the recitation of the Divine names confer the ethical character of those names upon the reciter, but also it has the power to have extraordinary effects in the world. This poem as a repository of the divine names is highly respected for its magical and healing properties. The epithet "Forgiving one" creates the conditions for genuine repentance, while the overwhelming force of the "Wrathful one" can cancel the depredations of oppressors. This is how the recitation of this verse of poetry is described by a famous commentator, the well-known Sufi reformer Aḥmad Zarrūq (d. 1493):

> One who recites this verse has 100 times the result of Friday prayer. The influences of knowledge appear to him. And for one who persists in reciting it, God drives from his heart the love of the world, and his soul's attachments weaken. The influence of divine assistance affects him, at the moment of his recitation of it, during sunrise and at midnight. For the destruction of an oppressor, it is recited in this fashion: "O Overpowering, O Wrathful, O Powerful Force! Take back what is mine from the one who wronged me and injured me," and God will take it back.[42]

It may be surprising that in his quotation, Omar has changed the first name, "Forgiving one" (*ghaffār*), to God (*allāh*), and he has dropped the second name, "Wrathful one" (*qahhār*), but this was probably out of respect for the power of the names; it is unlikely that he would forget the main point of the verse, and an informed reader would be able to restore the key terms anyway.

Translation 3.5.
DOCUMENT 15: QUR'AN VERSES, NO. 2

[A. INVOCATION] [PAGE 1]

"The First, the One, without beginning, and the Last, the Eternal, without end."[43]

[B. SERMON]

"Qarun was from the people of Moses" [Qur'an 28:76].

[C. SERMON]

"Woe to every backbiter and slanderer / who gathers wealth and counts it up. / He figures that his wealth will make him immortal! / But no! Let him be thrown into the Crusher. / And how will you know what the Crusher is? / It is the fire of God, blazing, / Which will rise above their hearts. / Indeed it will close over them / In outstretched flames" [Qur'an 104:1–9].

[D. PRAYER]

"Forgiving one, I've asked you for pardon and repentance; / Wrathful one, remove deceptions with your wrath!"[44]

[E. CONSOLATION] [PAGE 2]

"Did We not make you happy / and lighten your burden" [Qur'an 94:1–2]?

[F. REPENTANCE]

"O believers, turn to God with a sincere repentance" [Qur'an 66:8].

[G. ELECTION BY GOD]

"And when the angels said, O Mary, God has chosen you, and has purified you, and has chosen you above all the women of the world" [Qur'an 3:42].

DOCUMENT 16: QUR'AN VERSES, NO. 3

The last of the Qur'anic documents to consider, Document 16, is a straightforward combination of blessing invocations and warnings of punishment. This document, which has not been translated previously, was in the possession of Charles Sumner, the well-known abolitionist, and is included in his collected papers in the Harvard library. A note attached to it states, "Presented [to Charles Sumner] by Wm. W. Williams of Terre Haute, In." Wm. W. Williams (d. 1839) was a prominent businessman in Terre Haute (not to be confused with William

Williams, Republican congressman from Indiana), but nothing is known about his relationship with Sumner or how he came into possession of the document. The Arabic text is accompanied by an English translation from an unknown hand. This document was exhibited in Boston's Faneuil Hall on March 5, 1858, as part of a protest against the Supreme Court's *Dred Scott* decision, which had significantly undermined the rights of free Blacks. The protest was organized by Black abolitionists in Boston on Crispus Attucks Day, which celebrated the contributions of Blacks to US independence. This was a rare instance when one of Omar's documents (described in a broadside ad as "Arabic sentences written by a Black Man owned by Gen. Owen, of Wilmington, N.C.") was brought into national consciousness as part of an antislavery argument.[45]

Outline of Document 16

A. Invocations

    A.1. Blessings on Muhammad

    A.2. Blessings (Qur'an 1:1)

    A.3. Good formula

    A.4. The believers

B. Warnings

    B.1. Threat of hellfire (Qur'an 104:1–9)

    B.2. Defeat

The document begins with a series of invocations (Document 16, A.1–A.4), beginning with the blessing on Muhammad, followed by the first verse of "The Opening" chapter (Surat al-Fātiḥa) of the Qur'an, and the Good formula. There is also a brief phrase, "Those who believe," which occurs sixteen times in the text of the Qur'an in this particular form (in a slightly simpler form, it occurs over 180 times). Without connecting to any particular passage in the Qur'an, this phrase (also inscribed in Omar's Arabic Bible) recalls the presence of the community of believers addressed by the sacred text.

The quotations that follow include the now familiar denunciation of arrogant wealth and the threat of hellfire in chapter 104, already mentioned in

Documents 5 and 15 (B.1). The text concludes (B.2) with a mention of the title of chapter 105, "The Elephant." It is commonly understood as an account of the invasion of Arabia by an Abyssinian king in the year 570 with an army that included war elephants. The invasion was a failure, depicted in this chapter as the result of a miraculous attack by birds with divine inspiration. The reference to this text may be taken as another warning of divine punishment for those who fail to repent.

Translation 3.6.

DOCUMENT 16: QUR'AN VERSES, NO. 3

──────

[A. INVOCATIONS]

A.1. God, you by whom one blesses Muhammad!

A.2. "Praise be to God, the Lord of creation" [Qur'an 1:1].

A.3. "The Good is with God, and belongs to no other" [Good formula].

A.4. "Those who believe . . ." [Qur'an 2:62, etc.].

[B. WARNINGS OF PUNISHMENT]

B.1. "Woe to every backbiter and slanderer / who gathers wealth and counts it up. / He figures that his wealth will make him immortal! / But no! Let him be thrown into the Crusher. / And how will you know what the Crusher is? / It is the fire of God, blazing, / Which will rise above their hearts. / Indeed it will close over them / In outstretched flames" [Qur'an 104:1–9].

B.2. The Chapter of the Elephant [Qur'an 105 title]

Blessings and Talismans

BLESSINGS IN THE QUR'AN

Up to now, we have been considering the Qur'an in terms of the sermon format that Omar so frequently used. It is a form of argumentation, with a rhetoric that uses persuasion in the form of the warning and the promise. But the Qur'an can be read in several different ways. A small portion of the Qur'an is in the form of legislation or rules, and a certain amount of the text is devoted to stories, although there is significantly less narrative material in the Qur'an than in the Bible—and the Qur'an presumes that its audience is already familiar with those biblical stories. Major sections of the Qur'an are devoted to praise of God as the creator, which is spelled out in extended descriptions of the wonders of nature. And a good deal of the text of the Qur'an consists of prayers that may be incorporated into the formal rituals observed in Muslim communities, or in private devotions. Because the Qur'an is considered to be the word of God, the words themselves are understood to have power because of their divine origin.[46]

One way the power of the Qur'an was recognized became known as "the virtues of the Qur'an," a body of teachings derived from the hadith sayings of the Prophet Muhammad, describing the extraordinary results that may occur when one recites particular parts of the Qur'an. As an example, one may ask why Omar quoted the last two verses of chapter 2 of the Qur'an in Document 1. While one might come up with an explanation based on the contents of these two extremely long verses, the reason may be explained by their power as described by the Prophet in this hadith saying:

Ibn 'Abbās reported that while Gabriel was sitting with the Apostle he heard a creaking sound above him. He lifted his head and said: This is a gate opened in heaven today which had never been opened before. Then when an angel descended through it, he said: This is an angel who came down to the earth who had never come down before. He greeted and said: Rejoice in two lights given to you which have not been given to any prophet before you: Fātiḥat al-Kitāb [Qur'an 1, "The Opening"] and the concluding verses of Surat al-Baqara [Qur'an 2:285–86]. You will never recite a letter from them for which you will not be given [a reward]. (Sahih Muslim, Book 6, Hadith 30).

This vivid account, enlivened by angels, makes clear that the mere recitation of a letter from these two verses will provide a benefit; and since the two verses contain over 300 letters, the power of their recitation is obvious. It is for this reason that the analysis of Document 1, above, marked the inclusion of these verses as blessings rather than argument.

Much the same could be said about chapter 67, "The Kingdom" (*al-Mulk*), which Omar quotes in full as a preface to his "Autobiography," and in part as a sequel to the Document 1. Does it contain argument, or is it playing the role of blessing? Here is how one hadith portrays it: "It was narrated from Abū Hurairah that the Prophet said: There is a sura in the Qur'an, with thirty verses, which will intercede for its companion [the one who recites it] until he is forgiven" (*Riyāḍ al-ṣāliḥīn*, Book 8, Hadith 26). This pronouncement, which quotes the opening lines of chapter 67 to avoid any mistake, maintains that this text will intercede with God on the behalf of the reciter, until God forgives him—a major promise indeed. Based on that report, we see the quotation of chapter 67 in Omar's documents as an application of that blessing, rather than an argumentative sermon.

While the hadith-based accounts of the blessing properties of different chapters of the Qur'an were widely known, there were systematic local treatments of the subject in works written not far from Senegal during Omar's lifetime. One such treatise is *The Medicine of the Prophet,* by the noted woman scholar Nana Asma'u, which describes the influences projected by 44 of the Qur'an's 114 chapters. Omar quotes several of these examples at full length, including chapter 67 with very same Prophetic description cited above.

It is not always the case that the blessing properties of a chapter of the Qur'an are predominant. Nana also mentions two other chapters that Omar quotes, in both cases playing on the qualities of the title. The properties of chapter 97, "Destiny," are as follows: "Whoever reads Surat al-Qadr [Qur'an 97] one hundred times will have God put the most important of his names into his head so that he can pray for whatever he desires and have his needs fulfilled." That interpretation addresses the meaning of this chapter's title as "Power," stressing the forces that can be unleashed by its words. When Omar quotes it, however, it has to do with the acceptance of one's fate as decreed by God. Likewise, this is how she describes the effects of chapter 104, "The Backbiter": "Whoever reads Surat al-Humazah [Qur'an 104] will not be the subject of ridicule. If it is read for someone who is afflicted by the evil eye, he will be cured by God's permission. Whoever recites it frequently during extra prayer sessions will have his wealth and sustenance increased." But as Omar employs this chapter, it seems to be mainly in terms of the ethical critique of the slanderer and the arrogant miser mentioned in the text, rather than as protection against those types of individuals.

TALISMANIC DRAWINGS

Among the most striking aspects of the documents Omar composed are the complex geometric designs that occur repeatedly in the manuscripts. Indeed, the Arabic text also features emphatic markers mostly used for punctuation—two horizontal lines like an extended equals sign, a small circle, a figure resembling a cursive letter *l*, a squiggle, three dots clustered in a triangle, and a flourish. These figures are used at the end of quoted passages, to mark off verses of poetry, and to mark a new section of the text. One can also see several instances of the five-pointed star, typically known as the seal of Solomon, and associated with the esoteric "greatest name" of God.

The most common design found in Omar's documents is a version of a geometric pattern formed by symmetrical pairs of lines consisting of alternating hollow rectangles, overlapping in such a way as to produce a pattern of regular complex squares. Omar presented this pattern most frequently in a composition consisting of two connected groups of six squares, all arranged on two rows, with oblong extensions on the outside of each square. The pattern occurs four times, in Documents 1, 6, 9, and 12. In Document 6, this pattern is accompanied by two additional talismans (fig. 3.1).

The designs did not seem to attract much interest among the occasional readers of the manuscripts, although one commented that it might be an attempt to render buildings that Omar had seen someplace. Yet a cataloger of Document 1 used the word "amulet" to describe the pattern. Another version of this diagram is found in Documents 2 and 5, consisting of two joined squares formed according to the same design, functioning together as the middle letter of the Arabic word *faṣl*, meaning "section" (fig. 3.2).

Evidently, this figure is regularly used in West African Arabic manuscripts as a decorative separator, marking the beginning of a new section of text. It would not have been used in the Qur'an, which does not have any divisions marked as a *faṣl*. In this example, the vowel marks are carefully added to produce the indefinite form of the word *faṣlun*, "a section" (فَصْلٌ). What was the purpose and function of these designs?

Evidence indicates that this pattern was an abstract form drawing upon the occult powers of geometric shapes in the Islamic tradition, and it was also explicitly linked to the sacred text of the Qur'an to reinforce the text's reception. A remarkable example of this design is found in a Qur'an in the library collection of the University of Leeds (Arabic Ms. 301), probably copied in West Africa in the nineteenth century. At several key points in the text, specifically, the opening of suras 1, 7, and 19, more or less extensive versions of this pattern are prominently

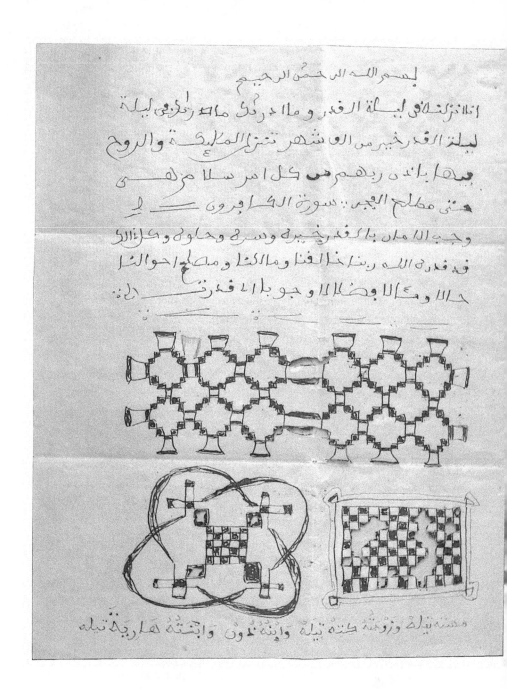

بسم الله الرحمن الرحيم

إنا أنزلناه في ليلة القدر و ما أدراك ما ليلة القدر ليلة القدر في ليلة

ليلة القدر خير من ألف شهر تنزل الملائكة و الروح

فيها بإذن ربهم من كل أمر سلام هي

حتى مطلع الفجر :: سورة القدر وروى ـــــ ل

وجب الأمان بالقدر خيره و شره و حلاوه و كل الـ

فد فدر الله رينا خلق الفنا و مالكنا و مصلح احوالنـ

حالا و مآلا و ضلالا و جوبا الا قدرتنـ ال :

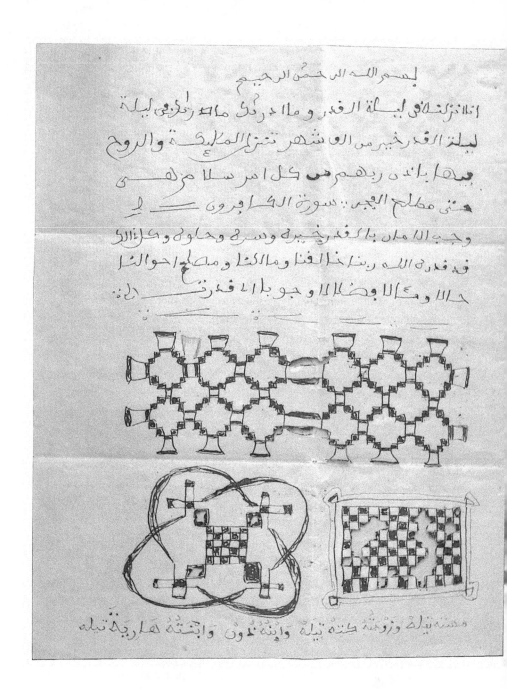

مسته نيله و زوجته خنته نيله و ابنته ثمون و ابنته هاريه نيله

FIGURE 3.1.

Second page of letter from Omar ibn Said to John Allan Taylor, August 1, 1853.
Three talismans are drawn at the bottom of the page. English version in Translation 3.3.
Spartanburg County Historical Association, Spartanburg, SC.
Photography © John L. Miller.

الحمد الله خلو الخلق لعباد ته حتى زرد اجعالهم

و افوالهم يا بها الله يس # امنوا توبوا الى الله توبة

نصوحا !

و يل اكل همزة لمزة الذ جمع مالا و عدده ه

يحسب ان ماله احلد ى كلا ليبذ ن ٠ فى الحطمة

و ما ا رئك ما الحطمة ذار الله الموقدة تطلع

على الا بيد ة انها عليهم موصدة فى عمد ممدة

لا يلف فريبس اى لوهم رحلة الشتا ء والصيف

فليعبدوا رب هذا البيت الذ ا طعمهم من جوع

و ءامنهم من خوف سورة الما عى

انا نزلنا اليه الكتا ب لتحكم بين الناس بما ارئك الله

الخير عند الله لا لغيره و من عمل صالحا و انفسى

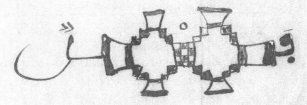

FIGURE 3.2.

Arabic text, with quotations from the Qur'an by "Old Morau," January 8, 1845.
A talisman is drawn at the bottom of the page. English version in Translation 3.2.
Ms 293, Charles F. Heartman Collection, New-York Historical Society, 100067d.
Photography © New-York Historical Society.

displayed. The pattern has been described as "transverse sets of a crenellating strapwork with their mirror-image, overlapping with vertical sets of the same."[47]

The same basic pattern can be found in architectural decoration in Cairo, in the Burdayni mosque, dating to 1616 during the Ottoman era. In this case, the horizontal lines are a dark red, while the vertical lines are black, making the geometrical construction of the design easily apparent (fig. 3.3). This composition also differs in that each central space is occupied by an eight-pointed star with each point divided into gold and black sections, and each connecting space contains a gold square balanced on one corner.[48]

More immediately relevant is a geometrical design on the inside cover of a magnificent Qur'an now in the collection of the Walters Art Museum in Baltimore.[49] Here the spaces contain a double concentric circle (fig. 3.4). It also appears that all four sides have been trimmed to form twin horn extensions, creating a visual impression similar to the "knife" patterns found on talismanic tunics from West Africa.[50] Yet another instance is a talismanic collection of snippets from Qur'anic verses (and a few words in Soninke), collected by Pierre Eugene du Simitière in the 1770s from an enslaved African Muslim in the Caribbean. It is accompanied on the reverse by a simplified version of the strapwork design.[51] These examples indicate that the strapwork pattern was well known in sacred contexts, both as an accent to the text of the Qur'an and occasionally in the mosque as well.

Beyond the purely decorative function, the reference just made to talismanic tunics opens up an important relationship between geometric forms and occult sciences.[52] It is important to recall that the Islamization of West Africa took place relatively recently, with Muslims overall becoming the majority in countries like Senegal only in the twentieth century, during French colonial rule. During this long process, which took place unevenly among various groups, the material symbols of Islam over time became Africanized and abstracted. Literacy and calligraphy were accessible to educated elites, for whom a text could have multiple meanings. Illiterates, whether Muslim or otherwise, could only see the Arabic script as a sign for Islam in general. The highly developed system of talismans (*ṭilism*) included magic squares (*wafq*), in which the sum of each row, column, and diagonal was the same number. The Arabic alphabet, like all the alphabets derived from Phoenician, assigned numerical values to each letter, so each magic square could embody a particular name of God or other important formula. This concept could be deployed both through textual forms embodying the Arabic script, or through simplifications into lines and other geometric designs. Square designs, whether explicitly filled with text or numbers or in

FIGURE 3.3.

Strapwork pattern in tile, Burdayni mosque, Cairo. "Mosquée d'El-Bordeyny: Développement de la mosaïque du mihrab," in Émile Prisse d'Avennes, *L'art arabe d'après les monuments du Kaire depuis le VIIe siècle jusqu'à la fin du XVIIIe* (Paris: A. Morel, 1877), plate 61.

FIGURE 3.4.

Strapwork pattern, Qur'an, nineteenth century, West Africa. The Walters Art Museum, Baltimore, MD. W.853.II, vol. 2, upper board inside.

abstract checkerboard form, are commonly known in West Africa by the Fulbe term *hatumere*, derived from the Arabic *khātim*, meaning "seal."[53] This broad category can include seal rings and objects inscribed with magic squares.

The practical embodiment of these practices can be seen in the example of talismanic tunics, robes that are covered with diagrams containing properties of protection and healing. One such robe, a nineteenth-century garment now preserved at the Musée du Quai Branly—Jacques Chirac in Paris, is covered with dozens of small renderings of diagrams, including simplified versions of the strapwork designs described above.[54] In addition, the same robe features examples of other patterns used by Omar, such as the lower left diagram in Document 6 (fig. 3.1). This pattern is obviously based on a seal design that appears several times on the same tunic.[55] The major difference is that Omar has introduced at the center a five-by-five-square *hatumere* or magic square in alternating black-and-white checkerboard format. In the same document, this figure is accompanied by a large rectangular nine-by-thirteen-square diagram enclosed in a box with small squares at the corners.

The exact significance of these diagrams can only be surmised, though it seems likely that Omar would have endowed the drawings with powers conferred by his mental equivalent of the recipe book that learned Muslims used as manuals for the production of such talismans.[56] It may be observed that two of the documents containing the double-six strapwork designs also focus on the names of the Owen family (Documents 9 and 12), with no other accompanying text except short Islamic blessings in Document 12. The Taylor family is also highlighted by name in Document 6, alongside a strapwork figure and two magic squares, but they are accompanied by quotations from two chapters from the Qur'an and the title of one other chapter. And in the earliest instance (Document 1), the name of General Owen is inscribed at the center of the strapwork figure, and then followed by a complex sequence of Islamic texts. Likewise, when we turn to consider the related *faṣl* markers, a similar variety of accompanying texts appears. Document 2 contains the Lord's Prayer, introduced by the Testing formula and a Qur'anic verse, while Document 5 has five Qur'anic passages and three Islamic formulas. Although the detailed application of such designs undoubtedly has its own complexity, it seems clear that they have talismanic functions of healing and protection, whether in isolation or enhanced by the proximity of scriptural texts, including from the New Testament.

At this point, we can add translations of two documents that are exclusively talismanic, one of which has no text except for the names of the members of the Owen family. Presumably Omar designed these documents as protective gestures. Document 9, housed with the John Owen Papers in the North Carolina State Archives, has a talisman like the one in Document 1 (in two clusters of six), though it is visibly damaged; curiously, it is identified as the Lord's Prayer in a pencil inscription. Document 12, from the Owen and Barry Family Papers at the New Hanover County Library, has the same talisman (in better condition), and it adds two Islamic formulas of blessing as an invocation, plus a signature.

DOCUMENT 9: OWEN TALISMAN, NO. 1

Translation 3.7.

DOCUMENT 9: OWEN TALISMAN, NO. 1

[TALISMAN]

My master is named Jim Owen.

Martha Owen	Thomas Owen	Betsy Owen
	Mary Owen	
Margaret Owen	John Owen	Sophia Owen
	Eliza Owen	

DOCUMENT 12: OWEN TALISMAN, NO. 2

Translation 3.8.

DOCUMENT 12: OWEN TALISMAN, NO. 2

In the name of God the Merciful the Compassionate; may God bless our master Muhammad.

[TALISMAN]

Master General Owen	Thomas Owen	Mary Owen
Sofia Owen	Margaret Owen	Liza Owen

My name is Omar ibn Said, but from my mother's side [she is] Umm Hānī Yarmak.

Taking Stock

As we pass the midpoint of this study, it will be useful to reconsider the problems initially addressed, and how far we have progressed in the first three chapters. We began with the dislocation of Omar ibn Said from his home in West Africa and his enslavement in the Carolinas. We have examined fully half of his documents, which can be divided into the "Autobiography," seven documents constructed as sermons, and a couple of talismanic compositions (although the talismans tend to leak over into the sermons). We have tried to articulate what cultural and literary resources are needed in order to understand Omar's situation, and a fundamental problem remains. The three audiences that he identified in his "Autobiography" (elite white enslavers, former companions at an African seminary, the general population of the United States) are either unable or unwilling to read his Arabic writings. He cannot really write, in the sense of addressing a reader, yet he continues writing; that is what scholars do. In the next chapter, we will focus on Omar's Bible and eight other documents that are primarily concerned with texts from the Bible. Writing those texts is a task he would never have imagined had he stayed in Africa. Examining how he wrote those documents, and what it would take to read them, will be the basis for addressing the question of the audience of these writings.

A Muslim in Church

THE OFFICIAL HISTORY of the First Presbyterian Church in Fayetteville, North Carolina, includes the following entry under the heading, "Notable Persons": "Moreau, colored adult, property of Governor Owen, baptized December 2, 1820. Dismissed to Presbyterian Church in Wilmington, North Carolina, July 11, 1837." This record of Omar ibn Said joining a church is followed by a highly imaginative account of his life as an "Arabian Prince" and would-be Christian missionary.[1] Following the transfer of the Owen family and its retinue to Wilmington, the records of the Presbyterian Church there include this brief notation: "1838—Morrow—servant to James Owen, Indian Prince."[2] While on the purely bureaucratic level, these official accounts seem to confirm Omar's embrace of Protestant Christianity, both enhance the seemingly ordinary mention of the date with fanciful descriptions of his origins. They disagree as to whether he was Arabian or Indian, but both confidently describe him as a prince, who has been dramatically reduced to servitude in his role as a Christian convert. This element of fantasy, which recurs in all accounts of Omar, raises questions about a fundamental feature of the narrative: To what extent can we describe him as a convert to Christianity? In short, who was Omar, really?

The Question of Conversion

The story of Omar's conversion is central to virtually every article that appeared about him, beginning with the 1825 *Christian Advocate*. Indeed, it seems likely there would have been no reason to give him any publicity had it not been for this story of a Muslim who receives Christian redemption. As we have seen, the white elites connected to Omar were unable and unwilling to recognize his desire to be free or to return to Africa, and they were happy to assert the contrary. Given the strong reliance on quotations from the Qur'an and Islamic literature in Omar's documents, it seems at best a considerable exaggeration, and at worst an outright falsehood, to say that he had turned his back on his Islamic training.

Of course, much depends on what one understands by the word "conversion." For some it means a complete transformation, and a total rejection of one's former religious beliefs. But in a social context, conversion is not defined only by the inner change of heart that had been associated with conversion narratives since Saint Augustine. As Katherine Gerbner has pointed out, "Conversion is always about power. In Protestant slave colonies, conversion was the first step toward wielding and exercising political and social authority."[3] While outward conversion to Christianity carved out a comparatively privileged space for Omar within the southern slave system, he clearly reserved his options and kept his loyalties to Islamic touchstones. The performance of conversion even conferred on him a certain celebrity within Protestant missionary circles. But the exaggerated nature of the claims made for his conversion become apparent when contrasted with the contents of his documents, and they are further undermined by incoherence and contradiction within the narratives.

Here are some several examples of the claim that Omar became a Christian and renounced Islam: "His master being a pious man, he was instructed in the principles of the Christian religion, which he received with great pleasure; and he seemed to see new beauties in the plan of the gospel, which had never appeared to him in the Koran."[4] On a similar note, "He has thrown aside the bloodstained Koran and now worships at the feet of the Prince of Peace. The Bible, of which he has an Arabic copy, is his guide, his comforter, or as he expresses it, 'his Life.'"[5] And again: "Gradually he seemed to lose his interest in the Koran, and to show more interest in the sacred Scriptures, until finally he gave up his faith in Mohammed, and became a believer in Jesus Christ."[6] These accounts are contradicted by Omar's own writings. In nine different documents, dated as late as 1855, Omar begins by reciting the formula, "God bless our master Muhammad," and he includes the Qur'anic invocation of God ten times. Overall, in the documents he quotes over twenty passages from the Qur'an and only six from the Bible. This is scarcely the result one would expect from the conversion narratives.

Moreover, willful ignorance about Africa's Arabic literature, enhanced by anti-Islamic sentiment, led to the claim that Omar's knowledge of Arabic was limited to the Qur'an—a text that could be safely dismissed as false prophecy. So accounts like the following were common: "For ten years he taught the youth of his tribe all that they were wont to be taught, which was for the most part, lessons from the Koran."[7] Although only a handful of Americans could read Arabic at all, nearly every description of Omar's writing assumed that it had to be the Qur'an, since no one knew of any other possibility. "It was found that the scraps of writing from his pen, were mostly passages from the Koran."[8] Keeping the Qur'an as a straw man kept things simple. Yet our analysis has shown that Omar quotes not only two Arabic grammarians but also three Muslim theologians and two Sufi mystics, not to mention the sayings of the Prophet Muhammad. Recognizing these sophisticated layers in Omar's writings would have complicated the simple story of his conversion.

Bible versus Qur'an

The obsession with Omar's conversion, envisaged as the outcome of a struggle between the Bible and the Qur'an, is evident from the earliest document, Omar's letter of 1819 addressed to the Owen brothers. The accompanying cover letter from John Louis Taylor to Francis Scott Key requested his assistance not only with locating a translator for the letter but also in finding an Arabic translation of the Bible to facilitate Omar's conversion. This was a time of increasing popularity for evangelical Christianity, in the wake of the Second Great Awakening of the early nineteenth century. The American Bible Society had been founded in 1816 to support international distribution of Bibles, and Key was a vice president of that organization from 1817 until his death in 1843. James Owen, an active member of the Fayetteville Presbyterian Church, was also on the board of the Fayetteville chapter of the American Bible Society. So the focus on the Bible in relation to Omar was understandable.

The narratives about Omar's contact with the Qur'an and the Bible play an important role in stories of his conversion. One account, the 1837 report by Rev.

Ralph Randolph Gurley to the American Colonization Society, indicates that Omar had an Arabic Qur'an in his possession. "I allude to Moro or Omora, a Foulah by birth, educated a Mahometan, and who, long after he came in slavery to this country, retained a devoted attachment to the faith of his fathers and deemed a copy of the Koran in Arabic (which language he reads and writes with facility) his richest treasure."[9] Where or how Omar may have acquired an Arabic Qur'an is unclear, and it is hard to imagine that such a thing could be easily found in the United States at that time.

Other early sources say that he had an English translation of the Qur'an. John Louis Taylor said as much in 1819:"His greatest delight, at present, is in hearing the Koran read to him in English; but it is with much difficulty he is made to understand it, and the little he does gather he probably owes to his familiarity with the original."[10] This observation contains an important additional point, which is that Omar's command of English was very poor. Gregory Bedell stated this frankly in 1825: "He speaks English more imperfectly than any African we have ever seen, but still can make himself intelligible."[11]

It is difficult to imagine that Omar would have found much satisfaction in listening to white southerners reading from George Sale's 1734 English version of the Qur'an, which is likely the only English translation available in the early nineteenth century; Thomas Jefferson had a copy of Sale's Qur'an. While not quite Elizabethan in style, Sale's version has plenty of archaic expressions that would challenge many experienced readers of English, let alone a novice like Omar. Moreover, it really was not possible to use such a translation for Islamic prayer ritual.

Nevertheless, the story of Omar's early use of an English Qur'an was persistent. Rev. Mathew Grier, in a frequently reprinted account from 1854, maintained, "Through the kindness of some friends, an English translation of the Koran was procured for him, and read to him, often with portions of the Bible. Gradually he seemed to lose his interest in the Koran, and to show more interest in the Sacred Scriptures, until he finally gave up his faith in Mohammed, and became a believer in Jesus Christ."[12] Some reprints made editorial changes to Grier's report, calling the Qur'an a gift from "Master" (i.e., James Owen) or altering the conclusion to read on a doubtful note that Omar "became an humble and, by all outward signs, sincere believer in Jesus Christ." In any case, the abandonment of the Qur'an and the embrace of the Bible became essential elements in the legend of Omar.

Poetry of Slavery and Conversion

Other literary resources would be brought to bear on the representation of Omar as a triumphant convert to Christianity through slavery. It is striking to see how the earliest published account of Omar's story concluded. Rather than offering an independent judgment, the author chose to end by quoting the immensely popular British poet William Cowper (d. 1800), famous for his anti-slavery poems. Instead of choosing one of Cowper's more overtly abolitionist poems, however, he settled instead on the closing lines from "Charity," where an African welcomes slavery, since it includes conversion to Christianity, and hence salvation.

> My dear deliverer out of hopeless night,
> Whose bounty bought me but to give me light;
> I was a bondman on my native plain,
> Sin forged, and Ignorance made fast the chain;
> Thy lips have shed instruction as the dew,
> Taught me what path to shun, and what pursue;
> Farewell my former joys! I sigh no more
> For Africa's once loved, benighted shore;
> Serving a benefactor, I am free,
> At my best home, if not exiled from thee![13]

Slavery becomes freedom through salvation.

This poetic conclusion was applauded by Frederick Freeman, an Episcopalian priest who wrote *A Plea for Africa* (1848) as a tract in dialogue form, supporting the Liberia colonization project as a gradualist solution to the problem of slavery. Freeman saw the case of Omar ibn Said (aka "the Prince") as evidence to support the American Colonization Society's position, with Omar's conversion to Christianity as compelling proof that slavery was not all bad. So he had one of the discussants praise the use of Cowper's poem as a perfect reflection of Omar's mind. "The gentleman who bought Prince [i.e., James. Owen], and used him so kindly, and instructed him, must have felt amply rewarded and greatly happy to find this poor Mahomedan become an humble follower of the Lord Jesus. And it would seem almost as if Cowper had written expressly to suit the case of Prince [Omar], speaking the very feeling of his heart, and almost his very words, in those lines."[14] Cowper's poems on slavery were indeed so popular that it was almost obligatory to quote one in every "slave narrative." Ralph

Gurley had already quoted the following verse from Cowper's "Charity" in 1837, as a comment on Omar's situation: "Oh, 'tis a godlike privilege to save! / And he that scorns it is himself a slave."[15] But Freeman does not address an ambiguity in Cowper's poem, what one critic calls "the paradox by which literal freedom becomes simply a precondition for 'voluntary re-enslavement to Christianity' in 'Charity.'"[16] The unanswered question is how freedom of religion is possible in slavery, when the enslavers have complete control over the religious activities of the enslaved. Even more remarkable is the assumption that a crisis faced by an African Muslim can be summarized by a British poet, when we know that Omar had access to a rich poetic tradition in West Africa, including in Arabic, that his enslavers could not even imagine.

Imaginary Documents

In addition to the eighteen Arabic writings by Omar that survive, there is credible evidence of at least a dozen more documents written by him, which have been mentioned in print by their owners but of which no trace remains; we will review this phenomenon in chapter 5. But there is also a seemingly similar situation, with dubious claims regarding the existence of documents in which Omar is supposed to have declared his fervent support for Christian missions in Africa. These imaginary documents, which are completely different in form and substance from Omar's actual writings, appear to be pious forgeries created to support the aims of the American Colonization Society.

The first occasion for mentioning these imaginary documents was in 1837, when Rev. Ralph Gurley submitted what was essentially a fundraising letter to the churches supporting the Liberia colonization project of the ACS. In this report, Gurley alludes to the crucial role that missionaries expected a chosen few enslaved members of the Foulah (Fulani) tribe to play in spreading the Gospel. The attempt to involve Abdulrahman ibn Ibrahima (another "prince" of Foulah origin) had fizzled out when he failed to convert to Christianity, and then died a few months after his arrival in Liberia in 1829. But hopes remained high that Lamin Kebe (also known as "Old Paul"), a formerly enslaved African of similar background, could lead the mission to success. Omar had been put in touch with Lamin in 1836, when he sent to Lamin the manuscript of his "Autobiography"; Lamin later turned that over to Theodore Dwight of the American Ethnological Society, who was also a strong supporter of missions to Africa. As early as 1819, ACS members had singled out Omar as a potential leader of the missionary project; John Louis Taylor had made this plain in his letter to Francis

Scott Key. By the mid-1830s, however, with Omar nearing his seventieth year, it was conceded that he was too old to send into the field. Nevertheless, there was still some benefit to be had by invoking the example of Omar's alleged enthusiasm for converting African Muslims to Christianity. That, at least, is how we interpret Gurley's highly improbable claim about letters from Omar to Lamin, passionately urging support for the ACS mission in Liberia. It was, in short, an irresistible fundraising device, so Gurley made up the contents of two letters that he deemed Omar should have written to Lamin.

Christian missions to convert Muslims were remarkably unsuccessful, so continued fundraising operations required a success story to justify continued requests for contributions. Here is how Gurley presents an imaginary document, quoted here in its entirety:

Moro is much interested in the plans and progress of the American Colonization Society. He thinks his age and infirmities forbid his return to his own country. His prayer is that the Foulahs and all other Mahomedans may receive the Gospel. When, more than a year ago, a man by the name of Paul [Lamin Kebe], of the Foulah nation and able like himself to understand Arabic, was preparing to embark at New York for Liberia, Moro corresponded with him and presented him with one of his two copies of the Bible in that language. Extracts from Moro's letters are before me. In one of them he says "I hear you wish to go back to Africa; if you do go, hold fast to Jesus Christ's law, and tell all the Brethren, that they may turn to Jesus before it is too late. The Missionaries who go that way to preach to sinners, pay attention to them, I beg you for Christ's sake. They call all people, rich and poor, white and black, to come and drink of the waters of life freely, without money and without price. I have been in Africa; it is a dark part. I was a follower of Mahomet, went to church, prayed five times a day and did all Mahomet said I must but the Lord is so good. He opened my way and brought me to this part of the world where I found the light. Jesus Christ is the light, all that believe in him shall be saved, all that believe not shall be lost. The Lord put religion in my heart about ten years ago. I joined the Presbyterian Church, and since that time I have minded Jesus' laws. I turned away from Mahomet to follow Christ. I don't ask for long life, for riches, or for great things in this world, all I ask is a seat at Jesus' feet in Heaven. The Bible, which is the word of God, says sinners must be born again or they can never see God in peace. They must be changed by the Spirit of God. I loved and served the world a long time, but this did not make me happy. God opened my eyes to see the danger I was in. I was like one who stood by the road side and cried Jesus, thou Son of God, have mercy; he heard me and did have mercy. 'God so loved the world that he gave his only begotten Son, that whosoever believeth in him should not perish but have everlasting life.' I am an old sinner, but Jesus is an old Saviour; I am a great sinner, but Jesus is a great Saviour: thank God for it. — If you wish to be happy, lay aside Mahomet's prayer and use the one which our blessed Saviour taught his disciples — our Father, &c.

Gurley supplies another supposed letter from Omar along similar lines, but this much will suffice. Ironically, Lamin dashed the hopes of the ACS when he returned to Africa, ostensibly as a Christian missionary, only to disappear into the hinterland at the first opportunity. The alleged correspondence by Omar is utterly unlike any of the actual writings from his hand. Its aim and flowery style, replete with dramatic contrasts, slips in a scriptural verse (John 3:16) in true ministerial fashion. It is all too obviously part of the missionary project advanced by Gurley.

The other imaginary document to consider seems to have been independently devised by a later missionary, George E. Post, in an article published in 1869; Post was still fantasizing about converting Africans through Arabic as Gurley had sought to do three decades earlier, thinking it would be much more efficient than having to learn many African languages. We discussed this article in chapter 3 as an example of an inability to read Omar's Arabic documents. Not only did Post misread the text, but he also ignored Omar's plea to return to Africa. In presenting his account of the imaginary document, Post provided a combination of vague descriptions and circumstantial details to lend verisimilitude to the story.

Toward the time of his [Omar's] death, which took place two or three years since [actually in 1863], his mistress gave him a blank book, requesting him to write an account of his life. He kept it for some time, and at length returned it to her, filled with Arabic writing. After his death it was sent to an Arabic scholar, who sent it back, saying that it was a collection of passages of Scripture, put together with no definite link of connection. This book was shown to me in the autumn of 1868, by Dr. Budington, of Brooklyn. I found it to contain the pith of the scheme of redemption, in a series of Scripture passages from the Old and New Testaments, and on the last two pages, the following appeal to his kindred, whom he names.

None of the children of the Owen family have mentioned any such document, nor do we know who the unnamed Arabic scholar was.

The reference to Rev. William I. Budington (d. 1879) brings in a real historical character, but Post is the only source for this claim. Here is the text of the supposed letter: "Salaams to all who believe on the Lord Jesus Christ. I have given my soul to Jesus the Son of God. O, my countrymen [of] Bundah [Bundu], and Phootoor [Futa Toro], and Phootdalik [Futa Jallon], give salaams to Mohammed Said and Makr Said, and all the rest. Come, come, come, come, come, come to Jesus, the Son of the living God. He shall enter Paradise forever. Amen." Here too, the style is that of a Christian preacher, completely unlike the texts written by Omar, who shows no signs of familiarity with biblical "schemes of redemption." It seems that Post in putting together the phrases just mentioned may have been imitating a phrase that occurs in the actual "Autobiography," where Omar wrote, "I sought knowledge in Bundu and Futa. The shaykh was called Muḥammad Sayyid, my brother, and Shaykh Sulaymaan Kumba and Shaykh Jibril Abdal." Post goes on to recount the story of Theodore Dwight and Old Paul, still making the case that Africa was to be converted to Christianity through Arabic, with Liberia leading the way. Given Post's unreliability in describing an actual document, his unconvincing account of an imaginary one can be safely consigned to the pages of the *Missionary Herald* where it first appeared.

Dissimulation

If the narratives of Omar's conversion to Christianity are not to be taken at face value, how should his religious position be understood? From a Muslim perspective, apostasy is viewed with great seriousness, and indeed the Mālikī school considers it a capital crime with minimal possibilities of recantation. But at the same time, there is a large dossier on forced conversion to Christianity among Muslims in Spain after the Reconquista, when the Catholic rulers of Castile and Aragon defeated the last Muslim rulers of Granada. There is a significant amount of discussion of this issue in Islamic texts, including Qur'an commentaries and legal writings. These discussions included the recognition that forced conversion could be excused if one remained a believer inwardly, performing outward conformity with another religion as a dissimulation, known by the Arabic term *taqiyya*. Contrary to a common understanding, the notion of dissimulation under persecution, the concept that one could conceal one's true faith if there is no choice, was not an option limited to Shi'i Islam. The case of the Spanish Muslims, known as the Moriscos, demonstrates how it was possible to accommodate to a hostile new religious order, much the same as the Marrano Jews, who were subject to a similar persecution. As Devin Stewart has pointed out, the practice of dissimulation implied a long-term "dramaturgy . . . [which] required a sustained performance involving hundreds of individual statements and actions of different types, many of which might have had little to do with expressions of belief or ritual practice per se."[17] It is likely that this type of dissimulative performance is the most appropriate way of understanding Omar's religious posture.

We base our conclusion that Omar's performance of Christian practices was dissimulation on aspects of his writings that contradict what would normally be expected of a new convert. But in thinking about Christianity and Islam in a competitive context, it is worth pointing out that this relationship is not symmetrical. That is, due to the historical relationship between the two traditions, Muslim sources have a great deal to say about the Bible and Christianity, while the reverse is not the case.

The Qur'an speaks in positive tones about the Torah, the Psalms, and the Gospel as originally authentic scriptures that were inspired by God and confirmed by the Qur'an. There is in principle no reason why Muslims should not consult the older scriptures if they are so inclined. Yet in practice, over the centuries a suspicion has arisen among Muslims that biblical writings have been distorted to a remarkable degree. This means that it is relatively uncommon for the Bible to feature as a standard reading or reference point for Muslim theologians, and there are some notable Muslim commentators on the Bible. But there is nothing in Islamic law that would forbid someone like Omar ibn Said from reading the Bible or listening to a Christian religious service. And while it is possible today to find friendly ecumenical gestures toward Islam on the part of some Catholic and liberal Protestant thinkers, evangelical Christians generally display hostility toward Islam that rules out any positive connection. The Qur'an was delivered to its audience some six centuries after the time of Jesus, so it goes without saying that it is not mentioned in the Bible. Islam tends to fall automatically into the category of false prophecy, and some Christian pastors have gone to the extent of publicly burning Qur'ans after conducting mock trials of the text for crimes against humanity. This historical relationship means that Omar's dissimulation has a smaller degree of internal tension than if he were an evangelical Christian pretending to be a Muslim.

We cannot read Omar's inner thoughts, but we can extrapolate from what he actually wrote. In fact, when he refers to his shift from Islamic to Christian practice, he uses the phrases "path of guidance" and "a great light," perhaps recalling that the Qur'an (5:44, 5:46) uses the same words to proclaim that there is "guidance and light" in the Torah and the Gospel. It is also possible that Omar was thinking of Qur'an 2:120, which rejects Jewish and Christian attempts to convert Muslims, declaring the superiority of Islam by saying that "the guidance of God is the [true] guidance." In that way Omar's reference to divine guidance could be read by Christians as affirming their religion, even as it could provide him ambiguous cover to declare his Islamic loyalty. If Omar was pretending to be something he was not, this pretense would have had consequences. If he was performing an imaginary identity for himself in church, then in his writings he could also summon the imagined but distant community that he greatly missed. But the form and meaning of the biblical texts quoted in his remaining documents will point to the audience that asked him to produce the documents, which they saw as evidence of his conversion and the benefits of slavery.

Omar's Unused Bible

What exactly was the Bible that belonged to Omar? Here we shall undertake a detailed analysis of Omar's actual treatment of the Bible in his writings, particularly since the Christian ministers and missionaries who knew Omar all regarded the Bible as a crucial element in his conversion. The Arabic version of the Bible that was obtained by Francis Scott Key had been published in 1811 in Newcastle-upon-Tyne, England, by Sarah Hodgson. The impetus for the publication came from Joseph Dacre Carlyle, professor of Arabic at Cambridge University. He was inspired by discussions that had been taking place in the British and Foreign Bible Society as early as 1798, in which missionaries became attracted to the potential of Arabic as a language for the evangelization of Africa.[18] For the text, Carlyle drew upon the Arabic version from the massive six-volume Polyglot Bible that had been produced in London in 1657, which for the Old Testament included the Arabic versions of the Torah translated from the Hebrew by the important medieval Jewish scholar Saadia Gaon (d. 942). The Arabic version of the Psalms had been translated from the Coptic Bible used by Egyptian Christians, also in the tenth century. When Carlyle died in 1804 while working on the New Testament text, the work was taken over and completed by another Arabic scholar from Cambridge, Henry Ford. The small number of copies printed, and their high cost, resulted in a relatively small audience for this translation, despite the support of Bible societies. It would soon be superseded by versions in a more modern style of Arabic that would appeal to Christian communities in the East. After Omar's death in 1863, his Bible came into the hands of Eleanor

("Ellen") Porterfield Owen Guion, daughter of John Owen. In 1871, she donated this Bible to Davidson College in Davidson, North Carolina.

Some reports from contemporary observers describe the way Omar would recite and translate from his Arabic Bible. According to one late report, "He has no copy of the Koran at present, but a few friends procured for him, after he became a Christian, a copy of the Bible in Arabic, in which he daily reads many chapters and which he translates with great aptness and force for his visitors."[19] Here is Mathew Grier's more extensive account:

> "Uncle Moreau" is an Arabic scholar, reading the language with great facility, and translating it with ease. His pronunciation of the Arabic is remarkably fine, and his reading is pleasant to hear, even when the hearer is wholly ignorant of the meaning of the words. His translations are somewhat imperfect, as he has never mastered the English language, but they are often very striking. We remember once hearing him read and translate the twenty-third Psalm, and shall never forget the earnestness and fervour which shone in the old man's countenance, as he read of the going down into the dark valley of the shadow of death, and using his own broken English continued, "me no fear, master's with me there." There were signs in his countenance and his voice that he felt the consoling influence of those words.[20]

This description displays the fascination that many felt upon witnessing Omar's command of an exotic language, despite their inability to understand or evaluate his knowledge of it. These observers enthusiastically praised Omar's grasp of the Bible, saying he was "translating with ease," before acknowledging his "imperfect" and "broken English." Was Omar actually reading aloud from the Arabic Bible, or reciting something else? It is difficult to say whether this account is wishful thinking or a reliable observation.

DOCUMENT 11: NOTATIONS TO THE BIBLE

The Bible of Omar ibn Said played a major role in his legend, as the major factor responsible for his conversion. Stories told about him emphasize that he constantly carried it. A photograph of the Bible at the Davidson College library shows it in very bad condition before restoration, strongly conveying the impression that it was handled a lot. It is therefore a matter of some importance to know if there is evidence in the Bible to indicate how Omar may have read it.

The evidence that exists can be summarized briefly, as seen below in the translations of the marginal comments that he made in the Bible.

There are several indications of Omar's possible dissatisfaction with the Arabic Bible, both for style and content. One minister reported, "This pious man is supplied with a copy of the Arabic New Testament. He says the translation is not good. Yet with the aid of the English he has learned much of God's word."[21] Since Omar was not in a position to evaluate the relationship of the Arabic Bible to earlier versions, his criticism may have been directed at its style. The Arabic Old Testament text found in his Bible probably dates from the tenth century, and it abounds with archaic expressions. Protestant missionaries found this translation to be difficult reading for Arab Christians, who increasingly became targets for conversion, as efforts to convert Muslims proved largely ineffectual, and evangelicals saw the Eastern churches to be badly in need of a new message.[22] So in a few years missionaries began to move to Arabic Bible translations with a more contemporary style. Omar too may have felt that the text was not easy, but it is not clear how his limited English could have compensated for that.

Further evidence is found in the form of comments that Omar has written in the front and back endpapers of the Bible, including several repetitions of the Good formula, Omar's own name, his customary signature, and a name in *'ajamī* that appears to be Mrs. Francis Bowen, the director of a school in Fayetteville from 1810 to 1831, and a member of the Episcopal Church of Fayetteville. She also presided over the establishment there of the "United Female Benevolent Society of North Carolina" in December 1819.[23] Two of Omar's comments have Islamic references. On the front flyleaf is a fragmentary quotation from the Qur'an: "Qarun was of the . . ." (Qur'an 28:76). As discussed in chapter 3, the complete verse evoked by these few words is a critique of arrogance and wealth that was quoted in Document 15 as part of a sermon; the Qur'an is particularly severe in its criticism of the gloating of the wealthy Israelite Qarun, and somehow that condemnation has come to mind in this brief scribble. The other comment relating to Islam is an adaptation of a line from the important theological and legal handbook, the *Summary* of Khalīl: "'Praise be to God, with much praise. He bestows bounties that overflow' with the good." This quotation has already appeared twice in the "Autobiography," where Omar cited it to show how he interpreted the New Testament. The appearance of this saying in the Bible is a confirmation of Omar's continued reference to Islamic theological arguments, especially in proximity to the biblical text.

TABLE 4.1.

Omar ibn Said's Arabic transcriptions of English titles of biblical books

FOLIO	ENGLISH TITLE OF BIBLICAL BOOK	ARABIC TRANSCRIPTION OF ENGLISH
4r	First Book of Moses, Genesis	*kitāb mūsā dhīnisiṣ*
22r	Second Book, Exodus	*kitāb al-thānī dhīnisiṣ**
37r	Leviticus	*alībitakas*
76r	Joshua	*dhushuā*
85r	Judges	*dhuzjis*
94r	Ruth the Moabite	*rūth baṣabā* (?)
96r	First Book of Samuel	*al-awwal kitāb sāmūl*
144v	First Book of Chronicles	*al-awwal kitāb kanakal*
168r	Ezra	*li-ʿizra* ["by Ezra"]
171v	Nehemiah	*niḥimyā*†
180r	Job	*dhūba*
189v	Book of Psalms	*kitāb sām*
230r	Isaiah	*aydhīʿa*
248v	Jeremiah	*zarimāʾya*
267v	Lamentations	*leman tays*
270r	Ezekiel	*ḥiziqiyāl*
296r	Joel	*dhoyil*
297r	Amos	*ʿīmaṣ*
300r	Jonah	*dhūna*
302v	Nahum	*nīham*
303r	Habakkuk	*ḥabaqak*
304r	Zephaniah	*zifʿināya*
311r	Matthew	*māsyuh*
322r	"The Good" (Good formula)	

322v	Mark	maʿk
329v	Luke	luk
341v	" . . . what those who . . ." (Qurʾanic phrase)	
342r	John	dhūn
351r	Acts of the Apostles	īʾakṣu dhībāsila
369v	1 Corinthians	al-kuwinsin
378v	Galatians	kalāsīn
380v	Ephesians	afīdhan
382r	Philippians	fīlībīn
383v	Colossians	kalāsan
385r	1 Thessalonians	taslūnī
387r	1 Timothy	timatī
390r	Philemon	fīlīman
390v	Hebrews	ḥibrū
394v	1 Peter	bitah
401r	Revelation	rebelesan

* The title of Genesis is erroneously repeated here in place of Exodus.
† The annotations to Ezra and Nehemiah consist only of short vowel marks added to the printed text.

Translation 4.1.
DOCUMENT 11: NOTATIONS TO THE BIBLE

––––––

[FRONT ENDPAPER]

"Praise be to God."

"The Good is with God" [Good formula].

"The Good is with God" [Good formula].

Mrs. Frances Bowen [*mis firasiṣ būmwā*].[24]

"The Good is with God" [Good formula].

[FRONT FLYLEAF]

"Those who believe" [frequent Qur'anic phrase].

"The Good is with God" [Good formula].

Omar ibn Said ibn Adam.

"Qarun was of the . . ." [Qur'an 28:76].

[ENDPAPER, 407V]

"Praise be to God, with much praise. He bestows bounties that overflow" with the good.[25]

My name is Omar bin Said son of Adam, but from my mother's side, [she is] Umm Hānī Yarmak. O God! May God refresh her grave.

The annotations to Omar's Bible provide frustratingly little indication of his interaction with the text. The most important evidence of Omar's use of the Bible remains in seven of the documents that are primarily devoted to biblical writings. While these do not contain any overt commentary, the way they are framed in each individual case is suggestive, and we will accordingly turn to those documents for clarification of this issue.

THE LORD'S PRAYER

Unsurprisingly, the most commonly quoted biblical text in Omar's documents is the Lord's Prayer, perhaps the best-known and most widely quoted lines from the New Testament. This prayer dictated by Jesus to his disciples has played a central role in Christian devotion over the centuries. We have translated it directly from the Arabic text, rather than using familiar English versions, in order to preserve the particularity of this version that Omar used. He has quoted it five times in his writings, either as a standalone text (in Documents 2, 3, and 10), combined with another biblical text (Psalm 51, in Document 18), or as the subject of a narration in the "Autobiography." Two of these examples (Documents 2 and 3), along with Document 18, contain introductory quotations of Islamic formulas, and one of them (Document 3) includes a talismanic drawing in the form of a text separator with strapwork decorations. The discussion of the Lord's Prayer in the "Autobiography" mentions it in the context of the change in Omar's religious practices after his enslavement in America, taking the place of the first chapter of the Qur'an as a defining religious practice. The overall impression throughout these documents is that Omar continues to apply Islamic writing practices, both verbal and graphic, in his treatment of this biblical text. At the same time, if we seek the appropriate category to classify Omar's quotation of the Lord's Prayer, it seems most fitting to describe it as a blessing text.

As we have already noted, the contents of the Lord's Prayer overlap significantly with the subject matter of "The Opening," the first chapter of the Qur'an. There is also a verbal connection between the Lord's Prayer and the Testing formula so frequently quoted by Omar, as in Document 2. The phrase widely translated as "lead us not into temptation" uses the plural form, "tests" or "temptations," in the Arabic version. Omar would have noticed that this word is related to the word "test" in his Testing formula ("he tests their words"). This is why we translate that phrase in the Lord's Prayer as "do not put us into tests."[26]

Translation 4.2.

DOCUMENT 2: THE LORD'S PRAYER, NO. 1

"Praise be to God, who created humanity to worship him, so he might test their actions, their words" [Testing formula].

"One who does good, does so to the benefit of his own soul; and one who does evil, does it against his soul" [Qur'an 41:46].

"Our father who is in the heavens, your name is sanctified. Your kingdom will come, your wish will be on the earth as it is in heaven. Our bread that is for tomorrow, give us today. And forgive us what we owe, as we forgive one who owes us. Do not put us into tests, but save us from evil, for the kingdom, and the power, and the glory are yours forever. Amen" [Lord's Prayer, Mt. 6:9–13].

Document 3: The Lord's Prayer, No. 2

This document is also preserved in the Davidson College library, probably arriving there about the time of the Arabic Bible. It is distinctive in its use of a Qur'anic invocation and blessing on the Prophet Muhammad to introduce the prayer of Jesus.

Translation 4.3.

DOCUMENT 3: THE LORD'S PRAYER, NO. 2

"In the name of God the Merciful, the Compassionate; may God bless our master Muhammad."[27]

"Our father who is in the heavens, your name is sanctified. Your kingdom will come, your wish will be on the earth as it is in heaven. Our bread that is for tomorrow, give us today. And forgive us what we owe, as we forgive one who owes us. Do not put us into tests, but save us from evil, for the kingdom, and the power, and the glory are yours forever. Amen" [Mt. 6:9–13].

My name is Omar ibn Said, but from my mother's side [she is] Umm Hānī Yarmak, may God refresh her grave.[28]

Document 10: The Lord's Prayer, No. 3

This is the plainest presentation of this biblical prayer. Preserved in the John Owen Papers in the North Carolina State Archives, for some reason this is mistakenly described as Psalm 23. This document varies slightly from the other quotations by including the full text of the opening verse, where Jesus tells his disciples, "So pray like this." In effect, this makes the document a quotation of verses from the New Testament rather than a performance of the prayer itself.

Translation 4.4.

DOCUMENT 10: THE LORD'S PRAYER, NO. 3

"So pray like this: Our father who is in the heavens, your name is sanctified. Your kingdom will come, your wish will be on the earth as it is in heaven. Our bread that is for tomorrow, give us today. And forgive us what we owe, as we forgive one who owes us. Do not put us into tests, but save us from evil, for the kingdom, and the power, and the glory are yours forever. Amen" [Mt. 6:9–13].

PSALM 23

The other more frequently quoted biblical passage in Omar's writings is Psalm 23 (Psalm 22 in the Arabic Bible), which also is an exceptionally popular and widely used prayer, particularly in the King James Version. As mentioned above, Omar was known for his rendition of this passage in his imperfect English. It is not surprising that Omar was drawn to the Psalms as an approachable part of the Bible; three of the six biblical texts that he quotes are from the Psalms. Commentators have frequently remarked that the literary style of the Qur'an is reminiscent of the Psalms for many readers of both texts.

Document 7: Psalm 23, No. 1

Omar presented this manuscript in 1855 to John Frederick Foard, an associate of the Owen family and a supporter of the colonization of African Americans in Liberia. Foard describes this document thus: "He announced the 23rd Psalm and read it, when I asked if he would kindly write it for me? he did so, and came with it for another interview. I was out visiting other friends and failed to see more of him, but the Psalm was written and left for me, which appears as written, with this communication."[29] The document and the scrapbook containing it were conveyed to the University of North Carolina Library by an official from the American Bible House. Again, Omar introduces this text with an Islamic invocation and blessing, and he also personalizes it with the date and the name of the addressee and a signature.

Translation 4.5.

DOCUMENT 7: PSALM 23, NO. 1

"In the name of God the Merciful the Compassionate; may God bless our master Muhammad" [Qur'anic and Prophetic formulas].

I write this letter in the year 1855 in the month of November, on the eleventh, Monday.

"The lord tends to me, he does not leave me lacking. He settles me on the green pasture and sets me by quiet water. He turns my soul to the paths of piety, and he guides me for his name's sake. If I travel in the midst of the shadows of death, I fear no evils, for you are with me. Your rod and your staff are my consolers. You have anointed my head with oil, your cup intoxicates me like wine. Your mercy and goodness will reach me all the days of my life, and I will live in the lord's house to the end of days" [Psalm 23].

I send this letter with a man called Foard.

My name is Omar ibn Said, but from my mother's side [she is] Umm Hani Yarmak, may God refresh her grave.

Document 13: Psalm 23, No. 2

This document is preserved among the Owen and Barry Family Papers in the New Hanover County Library in Wilmington. It is located inside the front cover of the writing journal of Eliza Henrietta Owen, daughter of James Owen. Like Document 7, it uses Islamic formulas to introduce the biblical text, and it concludes with a brief signature.

Translation 4.6.

DOCUMENT 13, PSALM 23, NO. 2

"In the name of God the Merciful the Compassionate; may God bless our master Muhammad" [Qur'anic and Prophetic blessings].

"The good is with God, and belongs to no other" [Good formula].

"The lord tends to me, he does not leave me lacking. He settles me on the green pasture and sets me by quiet water. He turns my soul to the paths of piety, and he guides me for his name's sake. If I travel in the midst of the shadows of death, I fear no evils, for you are with me. Your rod and your staff are my consolers. You have anointed my head with oil, your cup intoxicates me like wine. Your mercy and goodness will reach me all the days of my life, and I will live in the lord's house to the end of days" [Psalm 23:1–6].

OTHER BIBLICAL VERSES

Document 18: The Billheimer Verses

This document, the most recent one that has come to light, was written by Omar in 1856 and presented by James Owen to Gen. George B. McClellan at the Red Sulphur Springs resort in Virginia.[30] He in turn passed it on to Rev. Thomas Charles Billheimer (1842–1923), a Lutheran pastor from Pennsylvania, who in turn gave it to his son, Rev. Stanley Billheimer (1872–1964). The next owner, who remains anonymous, sold it to book dealer Ian Brabner, from whom it was purchased by the University of North Carolina Rare Book Collection in 2021. Like Document 8, it was presented to a prominent acquaintance at a hot springs resort. Among the documents containing biblical texts, this one is unusual in presenting two instead of just one. Like the majority of the biblical quotations, it is preceded by Islamic invocations and blessing formulas (A). In this case, there is an address line, specifying James Owen as the recipient. The date in English follows (B), and then comes a quotation of a Qur'an verse (C) that is also quoted in Document 8. It is a triumphal verse that alludes to the victory of the Prophet Muhammad over the unbelievers of Mecca. The rest of the first page (D) is occupied by Psalm 51 from the Bible (Psalm 50 in the Arabic version), the longest of the six biblical texts recorded by Omar. Traditionally ascribed to David like the rest of the Psalms, this powerful expression of repentance was often linked to the story of David's adulterous relationship with Bathsheba. It was a well-known text (called the Miserere from the first word in its Latin translation), often recited in church services. On the reverse (F) is another transcription of the Lord's Prayer, closing with a signature (G).

Translation 4.7.

DOCUMENT 18: THE BILLHEIMER VERSES

A. "In the name of God the Merciful the Compassionate; may God bless our master Muhammad" [from Omar to the gentleman (*sayyid*) named Jim Owen].

B. I write this letter in the year 1856, in the month of August [*a'qāst*], which means August [*ūkas*], on the fourth, Monday [*mandī*], which is what *ithnān* is called.[31]

C. "Help is from God, and victory is near, so bring good tidings to the believers" [Qur'an 61:13].

D. Psalm 50 [51], *sām*.[32] "Have mercy on me, O God, according to your unfailing love; according to your great compassion blot out my transgressions. / You wash away all my iniquity and you cleanse me from my sin.[33] / For I know my transgressions, and my sin is always before me. / Against you, you only, have I sinned and done what is evil in your sight; so you are right in your verdict and justified when you judge. / Surely I was sinful at birth, sinful from the time my mother conceived me. / Yet you desired faithfulness even in the womb; you taught me wisdom in that secret place. / Cleanse me with hyssop, and I will be clean; wash me, and I will be whiter than snow. / Let me hear joy and gladness; let the bones you have crushed rejoice. / Hide your face from my sins and blot out all my iniquity. / Create in me a pure heart, O God, and renew a steadfast spirit within me. / Do not cast me from your presence or take your Holy Spirit from me. / Restore to me the joy of your salvation and grant me a willing spirit, to sustain me. / Then I will teach transgressors your ways, so that sinners will turn back to you. / Deliver me from the guilt of bloodshed, O God, you who are God my Savior, and my tongue will sing of your righteousness. / Open my lips, Lord, and my mouth will declare your praise. / You do not delight in sacrifice, or I would bring it; you do not take pleasure in burnt offerings. / My sacrifice, O God, is a broken spirit; a broken and contrite heart you, God, will not despise. May it please you to prosper Zion, to build up the walls of Jerusalem. Then you will delight in the sacrifices of the righteous, in burnt offerings offered whole; then bulls will be offered on your altar. Hallelujah."[34]

E. The end.

F. "Our father who is in the heavens, your name is sanctified. Your kingdom will come, your wish will be on the earth as it is in heaven. Our bread that is for tomorrow, give us today. And forgive us what we owe, as we forgive one who owes us. Do not put us into tests, but save us from evil, for the kingdom, and the power, and the glory are yours forever. Amen." My name is Omar bin Said ibn Adam, but from my mother's side, [she is] Umm Hānī Yarmak. May God refresh her grave.[35]

G. The end. End ['ind].[36]

Document 14: Romans

The last of the biblical documents to consider is the only one in which Omar has quoted a text with theological implications regarding the doctrine of incarnation. The teaching that Jesus is the son of God is perhaps the most contentious aspect of Christianity as far as Muslims are concerned. The Qur'an is adamant in rejecting the anthropomorphic notion of God as father, and in Qur'anic Arabic, the word translated as "lord" (*rabb*) is reserved for God.

The document itself, preserved in the Eliza Owen scrapbook in the New Hanover County Library in Wilmington, is badly damaged, and only half of the brief amount of text that it contains is legible. The remainder of the biblical verse has been supplied from Omar's Bible.

It is not clear why Omar chose to quote this particular verse, which proclaims the divinity of Jesus and promises salvation through faith in him. The Islamic blessings at the beginning of the document would seem to be in conflict with that message; neither the doctrine of incarnation nor the resurrection of Jesus is acceptable in mainstream Islamic theologies. One possibility could be that Omar was asked to recite this verse as part of the baptism ritual that defined his entry to the Presbyterian church in 1820. Romans 10:9, with its strong emphasis on spoken confession combined with firm belief, may have been "the earliest form of the Creed" and "the formula of confession in baptism" for early Christians.[37] This verse is popular in modern gospel music, and it has played a role in Pentecostal conversion rituals.[38]

So it may be that Omar was simply recalling a particular phrase that he was asked to perform publicly in church. Yet it is hedged around by Islamic blessings, and the announcement of God's tests of humanity, that precede it. Those prefatory lines suspend the Christian confession of faith, rather than confirming it. Following this line of thinking, it seems appropriate to view this document as a historical record of what happened to Omar, not as a declaration of a change of faith.

Translation 4.8.

DOCUMENT 14: ROMANS

"In the name of God the Merciful, the Compassionate; may God bless our master Muhammad" [Qur'anic and Prophetic blessing formulas].

"Praise be to God, who created humanity to worship him, so he might test their actions, their words" [Testing formula].

"If you acknowledge with your mouth that Jesus is lord, and you have faith in your heart that God raised him from the dead, you are saved" [Romans 10:9].

Audience and Performance

Having completed our survey of Omar's biblical writings, the first question that arises is the overall religious character of this body of texts. The answer is that they remained remarkably consistent over more than three decades, although the biblical texts are not tied together into arguments as the Islamic texts are. Omar continues to display mastery of Islamic sources despite his protestations of forgetfulness in the "Autobiography." He quotes twenty-three different Qur'anic passages, amounting to thirty-one quotations if repetitions are included. In comparison, he quotes six different biblical texts, for a total of eleven quotations counting repetitions. Aside from scripture, Omar also quotes blessings and formulas (twenty-eight quotations), plus Prophetic sayings, Sufi poetry, and theological works, another fourteen quotations in all. It is apparent that he continued to write in terms of a scholarly tradition of West African Islam, including the 'ajamī method of writing non-Arabic words in Arabic script, long after his nominal conversion to Christianity. His performance included regular attendance in church, seated prominently in the Owen family pew; according to some accounts, it extended to participation in revival meetings.

From a formal and rhetorical point of view, there is little difference between Omar's biblical documents and those containing mostly Islamic materials. All the documents are explicitly or implicitly addressed to members of the white elite, whether visiting ministers, VIPs of different sorts, or the children of enslavers. All the documents remained illegible to their addressees, and Omar did not hesitate to include both stern sermons and talismanic blessings alongside triumphal Islamic declarations. The irony is that the only audience that could have read these documents was far away in both space and time.

As far as the biblical materials are concerned, the reader of Omar's documents is left to wonder why he quoted these particular texts. With the Lord's Prayer and Psalm 23, it is fairly obvious that the frequency of their performance in English would have made them familiar. Romans 10:9 may have played a role in Omar's baptism. Psalm 51, a classic expression of repentance, and Psalm 123, on the servitude of the believer, could easily have come to Omar's attention as popular standards in church services. Given Omar's sketchy engagement with the text of the Bible as a whole, his biblical citations seem to be a result of demands for samples of his Arabic, for the production of documents that were simultaneously exotic and familiar. When John Foard asked Omar for a copy of Psalm 23, he was evidently following a well-established pattern that we discuss in chapter 5. Jim Owen, as custodian of this unique resource, derived an undeserved fame from his enslavement of Omar. Nevertheless, the inability of anyone to read the Arabic left Omar on his honor to provide the right text. It seems that, for these six biblical passages at any rate, Omar was willing to look up the Arabic text and either recite it or copy it on demand (several of the biblical documents show interlinear corrections and insertions, probably the result of checking on unmemorized material). To this extent, he was curious enough, or compliant enough, to accede to requests for passages from the Arabic Bible.

To return to the question of Omar's religious identity, the weight of the evidence does not indicate that he claimed a Christian position in his Arabic writings. His use of biblical texts was restricted to a tiny sample, generally accompanied by Islamic formulas, and seemingly the result of requests that he embody the Bible in transcriptions; the resulting documents are so studied, so mute as to his interior state, that it is more credible to consider this as dissimulation. Who, then, was he? Omar remained a Muslim in church.

The Treachery of the Experts

The Missed Opportunity of a World Literature

The idea of a world literature was formulated by Johann Wolfgang von Goethe (d. 1832), inspiring other American and European voices who were critical of parochial and ethnocentric notions of culture. In 1827, Goethe declared, "I am more convinced that poetry is the universal possession of mankind, revealing itself everywhere and at all times in hundreds and hundreds of men. . . . I therefore like to look about me in foreign nations, and advise everyone to do the same."[1] Goethe was talking about developing paths to engagement with a newly emerging world of diverse cultures. He believed that "everywhere one hears and reads about the progress of the human race, about the further prospects for world and human relationships. . . . I am convinced a universal world literature is in the process of being constituted."[2]

In the two centuries since Goethe issued his call for world literature, this concept has been discussed and often criticized. Some saw it as an insincere mask allowing one to focus on European literature to the exclusion of all else.

Others dismissed it as an unrealistic task that was beyond the scope of normal education. After all, how many languages can anyone learn well enough to read poetry, for example? The point, as we understand it, is rather that the concept of world literature opens up the possibility of enlarging one's perspective by becoming acquainted with a culture different from one's own. It is a cure for a widely spread disease. Eurocentric prejudices have long excluded from literary consideration the languages of East Asia, the Middle East, and Africa, relegating them to the dustbin of barbarism. The nineteenth century saw the development of European colonial rule over much of these territories, and that conquest went hand-in-hand with the imposition of European languages and education on subject populations, an essential part of the "civilizing mission." When combined with ethnic nationalism in Europe itself, the focus on national languages has turned into a justification for racism, discrimination, and ethnic cleansing.

Indeed, in the century after Goethe's essay, the tide of imperialist ideologies would continue to rise. In his classic 1927 book *The Treason of the Intellectuals* (*La trahison des clercs*), the critic Julien Benda decried the complicity of intellectuals with racism and nationalism. In titling this chapter "The Treachery of the Experts," we allude to Benda's useful description of the power of racist and nationalist falsehoods that infect and overtake the custodians of knowledge production. When those given intellectual authority and respect are complicit in supporting systems like slavery, they are corrupted.

The call for a world literature was not widely heard. It coincided with the infancy of America's professional associations and expertise on Africa and the Middle East, which had a limited impact. This was almost fifty years after US independence from Great Britain, and nearly twenty years after the ban on the international slave trade. This was a time when American Arabists were reflexively assuming that the Qur'an was an inferior text, calling it "bombastic" and dismissing Muslim prayers as "random."[3] The first generation of published Black American poets such as Phillis Wheatley and George Moses Horton could have been seen as living proof of the universality of wisdom and literature, but as we have seen, the gatekeepers of American culture would not admit that.

What incentive did Americans have to learn the languages of Arabs or Africans? Everything was changing in the United States under Jacksonian politics: Americans wanted more democracy, continental expansion, and maritime commerce. The American Revolution had left as legacy the principle that all men are created equal, and all nations have the rights of self-determination. Theoretically, nothing prevented American experts from adopting an intellectual framework that would accommodate Goethe's call for a world literature.

Unfortunately, the expert community was limited by narrow intellectual horizons. In this chapter, we will examine the intellectuals who offered their real or imagined expertise to weigh in on Islam and Africa. The instrumental focus of using expertise to manage a slave-based economy was destructive to the larger aims of humanistic scholarship, and the fusion of colonization projects with missionary activities was also at odds with academic objectives. These are the main reasons why American experts failed to understand Omar ibn Said.

Civilizing Missions

What kind of efforts did US intellectuals make to understand Omar ibn Said and his writings? In early America, scholarship, Christian missions, and the intellectual underpinnings of slavery were deeply interconnected. The country's first academic societies followed the examples of French and British ethnological and geographic societies. The American Philosophical Society, by far the earliest, had been founded by Benjamin Franklin in 1743; both the American Ethnological Society and the American Oriental Society were founded in 1842.

Despite the limitations of this early scholarship, these societies included many of the scholars interested in Omar, and they generally were members of more than one society. Five of the sixty-eight founding members of the American Oriental Society (Bird, Cotheal, Hodgson, Salisbury, and Stuart) and three of the thirty-seven charter members of the American Ethnological Society (Dwight, Cotheal, and Hodgson), had been connected to the attempts to read Omar's documents.[4]

This was also an era profoundly affected by the Second Great Awakening, inspired by evangelical Christianity and signaled by events such as the founding of the American Bible Society in 1816. We should not be surprised that members of these learned associations often were also connected to missionary societies. The first issue of the *Journal of the American Oriental Society* contained numerous references, and a special appendix, on the scholarly activities of missionaries. Likewise, in the American Ethnological Society, "early debates revolved around the question of ethnology as a useful tool of missionary work versus ethnology as an end in itself, reflecting the division in the Society's membership between clergy and non-clergy." Both scholars and missionaries also belonged to the American Colonization Society (1817), known for being racist, as revealed by the project to send free Blacks to Liberia.

In the previous chapters, we have seen many examples of failures, misreadings, distortions, and outright lies in the depictions of Omar's documents.

Because of these overlapping professional boundaries, in evaluating nine-teenth-century writing about Omar, it is difficult to make a firm distinction between the academic amateurs and the missionary scholars. The shortcomings in their efforts were due to a lack of genuine scholarly expertise as well as ideo-logical limitations connected to slavery and colonialism. While these flaws can be found among both the missionaries, on one hand, and nominally academic figures, on the other, we will consider the two groups separately in order to clar-ify the forces at work, both when overtly driven by a desire to convert Africans, and when ostensibly inspired by scholarly inquiry.

Early American Attitudes toward Islam and Muslims

During the antebellum years, Islam was associated with barbarism, slavery, and violence. America's initial contacts with Muslim cultures occurred through con-flicts with the "Barbary pirates," a loose alliance of North African forces that demanded tribute from countries seeking trade in the Mediterranean. Barbary captivity narratives, depicting the sufferings of American sailors held in slav-ery, became popular among Americans in the second decade of the nineteenth century. As an example, in 1817, Captain James Riley, a former captive of Arab nomads in Algeria, published his memoir under the title *Sufferings in Africa*. The book was a best-seller and widely seen as validating America's long-standing fear of Oriental despots.

Islam had also played an important role in Christian apocalyptic thinking, starting with early colonial figures such as Cotton Mather and continuing up through the Millerites in the mid-1800s. For these evangelical Christians, the very existence of Islam, most prominently embodied by the formidable Otto-man Empire, was an anomaly they fervently opposed. Speculation about the coming Judgment Day focused on the Book of Revelation, treating its obscure warnings as coded predictions signaling the exact year when the Ottoman Empire would cease to exist, by divine command. Estimates for the date of this predicted event, deemed to be an essential step in preparation for the return of Christ and the resurrection of the dead, initially proposed 1697 but later shifted to 1840. Given the dominant role that apocalyptic thinking played among Amer-ican Christians, it should not be surprising that any discussion of Islam was nec-essarily based exclusively on the Bible. There would be no point in studying Ara-bic books on Islamic theology, because they could be dismissed as falsehoods and only a waste of time. Missionaries therefore had little incentive to become familiar with Islam, the Qur'an, or the principal Islamic power posing a problem for Christianity; that is, the Ottoman Empire.[5]

As a consequence, the whole topic of Islam in Africa was doubly marginalized; it was peripheral to the obvious center of Islam in Constantinople, it consisted primarily of Black Africans who were considered racially inferior, and no one knew very much about sub-Saharan Africa anyway. While the American Oriental Society proposed as its goal the study of the languages and cultures of Asia, Africa, and the Pacific, it is striking that the inaugural lecture of its first president, surveying the field of its inquiry, had nothing to say about sub-Saharan Africa apart from a few words on William Brown Hodgson's study of the Berber language. As a result, there was very little knowledge about Africa or Islam among Americans.[6]

What knowledge of Africa there was came from several sources. First, there were the enslaved Africans, many of whom came from the Senegambian region, where Islam has a strong and historical presence. Evidence indicates that some Americans were familiar with the presence of these enslaved African Muslims. Advertising runaway slaves under both their American and African Muslim names was common among plantation owners.[7] Missionary groups saw Islam as competing with Christianity for the "Negro" soul in Africa. This is what prompted Edward Wilmot Blyden, the first African American recipient of a PhD, later to travel to Africa and write his book *Christianity, Islam, and the Negro Race* in 1887.

Evangelical preachers who were familiar with foreign missionary work also brought information about Islam to their congregation. These preachers included supporters of the slavery system, and most had inherited old Western prejudices about Islam, which was labeled by inconsistently spelled names derived from that of the Prophet Muhammad. A rich tradition of polemics against non-Christian religions was typified by the very popular treatise of Dutch jurist Hugo Grotius, *On the Truth of the Christian Religion* (1627), which attacked three religious rivals: paganism, Judaism, and "Mahometanism."[8] These critiques were generic and made no distinctions between regional Muslim cultures; all were viewed as the same. Rev. Henry Bosman Covington (1830–85), for instance, would teach his congregation in Lincoln County, North Carolina, about Arabs and Muslims, arguing that Islam was a false religion: "Mahammadanism is very imperfect, and vastly impure in its motion and introduction, and has been extended ever since by the use of cursed weapons."[9] Like many observations of the time, Covington's sermon talks about Islam remotely, and the Muslim hypothetically, as if they did not exist already in the United States. Several years earlier, William Lancaster, a delegate to the 1788 North Carolina state convention to ratify the US constitution, warned his fellow delegates against using permissive language in describing who could become president of the United States. He did not trust the proposed wording of Article VI, Section 3, of the Constitution, that "no religious Test shall ever be required as a Qualification to any Office or public Trust under the United States." Lancaster cautioned that "in the course of four or five hundred years, I do not know how it will work. This is most certain, that Papists may occupy that chair, and Mahometans may take it."[10] To his mind, both Catholics and Muslims were eternal enemies of the nation, and were not meant to be American. Another delegate argued that even a Mahometan could seek office as long as he is elected by Americans. The amendment prohibiting religious tests passed with little dissent. In this debate, the Muslim example was an outlier, considered a remote possibility, but useful in probing the limits of constitutional rights.

Travel writing was another avenue for knowledge about Islam. Narratives by British explorers and colonial administrators such as Mungo Park and Thomas Thompson were widely read in America. Furthermore, a handful of Americans were also engaged as mercenaries in Egypt and reported their experiences. George Bethune English (d. 1828) became Muhammad Ali Pasha's chief of artillery during Egypt's conquest of northern Sudan in 1820, at which time he also converted to Islam. General English's memoir, *A Narrative of the Expedition to Dongola and Sennaar*, reads like an epic of conquest in Africa, even if it was written under the command of the viceroy of Egypt. English talks about leading an army of "Turkish cavalry, infantry and artillery, and a considerable proportion of Bedouin cavalry and Mogrebin foot soldiers . . . destined to follow the march of the army to the upper countries of the Nile."[11] His report ignores the cultural life of northern Sudanese Muslims, depicting a wasteland while exulting in Muhammad Ali's desire to conquer the sources of the upper Nile: "What was once a land occupied by nations superstitious and sensual is now inhabited by robbers and slaves."[12] His report placed African Muslims outside the fold of civilized nations or friends of the American Republic.

Missionary Interest in the Arabic Language

In the early nineteenth century, Arabic was seen as an exotic language that had little if any connection to America. Evangelical Christians were not interested in reading the Qur'an or Arabic literature in order to understand Muslim culture; they focused instead on trying to understand how Islam was depicted in the apocalyptic scenarios of the Book of Revelation, since that was the only reliable authority on the subject. It is true that some enslaved Africans were literate in Arabic, and this became noteworthy as a curiosity. Arabic-writing Blacks such as Abdulrahman ibn Ibrahima, Lahmen Kebby, and Omar ibn Said were mentioned in the popular press and introduced to church and professional congregations. Abdulrahman was even granted visits to members of Congress and the White House.[13] Some enslaved Muslims produced Arabic documents for various reasons, including pleas for public support; documents from some Muslim fugitives were even brought to the attention of former president Thomas Jefferson as collectors searched for someone who could read them.[14] These efforts were largely fruitless, however, since no one was able or willing to decipher what these slaves wrote.

The strongest reason for interest in Arabic was to learn it as a language that missionaries could use to spread the Christian message. Theodore Dwight, the editor of the *African Repository and Colonial Journal*, declared, "We believe that the study of this language [Arabic] should be neglected by none who propose to enter upon Missionary efforts in Africa, and that to all travelers in that country, a knowledge of it is of the highest importance."[15] Dwight asked readers of the *Methodist Review* why if a man like Omar was able to master a language (Arabic) so different from his own native tongue, Americans couldn't do the same. "Where is the youth, or even the adult, among the mass of our people who is able to do the same in Latin or Greek?"[16] Thompson, a former British governor of Sierra Leone, encouraged American missionaries to study Arabic before going to Africa, noting that the language represented a cultural bridge between Africa and the Middle East: "A man who intends to devote himself to Africa, might find means to prepare himself with a knowledge of the language by passing a few years previously in Palestine or Egypt."[17] Dwight proudly reported that he "found a few native Africans in the North"[18] who were able to read and write the language.

In the academic sphere, "it was the common opinion that there was no need to teach Arabic in our colleges."[19] And if some missionaries expressed interest in using Arabic to export Christianity, none wrote of using it to import foreign cultures; the inclusion of an exotic language like Arabic in the category of literature was still unthinkable. Thus, Jonas King, contemplating a missionary career, asked himself, "Can I give up all prospect of literary distinction in America, and turn my knowledge of Arabic already acquired to immediate practical use in instructing the ignorant, far from my friends and native land?"[20] As a result, there was no expert in America like Friedrich Rückert (d. 1866), the German professor of oriental languages who translated many classical Islamic texts such as the *Māqamāt al-Harīri*. No American expert came close to the French scholar Silvestre de Sacy (d.1838), who authored the two-volume *Grammaire arabe*. An exceptional case was Ralph Waldo Emerson, whose significant engagement with Persian poetry began in 1841, and was summarized by his lengthy essay on that subject for the *Atlantic Monthly* in 1858.[21] Such candid appreciation of non-European literature was uncommon, however. The American experts, to the extent they discussed Islam and Africa at all, were mostly preoccupied with dismissing the merits of African and Muslim cultures and endorsing the racist underpinnings of slavery.

In practice, some American writers, such as Thomas Bluett and Thomas Thompson, undertook open-minded case studies of enslaved people and the ideas of intelligence, literacy, and education among the peoples of Africa. Some even overcame anti-Islamic prejudice enough to express admiration for the Qur'an. Tayler Lewis (1802–77), a professor of Greek at the University of New York, took up the study of Arabic seriously. In commenting on a Qur'an manuscript from West Africa, he confessed, "I could not help feeling a wonderful interest in this strange book," and he even acknowledged "the literary excellence of the Koran."[22] Figures like Dwight, Blyden, and Thompson nevertheless always qualified their momentary enthusiasm for things African and Islamic with unquestioning support for the colonization of Liberia and the Christianization of Africa by that means.

There was also a limit to what literate Blacks could provide in terms of expertise on Arabic, Africa and Muslims. African-born Blacks who knew Arabic, like Omar and Abdulrahman, were much older than the average enslaved African and had been removed from Africa for many years; their command of English was weak, and both disuse of Arabic and the trauma of enslavement eroded their ability to express their viewpoints through that medium. In addition, none of these figures was seriously interested in furthering the aims of the missionaries, though Abdulrahman and Lamin pretended to support them, as a stratagem to return to Africa.

Therefore regional language competence and specialization in both Africa and Muslims were hardly to be found in the United States. Pioneers in the field of Africa and the Middle East included a few amateur scholars or political appointees, but most were missionary workers who spent time in these regions. These experts were often affiliated with the American Colonization Society, the American Ethnological Society, and the American Board of Commissioners for Foreign Missions. Their stories and reports were published in their newspapers and periodicals, such as the *Methodist Review*, the *African Repository and Colonial Journal*, and the *Christian Advocate*.

The Role of Proslavery Missionaries and Clergymen

The possibility of using free Blacks from the United States to spread the Gospel and establish trade partners dominated the thinking about Africa. A consensus on establishing an American colony where freed American Blacks could be returned as missionary workers found support among both proslavers and missionaries. For proslavers, this compromise would help get rid of free Blacks, whom they saw as a threat to southern slavery. Missionaries considered such a move an opportunity to bring the light of the Gospel to Africans. Likewise, the notion of creating a colony of American Blacks within Africa gained backing both from the American Colonization Society on the national level, and from state and local associations formed to support the same purpose. It was an unusual example of outsourcing a colonial enterprise to private groups motivated by religious aims.

It is sometimes forgotten that prior to the eighteenth century, enslavers were reluctant to permit conversion to Christianity, fearing that the new religious identity would confer freedom from slavery. The Second Great Revival that climaxed in the early nineteenth century furnished much of the impetus for converting Blacks, on the theory that this would provide stability for the slavery regime. The compatibility between Christianity and slavery became a divisive argument for southerners in the ensuing years, leading the enslaving elites to adopt new strategies for reconciling Christianity with slavery. A consensus developed among southern planters around the imperative to Christianize enslaved Blacks. William Capers, a South Carolina Methodist preacher and a longtime editor of the *Southern Christian*, told the enslavers that, "if Negroes could not be trusted with the gospel, Christianity might be 'at war' with slavery," but if they can be made "true Christians within the structures of Southern society, they would be living proof of God's favor, and conscience might be satisfied."[23] Many planters found in Capers's proposition a face-saving solution for the institution of slavery, and they followed his advice methodically. Two results emerged from enslavers' tactics in countering the abolitionist movement: they welcomed proslavery missionary experts and clergymen onto their plantations, giving them access to their human property, and they captured and disseminated photographic representations of enslaved Blacks that were designed to humanize the institution of slavery.

The mishandling of Omar's documents by the experts (whether academics or missionaries) was the result of the compromises that characterized the disputes over slavery during the antebellum era. The enslavers who controlled Omar only showed his writings to experts who exhibited proslavery sentiments. In return, these experts and their professional associations, religious or secular, used that access to showcase their familiarity with Africa and Muslim cultures. This transactional exchange of interest between enslavers and proslavery experts was the raison d'être for the systematic distortion of Omar's writings.

Proslavery clergymen maintained close relationships with enslavers such as the Owens, who provided them with access to Omar's "conversion story" so they could publish it in their journals and present it on fundraising tours. Most accounts of Omar's life story come to the present through these supporters of slavery. As we have noted in previous chapters, James Owen was a prominent member of the Fayetteville Presbyterian Church and a board member of the Fayetteville chapter of the American Bible Society. Proslavery missionaries and clergymen such as Mathew Grier, Ralph Gurley, and Gregory Bedell navigated this amicable arrangement with ease as they interviewed Omar and reported about him in antiabolitionist and Christian journals. They reconciled slavery with Christianity and fabricated lies in advancing this goal. This group's legacy lingered into the period after the American Civil War, when many southern experts defended the "Lost Cause" by reviving their old racist rhetoric.

A striking example of the experts' role in reconciling southern antipathy toward Christianizing Blacks was Charles Colcock Jones (d. 1863), a Georgian planter and pastor. Jones was a Princeton educated academic and professor of church history and polity at Columbia Theological Seminary in South Carolina; he also acted as the corresponding secretary to the board of domestic missions of the Presbyterian Church.

Jones advocated spreading the Gospel among enslaved Blacks but had no sympathy for the abolitionists. He believed that the Gospel would maintain a slavery-based society without causing conflict and war. Religious instruction for Blacks, in his view, "must be an entirely different thing from the training of the Caucasian." This approach will awaken Blacks' powers "to call into action that peculiar capacity for copying the habits, mental and moral, of the superior race," he wrote in his 1842 book, *The Religious Instruction of the Negroes*. Jones was aware that the enslaved Africans included practicing Muslims, and he saw a way to bring them into Christianity by claiming the two religions were ultimately the same: "The Mohammedan Africans remaining of the old stock of importations, although accustomed to hear the Gospel preached, have been known to accommodate Christianity to Mohammedanism. 'God,' say they, is Allah, and Jesus Christ is Mohammed—the religion is the same, but different countries have different names."[24] If this was an acceptable strategy to Jones, it would be ironic, given that such erasure of the difference between Christianity and Islam would have been anathema to Protestant ministers.

Was Jones alluding to the situation of Omar ibn Said in referring to Muslim slaves? It is not clear, but evidence connects Jones to the Owen family later. His wife, Mary Jones, received one of Omar's writings (Document 8) from James Owen in July 1857 while she and her husband were on vacation at the hot spring in Virginia.

Likewise, James Owen gave Document 18 to Gen. George McClellan, whom he met at Red Sulphur Springs, Virginia, in 1856. McClellan then passed it on to Rev. Thomas Charles Billheimer, a pastor at Gettysburg Seminary in Pennsylvania. Omar was well over eighty years old, and it can be assumed that he was unable to travel with James. Both Jones and Billheimer wrongfully identified their documents as the Lord's Prayer instead of a sura from the Qur'an. We have learned from Jones's letters to her children during those days in Virginia that they were disappointed in the healing powers of the hot spring; "Your dear father has not derived the advantage we anticipated. It was two weeks yesterday since we arrived here," she wrote to inform one of her children. And her husband was even advised by his doctor to refrain from the baths for a few days due to the continuous decline in his health.[25] Charles Colcock Jones must have been also hoping to reap some healing mysteries from Omar's copy of the Lord's Prayer.

Unfounded lies about slavery flourished among other missionary experts, as can be seen in the writings of John Leighton Wilson (d. 1886). A graduate of Columbia Theological Seminary, and a representative of the American Board of Commissioners for Foreign Missions in West Africa, Wilson eagerly promoted the lie that Omar was a criminal outcast sold into slavery by his own people. In another stunning display of arrogance, Wilson's 1855 book on West Africa rejected enslaved Blacks as credible sources on Africa because, he argued, they had no knowledge of the country, except of the particular district from which they came. Besides, it took so long to learn English well that they would be unable to impart any information they had.[26] Wilson presents himself as an expert on Africa since he "spent between eighteen and twenty years" there.

Omar makes an appearance in Wilson's book when the author talks about the Foulah people, one of the targets of missionary groups. Wilson maintains that they never participated in the slave trade, except in a few cases when disposing of criminals by selling them off instead of putting them to death. Then Wilson claims that Omar was one of these condemned Foulah people: "There is still [one] living in Wilmington, North Carolina, by the name of Moro, now eighty-five years of age. He has had opportunity to return to his country, but has always been adverse to returning. He was expelled from his own country for crime, but found the Savior here, and loves the country where he has found so inestimable a treasure."[27] Like most of the clergy who took over Omar's story,

Wilson provides no evidence to back his claims. He was evidently unaware that selling Muslims into slavery was legally prohibited in Senegal during the rule of Almaami Abdul Kader (1776–1807), which includes the date of Omar's capture. The selling of a fellow Fulbe into slavery is inconceivable according to both oral and written Foulah history. Omar also makes clear that he was sold into slavery by an invading, non-Muslim army that killed his fellow townsmen and captured him. Wilson's account of these events remains untrustworthy.

JOHN FREDERICK FOARD, DEFENDER OF SLAVERY

John Frederick Foard (1827–1909), a planter and physician, embodies the contradictions of proslavery and the hypocrisies of the experts. While he was an active advocate of resettling Blacks in Africa, he was a collector of Omar's Arabic documents. He had in his possession Omar's Document 7, which he formally dated 1856, although Omar actually inscribed the date of document in Arabic as 1855. Like many of his colleagues, who had earlier been advocates for the American Colonization Society, Foard became a leader of the white supremacist movement in the New South. Foard positioned himself as a champion of the "Negro Problem" in the late nineteenth century.

With the rebirth of white supremacist movements early in the twentieth century, Foard updated and published the third edition of his *North America and Africa* booklet to include Omar in 1904. The first two editions of the sixty-seven-page pamphlet, printed in 1875 and 1877, did not mention Omar. The 1904 edition added a supplement section to advertise for Foard's monthly magazine, plus a section on Omar, "A true story of an African prince in a Southern home." The section on Omar is very telling, demonstrating the revisionist approach of the southern elite and their attempt to control the narrative of slavery. This updated version has three main purposes.

First, Foard is remaking Omar's image to both retroject and project his racist vision. He is publishing the story for the first time, almost a half-century after receiving Omar's Arabic document. In the intervening years, he was never interested in seeking a translation, or knowing the real content of the document. But the turn of the century was a reckoning and awakening moment for white supremacist groups throughout the South. They rebranded southern slavery as a model institution, compared to the new colonialism that European nations were building in Africa. And Black Africans, including "Prince Moro," were depicted as finding peace and salvation in southern slavery. Here is how Foard romanticized Omar's story:

When America was discovered, England, Spain, Portugal, and other modern nations were perpetuating African slavery by buying captive prisoners of war, and non-combatants stolen for the trade. About seventy-five years ago a slave-ship landed and sold a cargo in or near Charleston, S.C. Among the number was a son of a King of the Malays or Melis, of Central Africa. Not willing to become a slave and not knowing the English language, he ran away and lived in the forest and swamps, until he was captured near Wilmington, N.C., and lodged in jail, and advertised and sold to General James Owen, at a large price.[28]

While Foard builds on previously circulated narratives, he clearly elaborates the tale.

Second, Foard attributed Omar's willingness to convert to Christianity to the generosity of the southern enslavers and their treatment of him as a family member.

General Owen was a brother of one of our former governors by that name, bought him as a curiosity, who built for him a house on his lot near his mansion, supplied all his wants, and gave him the liberty of the city; the only service he did during his natural life was to do shopping and carry messages for the family when needed; giving him time for reading and study. Having been well educated in his native language, soon adapted himself to the language and customs of the best people around him, became a devout Christian and a member of the First Presbyterian church with the Owen family, while he lived being called "Uncle Moro," and highly respected by all of both races of the city and many visitors.[29]

Again, the portrait of slavery on the plantation is idyllic.

Third, there is an aura of fixation in Foard's remarks on Omar's regal bearing, his hands, color, and norms of speech. Foard is using these disarming techniques to support his claim of Omar's royal origin. But the fact of Omar being a Black African was too evident for Foard to deny:

In the fall of 1855, the writer was a lay member of the North Carolina Conference of the M.E. Church, South, which met in Wilmington, and with others enjoyed the hospitality and kind attention of Miss Ellen Owen, daughter of Governor Owen, for nearly a week. When the name and history of the ex-Prince were discussed—Miss Ellen proposed sending for "Uncle Moro." He was received in her splendidly furnished parlor and introduced to each visitor, by receiving the right hand of each one between both of his and giving a hearty shake, after which, he was seated among his guests. He was a fine looking man, copper colored, though an African, well dressed, in a black coat reaching below the knees, as worn by the nobility of foreign countries of his day; sat very erect in his chair, with hands opened and resting on his legs. He conversed for a short while gracefully, after which, Miss Ellen handed him the family Bible and asked him to read a lesson in his native language. He announced the 23rd Psalm and read it, when I asked if he would kindly write it for me? he did so.[30]

Foard and other white supremacist leaders inherited the legacy of the proslavery clergymen of the antebellum era, and they were adamant on transforming Omar into a fictionalized legend, divorced from both Blackness and Africanness. Their success seems to be evident: Omar's story as well as his "Autobiography" went missing for more than a half-century. And the newer generations of North Carolina historians were unable to free themselves from the blinders of antebellum fantasies.

Louis T. Moore, arguably North Carolina's most popular amateur historian of the twentieth century, made Omar a central piece in his stories of the Cape Fear region.[31] His first popular piece on Omar, published in 1927, supplies Omar with Arabian roots: "Some thought occasionally that Moreau was of negro extraction. He always emphasized that fact that he was an Arabian and not a native of Africa." Omar, he observed, never disclosed the story of his capture. "He would only say that as a result of a conflict, he was captured and sold into slavery by some of the African tribes with which he had come in contact." Much of the story also talks about the Owens, and their benevolence toward Omar. So, "the grateful slave" declined his freedom. He declared that he was "willing to live and die under the good influence of a master." As this story gained popularity among southerners, Moore produced more fanciful tales about Omar, certainly from imagination rather than from facts.

One of Moore's embellished Omar tales is "Prince Slave of State's Governor."[32] By his own acknowledgment, Moore saw the story as coming from Arabian Nights tales, except that, in his words, "it is a fact and constitutes a reference to one of the most glamorous and admirable characters of the history." Moreau, the Arabian prince, was kidnapped from his homeland by some African tribes who sold him into slavery, and he was happy to be "a prince of a foreign nation . . . owned by the ruler of a State." The happy ending of this "Arabian nights tale" in North Carolina is that, because of the friendly treatment that he received from the ruler of North Carolina, Prince Moreau was said to be responsible for the spread of Christianity in his homeland of Arabia.

Experts' lies are always consequential, whether revered or reviled. In Omar's case, they have been revered for so long that they have obscured the man and his legacy.

THEODORE DWIGHT, AMATEUR AFRICANIST

No discussion of antebellum experts' engagement with Islam, Arabic, or Omar will be complete without considering a leading supporter of African missions in his time, Theodore Dwight Jr. (1796–1866). Dwight was the most prominent collector of African manuscripts produced under American slavery. A survey of the collections at the Library of Congress indicates Dwight's conspicuous engagement with West African Muslim writings throughout the antebellum era.[33] Due to his efforts, Omar's "Autobiography," Shaykh Sana See's papers, and the story of "Old Paul" (Lamin Kebe, known also as Lahmen Kebby) were preserved. Dwight was the first secretary of the American Ethnological Society and editor of its distinguished magazine. But where do we locate Dwight's position in the discourse on Africa?

Dwight studied theology with his uncle, Yale president Timothy Dwight, but never became a minister. Far from being a specialized scholar, he spent most of his life in New York City, writing for the general public in newspapers and magazines, on topics such as travel in the United States, local and ancient history, and public education, of which he was a great supporter. Although fascinated by languages, especially those of Native Americans, he was a generalist and a philanthropist rather than a scholar.

Dwight's writings and correspondence reveal the dilemma of a writer who is torn between the two camps of slavery and abolition. Like virtually all American intellectuals at the time, he was a promoter of spreading the Gospel among African Muslims and held the standard views on Islam as an inferior religion. He once characterized Islam in Africa as the "religion of the false prophet," and argued that the Qur'an's doctrine of the attributes of God and its moral principles were copied from the Hebrew Scriptures.[34] In this, he was affirming views that went largely unquestioned. What made Dwight distinctive was his genuine admiration for African culture, which he attempted to study with the meager resources then available.

Dwight's introduction to Omar came through Lamin Kebe (ca. 1785–1840), a learned West African scholar who spent over thirty years enslaved in South Carolina, Alabama, and other southern states. Omar had sent his 1831 "Autobiography" to Kebe, who in turn passed it on to Dwight in 1836. After getting his freedom, Kebe moved to New York with the American Colonization Society, while waiting for a vessel to take him to Liberia. His interviews with Dwight in 1834 and 1835 confirmed Dwight's belief in global literature and the plausibility of borrowing good practices from the people of West Africa. In his published accounts, Dwight tells his readers that while geographers of Europe have been exhausting their scanty resources, and sacrificing their lives to reach the banks of the Niger, Americans could learn all this at once from Kebe, "a man who has been living despised, and a slave in our own land, [but is] in possession of not a few of the secrets thus anxiously sought for by the learned."[35]

Dwight talks about receiving from Kebe a catalog of about thirty books in Kebe's own language. He then criticizes a French scholar's unfavorable account of the Sereculah (Sarakhule) language, because the language, in his view, is "agreeable, sonorous and easy to the organs of speech." Dwight urges his contemporaries to take lessons on good education from Kebe, noting that his mind shows some of the traits of a "professional school-master, and his opinions on pedagogy, claim some attention, as they are founded on experience, and independent of those current in other countries." Kebe was against allowing children to dictate to their parents which school they should attend: "It is very wrong to do as your children do in this country," which is allowing children to change their school if they are unhappy there. Dwight also provided a vocabulary list of the Sereculah language. This work established a blueprint on how Arabic could be used as a language of culture and a source of learning about Africa.

In an 1860 letter from Stephen Allen Benson, the president of Liberia, one senses Dwight's request for respect for African Muslims, attention to their intellectual well-being, and the need to utilize Arabic to mutually benefit both Muslims and Christians. Benson's response notes, "I fully Concur with you in the opinion you express, respecting the intellectual Constitution of some of the Mohamedan tribes east of us; and the incalculable good that might be effected, by Circulating—through Liberian or native agency—among them, publications, however small, in the Arabic language, descriptive of Civilized Countries; illustrated by small maps &c &c, with information Concerning the Customs, Arts, Sciences, and Christianity of those Countries."[36] Dwight was an enthusiastic leader of the American Colonization Society, but he was disappointed by most Americans' disregard for African cultures. He was a lucid sympathizer with Africans and their Arabic writings.

Enslavers' Photographic Representations of Omar

Photographic representations of Blacks were politicized in support of both slavery and abolition. The 1850s witnessed the weaponization of photographic representation in the antislavery movement. Frederick Douglass's popular autobiography of 1845, the publication of *Uncle Tom's Cabin*, and the appearance of the famous photograph of the fugitive Gordon fueled the antislavery narrative. *Uncle Tom's Cabin; or, Life among the Lowly* (1852) showcased the inhumanity of slavery while asserting the healing values of Christian love among the enslaved. The widely circulated image of the Black fugitive Gordon (also known as "whipped Peter," 1863), showed the scarred back of the formerly enslaved Peter, thus providing patent evidence for the cruelty of slavery. This moment also demarcated the time of the *Dred Scott* decision (1857) in which Roger B. Taney (d. 1864), the chief justice of the US Supreme Court, defended slavery, writing that a Black man has "no rights which the white man was bound to respect." This moment saw photography as a new, poignant material culture of objective proof in which Omar's personal portraits were captured by a polarized politics. Omar's extant portraits were products of proslavery politics designed to undermine abolitionism.[37]

Enslavers embraced the new medium of photography to counter the growing popularity of the abolitionist movement. They collected dehumanizing images of Blacks from their plantations to support the work of racist pseudoscientists who were claiming the inherent inferiority of Blacks. Showing Blacks as exotic primitives was the sole object of the photographic salon established in Columbia, South Carolina, by Louis Agassiz (1807–73), a Swiss-born Harvard University biology professor. In 1850, this pseudoscientist collaborated with South Carolina enslaver Robert Gibbes to prove, by taking naked pictures of Gibbes's enslaved subjects, his racial theory of the inferiority of Blacks. At the annual meeting of the American Association for the Advancement of Science, held in Charleston, South Carolina, in March 1850, Agassiz worked hard to validate his findings among his colleagues.[38]

Meanwhile, enslavers also collected images of their captives to demonstrate how slavery subtly asserted its Christianizing mission over the enslaved heathens. These commissioned, splendid photographic portraits of Blacks were used to advance a proslavery narrative of the benevolence of slavery. Omar's function in the Owens's household throughout his life was to be one such living proof. His extent portraits also fit these patterns of coercive representation. Two decades after his death, a local source was still reporting that Omar's "photograph is valued by all the surviving descendants of Governor and General Owen as that of a cherished member of their household and friend."[39]

One of Omar's extant images (fig. 5.1) neatly fits this category. This portrait is currently housed in the Beinecke Rare Book and Manuscript Library at Yale University. The photo is an ambrotype, a photographic process that was introduced in the United States in 1854, following the daguerreotype, an earlier version of photographic processing. The newly introduced ambrotype photographic style gained popularity because it was cheaper and faster to produce. The presentation of Omar obscures his condition as an enslaved person. It features him wearing a dark suit with a matching headwrap and resting his left elbow on a newel post, with one of his curled hands grasping his cane from beneath. A paper label written by an unidentified collector carries this inscription: "'Uncle Moreau' a slave of great notoriety, of North Carolina, a scholar who once wrote me a letter in Arabic & sent me his picture, a sketch of his life was in the *Congregationalist*, also the *American Missionary*." It is no doubt the ideal portrait of Omar that James Owen would take with him to show friends and acquaintances in his travels to Virginia hot springs, where Omar's Arabic manuscripts, recognized as Lord's Prayer blessings, were distributed to friends and business partners.

The second photographic portrait of Omar (fig. 5.2) belongs to the same category of coercive representation. The photo, dated 1855, is found in the North Carolina Collection Photographic Archives at UNC–Chapel Hill. The portrait is cased in an ambrotype with gold overlay and embossed leaf designs around the edges. Omar is wrapped in a dark woolen, waterproof coat, of a quality usually reserved for aristocracy. The coat is tightly buttoned, concealing any part of the body, his arms immersed in the sea of the coat's rolls. He wears a cap identical to a type of West African hat worn by some of the enslaved.

The third portrait of Omar that we consider (fig. 5.3) belonged to Alfred Moore Waddell (d. 1912). This portrait is in the DeRosset Papers in the Southern Historical Collection at UNC–Chapel Hill. Waddell, a white supremacist who married into the wealthy DeRosset family in Wilmington, was a Confederate veteran and southern politician. In 1898, he was a leader of the Wilmington Insurrection, in which the elected government was overthrown and many Blacks were massacred.[40] Waddell, the new mayor of Wilmington, became the public face of the "Lost Cause," a movement that erected Confederate monuments throughout the South.[41] Omar's photo with the white background seems to be copied from an ambrotype original portrait. Waddell comments extensively on the back of the photograph, imposing his own rhetoric over Omar's silence:

Uncle Moro' (Omeroh), the African (or Arab) Prince whom Genl. Owen bought, and who lived in Wilmington N.C. for many years, and died

in Bladen Co. in 1864, aged about 90 years. This old man's history was extremely interesting. Born in the region around Timbuctoo and the son of a King or Chief, he was taught to read & write Arabic, & having committed some offence he was banished by his people who were named by some writers Malis, or Mellès, and, by Stanley, Malais. He was captured and sold into slavery to a ship which brought him to South Carolina, where he was purchased by a young upcountry planter, who treated him harshly, and he ran away, wandered over the line into North Carolina, was found ill at a negro cabin, was arrested as a runaway slave, put in jail at Fayetteville, and, having attracted attention by writing on the walls in Arabic, was released by Gen. James Owen on bond, afterward bought by him from the S. C. planter and treated as a pensioner and friend the remainder of his life. Although a devout Mahometan he became a devout Presbyterian, and lived befriended & respected by everybody until his death in 1864, at the age of about 90 years. He is buried in the family graveyard of the Owens in Bladen County N.C. It was said that he was a Free Mason. He was a short, "Mustee"-colored man, polite, and dignified in his manners. I remember him very distinctly.

Waddell signed the picture and dated it 1904.

Waddell's note is rife with inaccuracies. He was echoing the legend of Omar, an image that was developing in the late nineteenth century and early twentieth century among southerners opposed to Black progress. In their view, for Black progress to be aborted, stories of esteemed, respected, or literate Black figures must be dismantled. Iconic Black figures in the southern press such as Omar ibn Said must then be Arabs, not Black Africans; they must be from a romanticized "Timbuuktu," not Futa Toro; Omar has to be a Mustee, a colored man, and a loyal slave, not a Black African.

After Reconstruction, deforming or hiding Omar's persona became another element supporting the white supremacist narrative. Waddell's systematic denial of Omar as a literate Black enabled defenders of the "Lost Cause" such as John S. Kendall to argue, as late as 1939, that scholars could never know what it was like to be a slave: "We do not know. The slaves themselves never told," he wrote. Kendall goes on to argue that Blacks, whether enslaved or free, had no literary gifts. "If they were capable of self-analyses to the degree of distinguishing their sentiments in one estate from those in the other, they have omitted to set down the result in writing."[42] Obviously, the absence of Omar's "Autobiography" and the preponderance of lies made Kendall's statement plausible.

FIGURE 5.3.

Albumen print of Omar ibn Said, 1850s. DeRosset Family
Papers (00214), Southern Historical Collection, Wilson Library,
University of North Carolina at Chapel Hill.

Amateur Scholars

Arabic experts were few and not professionally trained, since learning the language required industrious, self-guided, and solitary study. Unlike France, Germany, and England, England's North American colonies had no long tradition of oriental studies, and the only reason for thinking about Arabic was in connection to the study of the Bible. Ernest McCarus pointed out the connection between teaching Arabic and teaching Hebrew in America, beginning at Harvard in the eighteenth century, Yale in 1700, Dartmouth in 1807, and Princeton in 1822.[43] Interest in the Hebrew Bible and Semitic languages was the driving force for the inclusion of Arabic studies at several seminaries in the New England region. The methodology of teaching Arabic was poor and lacking in materials. The Ivy League schools that taught Arabic focused on grammar and translation to understand Arabic texts.[44] Students had little incentive to pursue such subjects, however. When Edward Salisbury was appointed professor of Arabic at Yale in 1843, without a salary, during the thirteen years that he offered Arabic courses, only two students signed up.[45] Others came to the field of Arabic through their missionary work in the Middle East or North Africa. It fell to these dispersed experts to interpret the Arabic writings that were found among enslaved Africans, including Omar.

Typically, scholars known to have studied Arabic only dabbled in the subject and never acquired much proficiency. This was the case with Peter du Ponceau, one of the pillars of the American Philosophical Society, and renowned for his interest in Native American languages. He is mentioned as an Arabic scholar, but his philological notebooks reveal that he had barely looked at the Arabic alphabet, much less studied the grammar.[46] Moses Stuart, a Yale-educated professor of biblical studies at Andover Theological Seminary from 1810 to 1848, was the first scholar assigned to translate one of Omar's documents. Unfortunately, he was not in the least qualified to read them.

It is undeniable that Omar's knowledge of Arabic fascinated Americans who came to know about him and his strange ability. Yet there is something childish in this wonder. No one had the slightest ability to evaluate Omar's command of the language, but it was standard practice for his observers to praise the beauty of his handwriting and the eloquence of his composition. It was as if learning Arabic was a switch that could be flipped to confer a sudden and total knowledge of the language and its complexities. No one seemed to entertain the notion that, like Ancient Greek, Arabic was a difficult language that required years of study to comprehend its more difficult works. Without any knowledge of Arabic literature, no one knew enough to be curious about what Omar was writing. So the admiration of his documents was a kind of fetishizing without any other intellectual engagement.

As we have seen, among the experts involved with translating Omar's documents was Alexander Cotheal, an amateur Arabist who was the treasurer of the American Ethnological Society. Another translator was Rev. Isaac Bird, who worked for the American Board as a missionary. Bird spent more than thirteen years in Jerusalem, Beirut, and Syria, and became, during the last part of his life, a professor of sacred literature at the Theological Seminary in Gilmanton, New Hampshire. He was the second translator of Omar's "Autobiography." Dwight also reached out to him to help with translations of other Arabic documents of enslaved Africans.

An examination of the available translations of Omar's documents reveals some translators who provided limited but acceptable translations, such as Cotheal and Bird; other scholars like Stuart decided not to translate a language of which they had insufficient knowledge. But a separate category must be reserved for William Brown Hodgson, who knew Arabic well but misused his knowledge in the service of slavery. We will use both Stuart and Hodgson as examples of scholarship that fell short.

MOSES STUART: THE DANGER OF LITTLE LEARNING

Professor Stuart never provided a translation of Omar's 1819 letter to the Owen brothers. It had been entrusted to him by Francis Scott Key, who was seeking a translator at the request of John Louis Taylor. The consequence of Stuart's failure to respond was profound: Omar's request to be returned to Africa was never related or mentioned in any of the newspaper publications about Omar during his lifetime. Why didn't Stuart answer Key? Either Stuart did not want to translate the document, or he could not, or both. The record indicates that whatever the reason, it was accompanied by racism and support of slavery.

Stuart believed in the inferiority of Blacks and the need to send free Blacks back to Africa. According to some reports, he even prohibited his students from attending abolitionist lectures.[47] In 1850, he published a pamphlet in defense of Daniel Webster's famous proslavery speech, "Constitution and the Union." Stuart's pamphlet *Conscience and the Constitution* viewed slavery as a historical reality rather than judging it by a moral principle. He believed that good Christians could also be enslavers, claiming that "there are thousands of masters and mistresses of exemplary Christian lives and conversation." He also maintained that good Christians should avoid joining the abolitionist movement, because "Christ purposely and carefully abstained from meddling with those matters which belonged to the civil power. Slavery was one of these." His pamphlet ended by reinstating the colonization argument of resettling Blacks in Africa to avoid integration, manumission, or conflict.

Stuart published a *Grammar of the Hebrew Language* in addition to articles on biblical interpretation, but Arabic was not one of his areas of research or teaching. His papers at Yale University contain his notebook on Arabic grammar. A close examination of the contents reveals it to be his personal notes, which he labeled "Arabic grammar lessons of Alif, Waw, Ya, and Sin and Sah." On the first page, on the right at the top, one reads, "De Sacy, Gram. Arabe, vol. I." What follows are a series of elementary lessons of grammar with page references to De Sacy's *Grammaire arabe*, first published in Paris in 1810 in two volumes.[48] Stuart was learning Arabic by copying from a textbook, starting with the alphabet, and reaching the intermediate-level discussion of adjectives on the last page of the notebook. His selective and superficial interaction with the two volumes was inadequate to learn the language. In all, his efforts take up less than thirty-two note-taking pages in De Sacy's two volumes.

Stuart's Arabic did not qualify him to judge Omar's work, which covers both classical and Qur'anic Arabic, harkening back to eleventh-century Islamic scholarship. Stuart's level would barely place him into a second-year class today. It makes perfect sense that he avoided dealing with the letter, since he could not decipher the text. But honesty would have required from him to admit his limits. He remained silent, choosing to bury the document in oblivion in the Yale library, so that Omar's plea to be returned to Africa remained unheard.

Perhaps Stuart was following his own advice to theological students, which he presented in the preface to his 1835 *Grammar of the Hebrew Language*, that they should "drink deep, or taste not."[49] This is a line that he borrowed from Alexander Pope, on the danger of "little learning." We are not sure which is more dangerous, a little learning or the failure to admit it! Stuart chose the latter, and the damage was done. It seems from the historiography of Omar's documents that Stuart's sabotage conferred an air of illegibility on every text written by Omar. It would take seventeen years until the first attempt to translate the "Autobiography" was made by Cotheal in 1848.

WILLIAM BROWN HODGSON, THE
SCHOLARLY ENSLAVER

Perhaps the most important amateur scholar of Arabic connected to Omar was William Brown Hodgson (1801–71), the first Arabist in the US diplomatic service.[50] Educated privately in the study of Greek and Latin classics, Hodgson sought a position at the State Department in 1824, with an application supported by Francis Scott Key, an old family friend. Francis Scott Key has already figured in the story of Omar as the person responsible for acquiring an Arabic Bible, which the Owen brothers requested for their project of converting Omar to Christianity. Key was also a long-time officer of the American Colonization Society, another indication of the close-knit networks that characterized American society at that time.

Hodgson joined the staff of the secretary of state, Henry Clay, and soon attracted the attention of US president John Quincy Adams. Acutely aware that the American diplomatic corps lacked any speakers of Arabic to assist in negotiations with the Barbary pirates, Adams saw Hodgson as a potential translator, and offered him $600 a year if he would go to Algiers and learn Arabic and other useful languages. Hodgson accepted this proposal and made significant progress in learning Arabic, Berber, and the Mediterranean creole known as Lingua Franca. He took part in diplomatic missions to the Ottoman court in Istanbul and to Cairo, handling various other assignments in different countries as he rose through the ranks. In 1841 he was heading to Tunis to assume the position of US consul there. During a stopover in Paris, he met an immensely wealthy heiress from Georgia, Margaret Telfair, and they were married the next year with the understanding that he would give up his diplomatic career. Hodgson then found himself in the position of owning several large plantations near Savannah, and over 600 enslaved Africans, many of whom, the legend has it, he could converse with in their own languages.

Hodgson displayed considerable ambition and entrepreneurship with his scholarly talents. At times he seems to have exaggerated his accomplishments; while there is no doubt that he was a regular member of the British and French Geographic Societies, his claim to be an honorary member of the Asiatic Societies of England and France has no confirming documentation.[51] But he was a founding member of both the American Oriental Society and the American Ethnological Society. Hodgson collected a significant number of manuscripts in Arabic and other languages, describing them in a privately printed catalog before he sold them to the British Museum.[52] A Berber translation of passages from the Gospel of Luke, which Hodgson had his assistant Ben Ali compose, was also sold to the British and Foreign Missionary Society.[53] This translation was "said not to be easily legible," however, since Hodgson created four new letters for the Berber language based on variations from the Arabic script, letters that would have been wholly unknown to the intended audience.[54] It also appears that, on the eve of the conquest of Algeria, Hodgson contracted to provide to the French government materials on the geography of North Africa, plus an anonymously published dictionary of Lingua Franca written by Hodgson himself. The frequently repeated assertion (unsubstantiated, it turns out) that Hodgson was one of the first Americans to receive the French Legion of Honor, may be a slightly distorted version of honors that he received from the French government, one in the 1830s and another in 1855, the latter signed by Napoleon III.[55] The alternative view of these moonlighting activities was the suspicion that he was spying for the French. To say the least, he seems to have been opportunistic.

As a prominent plantation owner, Hodgson was a close collaborator and friend of the South Carolina politician James Henry Hammond (d. 1864), one of the most public defenders of chattel slavery in the nineteenth century. There is an extensive record of their correspondence during the contentious years leading to the Civil War. In this correspondence, Hodgson provided expert advice to Hammond on issues ranging from selling and buying slaves to the politics of opposing the abolitionist movement.[56]

In the era before the rise of research universities, Hodgson, like other amateur scholars, presented his views in lectures to learned societies and short articles for journals. His writings exemplify the gamut of what was wrong with the experts. He combined the new planter gentry's greed with the arrogance of the civilizing missionary and a self-indulgent aspiration to be recognized as a prominent scholar. Through his career, he displayed a readiness to depict Islam as the de facto enemy of Christianity and Blacks as naturally inferior, in the process drawing upon the full range of pseudoscientific racial theory.

As a scholar, Hodgson made it clear that his expectations of the writings of enslaved Africans were low. When the American Philosophical Society reached out to him in 1837 to translate one of Abdulrahman ibn Ibrahima's Arabic notes, he did so, commenting that, "instead of writing the Lord's Prayer, he wrote Mohammad's invocation. Judging from the capacity of other Muslims, I imagine it would have been difficult for the Prince to have made a version of our Prayer and he therefore wrote his own."[57] When he heard that an Arabic manuscript had been sent to the American Ethnological Society from Liberia, he wrote to Theodore Dwight, "My curiosity has been much excited to know its contents. I do not suppose it is anything more than some Koranic extracts by a Mandingo Maalim [scholar]. Could you do me the favor to inform me what its subject is?"[58] Here he criticized the contents of documents before even reading them.

As early as 1829, from his diplomatic post in Algiers, Hodgson wrote an article for the American Colonization Society about the Fulani people of West Africa (also called Fellata, Foulah, etc.). In it he offered speculations about Fulani racial and linguistic origins, as a basis for strategic assessments of their usefulness for the Liberia project supported by the ACS. He saw Liberia, an American colony located "on the confines of Islam," as "destined to become a great empire," and designed to serve as a base for suppressing the international slave trade—an objective that had no connection whatever to the abolitionist cause in the United States. Hodgson therefore proposed mounting a scientific expedition to West Africa to support colonization, as a joint effort with the American Philosophical Society; he even offered to contribute $100 of his own funds to the cause. This combination of racism, imperialism, missionary projects, and amateur scholarship would continue to characterize Hodgson's writings for the rest of his life.

Hodgson's 1843 essay "The Foulahs of Central Africa" is a showcase of all the tropes of nineteenth-century racism.[59] He began with speculation on racial hierarchies, claiming that "the Foulahs are not negroes," by reason of an allegedly distinctive skin color that placed them between Arabs and Africans. He also introduced the notion that the Foulahs in some sense believe themselves to be white, evidently because he considered them morally superior to other Africans. He stressed the potential political dominance of the Foulahs in West Africa, and their ability to suppress the international slave trade. Hodgson maintained that Christianity is the best hope for bringing civilization to Africa, but he observed that Islam could be useful as an intermediate step, by effacing non-Islamic practices. Yet overall, "in Africa—in the land of the degraded negro—the gospel now stands face to face with the Koran." Thus Hodgson threw his support to the translation of the Bible into Arabic to aid conversion.

To assist his analysis, Hodgson then called on two scientific theories believed to support racial hierarchy: the linguistic division of social groups assumed to be racially distinct, and "craniology," a biological pseudoscience that, like phrenology, purported to classify different races according to the size and shape of the skull. Hodgson particularly appreciated the craniological contributions of his colleague Dr. Samuel Morton of the American Philosophical Society, on one occasion presenting this research personally before the National Institute in Washington in 1844.[60] Morton's collection of over a thousand human skulls, which is still preserved in Philadelphia at the Penn Museum, has in recent years become an embarrassment to the organization, which is seeking to repatriate at least 200 skulls of African Americans to cemeteries for burial.[61] The incompetence of this pseudoscientific doctrine in biology is matched by the ludicrous linguistic speculations in which Hodgson and his peers felt free to indulge. On the basis of the flimsiest similarity, these scholars proposed that the origin of the Fulani language can be considered to be Malay, another effort to portray them as non-African.

Hodgson's last publication, an essay on "the science of language," was delivered to the Georgia Historical Society while the Civil War was still being fought and was published in 1868. It is an essay filled with bitterness and diatribe. He lamented the Emancipation Proclamation and the defeat of the Confederacy, denouncing from the outset the new norms forcing slaveholding southerners to approve and admit "political equality, [and] the voices of a barbarian race."[62] He insisted on the connection between the doctrine of race and that of language, arguing the superiority of the races speaking the Aryan tongues. He protested that "the supremacy, of God's ordination, man now proposes to overrule, by the bayonet, in favor of the exotic, inferior, race. It may be foreseen, that such a sacrilegious attempt to degrade the nobler race will be punished by the eternal law of retributive justice."[63] In the rest of the paper, Hodgson swings back and forth between rage and rant, arguing from what he terms "comparative philology" that language determines race, that grammar is determined by birth, and that Blacks therefore speak a low "patois" instead of a civilized language.

Hodgson's racist views were on full display in his antagonistic relationship with Omar. Most revealing of the tension between the two was Hodgson's failed attempt to hire Omar as a research assistant on the language and culture of the Fulani people. On two separate occasions, in 1843 and 1845, Hodgson wrote to a French colleague, Armand d'Avezac, boasting that Omar would provide the data to permit Hodgson to write the fundamental account (known as a "notice" among scholars of the time) of the Fulani. In a letter read to the Ethnological Society in Paris in September 1843, it was reported, "Mr. William B. Hodgson writes from Savanna to Mr. d'Avezac that a Fulah prince, named Omar, is currently a slave in the United States, and may provide valuable information for the drafting of a developed Notice on his nation."[64] Two years later, d'Avezac wrote a lengthy article in the journal of the same society, in which he added, "And while this is printing, Mr. Hodgson tells me from New York that he will take advantage of the presence, in the United States, of a literate Foulah with whom he has already started a correspondence in Arabic, to obtain the elements of an ethnological notice, a vocabulary and a grammar essay."[65] Despite these declarations, Omar declined Hodgson's offer some time later. Omar may have distrusted Hodgson, and he probably needed the support of Jim Owen to refuse Hodgson's proposal.

Twelve years later, Hodgson was still angry with Omar, as he revealed in an article about an enslaved African who had copied out parts of the New Testament in English, but written in Arabic script. Scholars today would call this an ʿajami, or aljamiado, form of English (Hodgson wrongly considered this a unique case, not having bothered to examine Omar's brief Bible annotations). In remarks dripping with sarcasm and racist stereotypes, Hodgson ridiculed Omar's work ethic and his command of English.

> The Foolah African Omar, or Moro, as he is familiarly called, is still living at Wilmington, North Carolina. Betwixt himself and his indulgent master, Governor Owen, there has not existed other than the relation of patron and client. If the negro paradise is found in exemption from labor, Omar, with many others of his Southern brethren has already entered its portals. He has rejected advantageous offers to return to Africa. "White mon catchee one time, no catchem two time." Being desirous of investigating the philologic question of the Foolahs, which has long interested science, I offered him liberal pay and maintenance to place himself under my protection for a limited time. He declined the offer, and I suffered the ban of the "white mon."[66]

Hodgson concluded his comments with faint praise of Omar's accomplishments. "Omar is a good Arabic writer, and reads the Bible in that language with some correctness and intelligence. I have received letters from him in that language, expressing grateful sentiments towards his master, very creditable to his nature."[67] This exchange reveals a mockery and meanness that is only partly masked by the closing words of polite condescension. Hodgson's imitation of pidgin English ambiguously uses the words "catchee" and "catchem" as synonyms for deception—what the Nation of Islam leader Elijah Mohammed would later call the white man's "tricknology." Yet Hodgson was probably aware, but did not care, that these terms were also used to mean capture for enslavement.[68] He was too deeply immersed in the racism of his time to question it.

One additional comment is necessary on Hodgson's self-image as a scholar of Arabic, which he clearly ranked as his highest academic accomplishment, to judge from his formal portrait now held by the Georgia Historical Society (fig.

5.4). The painting was completed in 1875, several years after Hodgson's death, by the express wish of his widow; the painter was Carl Brandt, a German artist who prepared several paintings for the society. The portrait of Hodgson is opulent, showing him in his library in elegant clothes. Beside him on a table are a couple of bound books, and an open book, the pages of which he is gripping with one hand as he confidently gazes at the viewer. Pinned down by the books, a scroll artlessly spills over the edge of the table. A red wax seal on one side enhances the scroll's official appearance.

On inspection, the scroll turns out to have an Arabic inscription in a Maghrebi hand, most of which can be read with a little effort, though there are problems with the text, which is in prose rather than rhyming poetry. Although one might have expected a quotation of a well-known author here, it seems instead to have been written as a comment on the character of Hodgson himself. Part of the text on the right is covered by the painting's frame, and the lower section is partly concealed by the last loops of the scroll, so parts of it cannot be seen. The Arabic script may not have been accurately rendered by the German painter. Nevertheless, it seems appropriate to consider what this scroll appears to say about Hodgson and his knowledge of Arabic, even if it is fragmentary, since it seems to make sense as a continuous composition. The selection of such a text for Hodgson's portrait could only have been made by Hodgson before he died. Here is our translation, following the line structure of the original:

> . . . and we seek his aid.
> . . . the compassionate. The master, the man, had no successor
>   for us.
> I saw not his equal in sound thinking.
> The heart rejoices from love of him, and he is not forgotten.
> No one in his time resembled him.
> The world is in love with him. Is he not a leader?
> He deserves this encomium, and he surpasses
> The magic of explanation.[69]

One has the distinct impression that here Hodgson has written his own eulogy—who else could this be about? It is as if an Arab court poet had been commissioned to write his praises, in the most extravagant terms. Hodgson indeed had an expansive view of his own abilities. From today's perspective, his limitations are all too apparent.

FIGURE 5.4.

Portrait of William Brown Hodgson, by Carl Ludwig Brandt, Savannah, 1875.
Georgia Historical Society, Savannah, GA, portrait collection, HS 1361-AF-084.

The Failure to Read Omar's Documents

The experts, whether academics or missionaries, were the intermediary between Omar's Arabic documents and his American audience. The Owen family mostly gave Omar's documents to visiting dignitaries and clergymen, none of whom could read them. These individuals then sometimes reached out to Arabists for translation, despite these translators' inadequacies in competence and ethics. They were not converting a message from one language to another within the conventions of translation, practicing instead a systematic disregard for Omar's original texts. Sometimes pseudo-translations were used to substitute new meanings, rendering the original text even less recognizable.

These experts allowed their enthusiasm for slavery to govern their interpretation of Omar's writings. Some were allowed to insert their own proposed translations and comments, saying what they wanted about the original text regardless of its real meaning. Such was the case with Mary Jones, who was given Omar's rendition of the Qur'anic Chapter of Help (Sura al-Nasr, Document 8). Jones, the wife of Rev. Charles Colcock Jones, a prominent theologian, then mislabeled the document as the Lord's Prayer. Furthermore, the collector who later acquired the document took the liberty of writing the following description on the back of the document: "The Lord's Prayer written in Arabic by Uncle Moreau [Omar] a native African, now owned by General Owen of Wilmington, N.C. He is 88 years of age & a devoted Christian. This document was given to Mary Jones, at the Rockbridge Alum Springs, Rockbridge County Va. by Genl Owen on July 27, 1857." The description is concerned with recording the collection history rather than presenting an accurate account of the document's content.

This haphazard treatment of the documents resulted in the survival of only eighteen documents, of which eight were saved by families, six by clergy or intellectuals, and four by collectors. The lack of interest in preserving Omar's documents is evident in descriptions of at least a dozen documents written by Omar that can no longer be located. In chronological order, they include the following items.

- John Louis Taylor, in his 1819 letter accompanying Document 1, stated, "I have others in my possession, but the one selected is the best and neatest display of penmanship."[70]

- Of Omar's missing 1825 autobiography, Gregory Bedell remarked, "What has become of it we do not at present know."[71]

- The same year, Ralph R. Gurley, editor of the *African Repository*, claimed that he "became possessed of some of his [Omar's] beautiful writing in the Arabic language."[72]

- William Brown Hodgson referred to his Arabic correspondence with Omar in a letter cited by his French colleague Armand d'Avezac in 1845, and again in an article published in 1860.[73]

- Alexander Cotheal, in the 1848 preface to his translation of the "Autobiography," mentioned "a letter shown to me by Mr. Hodgson, rcd. by him from a slave by the name of Omar two years since."[74]

- In 1846, an editor of the *Providence Journal* noted that he had received a manuscript by Omar that was "not only an accurate but also an elegant version in Arabic of the Lord's Prayer and the twenty-second [i.e., the twenty-third] Psalm."[75]

- The unidentified collector of the 1855 ambrotype photograph of Omar (fig. 5.1) mentioned that he also received an Arabic letter along with the photo.

- Perhaps the oddest example is the Arabic letter that Omar wrote to a Chinese Muslim named Yang, which had been arranged by US missionary Dyer Ball while stationed in Canton in 1858.[76]

- William Plumer, in an 1863 article on Omar, wrote, "I have now in my possession a letter written by Meroh in Arabic, bearing all the marks of expert penmanship."[77]

- Also in 1863, Theodore Dwight showed to Rev. Daniel Bliss, of the Syrian Protestant College, "some Arabic manuscripts from the pen of the slave."[78]

- In an unsigned obituary of Omar that appeared on August 9, 1863, the author remarked that "he gave us a specimen of his composition in Arabic, which though not equal in beauty to others we have seen written earlier in life, does credit to his penmanship of that ancient language."[79]

- In 1868, former Yale professor of Arabic Edward Salisbury made a presentation to the American Oriental Society on an Arabic manuscript written by Omar that had been entrusted to him for explanation.[80]

- As late as 1880, an unnamed missionary wrote to Thomas Owen (son of James Owen), "I have one of Omeroh's manuscripts framed and hung in my study."[81]

Despite the words of praise found in these accounts, no one knows what happened to these documents.

Consider the case of Document 17, a mere signature of Omar that reads "Omar ibn Said [ibn] Adam." The fate of this document demonstrates a callous indifference to the preservation of his writings. Again, the complete text of Document 17 is the following, written on two lines:

Translation 5.1.

DOCUMENT 17: SIGNATURE

Omar ibn Said [ibn]
Adam

This document was acquired by Simon Gratz, a collector of signatures who lived in Philadelphia; it seems to have been cut out of a larger piece of paper with additional text, as it is missing the second "ibn" on the right-hand edge of the document. The autograph collector was not interested in the rest of the text, so he evidently destroyed the document, since it was irrelevant to his purpose. An unnamed intermediary who previously handled the document added to it his own account of Omar: "This is the autograph of an old slave of Gen. Owen of NC who was the son of an Arabian merchant (the name is an Arabic [one]). He was taken, sold into slavery, became a Christian, and blessed God for the grace in which he stood. I have seen him sitting as was his custom on the front seat in the Presbyterian Church in Wilmington and all respected old Uncle Munroe as he was called." The reminiscences of the collector take priority over the text itself.

Our understanding of this expert mentality requires consideration of the nature of the choices made. Contrasting these examples with other expert viewpoints highlights the character of treachery. It certainly helps us better understand the missed opportunities for seeking a world literature, as an alternative to dominant racist narratives. Only through this comparative framing will we see proof that antebellum experts had other options, demonstrating that they deliberately chose to support a proslavery ideology.

Conclusion

IN A LATE ACCOUNT OF Omar ibn Said published in 1884, we read, "Omeroh used to write quaint sentences in Arabic on paper and nail it on the pine trees around Owen Hill, telling the neighbors they must not take him away from his good master. The neighbors were never any the wiser, for Uncle Moro's Arabic was unintelligible to them."[1] Some four decades later, Louis T. Moore presented an embellished version of the same story.

> Prior to his mastery of the English language, tradition says that the Arabian prince would spend a great portion of his hours at Owen Hill, writing quaint sentences in Arabic on paper. He would then nail the messages to the pine trees on the plantation. Later when asked the contents of the messages he had thus placed, he replied with a good natured chuckle that they were appeals to the neighbors not to take him from his good master. Until they were informed by Moreau, the neighbors were none the wiser because of the printed messages. The Arabic was as unintelligible to them as Sanskrit.[2]

Can we take this kind of report seriously? The arguments presented in this book propose that Omar ibn Said and his writings need to be understood in relation to the African Muslim culture he grew up with, rather than being seen through the self-justifying narratives of white enslavers. That is the only way to restore his voice, so that we can hear him speak, instead of just hearing the Owen brothers.

But is there anything that this story can really tell us about Omar? The claim that Omar welcomed slavery and declined to be freed is hard to believe. The ubiquity of this fiction only proves the stubborn persistence of Lost Cause propaganda in romanticizing the Old South. In a way, the story encapsulates the fascination with Omar's strange talent, the allure of his foreign knowledge; but its potential danger is neutralized by the reassurance that he poses no threat to the economy of enslavement—he just wants to stay with his master. This is why he was regularly asked to write as "quaint sentences in Arabic" a familiar piece from the Bible, rather than anything (like the Qur'an) that might prove challenging. While this paternalistic fantasy may seem ludicrous, one might argue that it contains fragments of credibility that may be considered, as we now evaluate the results of this inquiry.

Although the praise of slavery must be rejected, it remains true that Omar's writings praise the Owen family for their good treatment of him. This acknowledgment is consistent with his principled acceptance of his destiny as divinely decreed. We have argued that this was Omar's stoic response to "great harm" rather than a celebration of enslavement. A more pertinent question addresses the depiction of Omar nailing his Arabic documents to pine trees all over the Owen estate, to the mystification of his neighbors. We have also proposed that Omar's writings must have priority over the tales of others, yet we have seen evidence that many of his known documents have disappeared through neglect. How many other documents, now lost, did he actually write? If hidden manuscripts written by Omar come to light (and we hope this book will stimulate the search to discover lost documents), might they tell a different story?

The method that we have employed, by systematically analyzing all of his writings, has identified characteristic formulas and terminology that firmly link Omar to the African Islamic environment. His quotations of Arabic theological and mystical texts conclusively demonstrate his lasting engagement with his Islamic training. We expect that any newly discovered documents that appear will conform to the style and content of his known writings, including mostly Islamic references, sermons, and talismans. His limited use of his Bible, as indicated by his meager annotations of it, refutes the claim that he embraced Christianity by rejecting Islam. At the point in his "Autobiography" where he apologizes for forgetting his Arabic, no one realized that he was quoting the *Summary* of Khalīl, a masterwork of law and theology for the Mālikī school (although William Brown Hodgson, who owned a copy of this text, could have recognized it if he had made the effort).[3] Omar's description of his former Islamic life, and his present attendance at the Presbyterian church, have a matter-of-fact quality of historic accuracy, not the triumphal declarations of salvation that one would expect from a convert. In the absence of any concrete evidence to the contrary, we have rejected the imaginary documents concocted by missionaries, implausibly presenting Omar as a proponent of Christianizing Africa. Like the attempts to portray Omar as an Arab or Indian prince, the conversion stories impose the proslavery narrative in place of his real story.

Bringing the tools of Arabic and Islamic studies to bear on Omar ibn Said has led us to see racism and missionary projects as the most powerful obstacles to understanding Omar's writings. Revisiting the debate over slavery and abolition during the antebellum era is required for any attempt to understand enslaved Muslims. There was a superficial difference between proslavery experts and abolitionist experts, but under the surface, the arguments on both sides were based on racist assumptions that reinforced the foundations of slavery. The American Colonization Society managed to combine racist views of Blacks with the ostensibly magnanimous project of sending them to Liberia. Among the commonly expressed fallacies of the day was a supposed incompatibility between Africa and Islam, between Blacks and Muslims. Scholars minimized civilizational elements of literacy and Islamic scholarship in their accounts of Blacks. Groups like the Fulbe were called white, on the bizarre grounds that their literacy proved they were not really Africans. Old Paul (Lamin Kebe) was aware of these normalized lies against Africans when he told his interviewer, Theodore Dwight, that "there are good men in America, but all are very ignorant of Africa."[4]

To get past these limitations, we argue that it is past time to recognize that Arabic is an American literary language, and that Africa is a source of American culture. Standard works of scholarship on Arabic in the past have been reluctant to admit that either of these two claims have any validity. As an example, the multivolume history of Arabic literature, written in German by Carl Brockelmann in 1943, demonstrates the classicist "golden age" mentality, focusing mainly on what are deemed major authors of the Middle East, only occasionally acknowledging peripheral developments. The third and final volume does present accounts of the prominent Syrian writers who emigrated to the Americas at the end of the nineteenth century.[5] Likewise, the survey *The American Language*, by noted critic H. L. Mencken, in its fourth edition in 1949, drew attention to the presence of Syrian authors in New York City who wrote in Arabic.[6] From neither of these sources might one guess that, a century earlier, Africans exiled to slavery in the Americas continued to use Arabic. In fact, the habitual omission of most of Africa from surveys of Arabic literature, half a century after Brockelmann, led to a multivolume project aiming at a comprehensive overview of *Arabic Literature of Africa* to make up for that neglect.[7]

The Arabic writings of enslaved Muslims have become an emerging field of study in the scholarly quest to understand the realities of slavery. It is an expanding area as scholars continue to discover more documents and expand the pool of writers beyond the English-speaking world. As in any discipline, new findings challenge old beliefs and call for new research methods and tools. Working on Omar's documents has given us a sense that many challenges lurk ahead, and that scholars should be attentive to some of the lessons that we have learned from writing this book. We need to know more about people in the Caribbean, South America, and beyond. We should learn from the diverse linguistic and cosmopolitan backgrounds of many enslaved Muslims, such as Salih Bilali in Georgia, Muhammad Kaba Saghanughu in Jamaica, Mahommah Gardo Baquaqua in Brazil and New York, and Rufino José Maria in Brazil, who were also writing in Arabic. A larger pool of Arabic materials of enslaved people in the New World will help us to assess the transatlantic slave experience more accurately. This will show not only how the oral traditions of Africans became part of America's popular culture but also how their writings, including Arabic, could actually develop into a literary tradition on this side of the Atlantic. The issues arising from this research are worth mentioning due to their methodological implications for the study of the Arabic of American slavery.

One question is how to deal with nonstandard uses of language in the texts. We ponder the question of what happens when unfree people are forced to write, not as a form of communication but as a form of exotic performance and cultural entertainment. In writings produced by enslaved writers on command, the writer is less concerned with grammar and rules of speech. Despite their nominal address to an uncomprehending enslaver, they are texts without a normal audience, in the mind of the writer. If the traditional role of an audience includes safeguarding cultural norms and enforcing grammatical conformity by censoring deviant forms of speech, the absence of an educated audience frees the writer from the nuisance of grammatical rules and regulations.

We are reminded of the many stories about the clash between Bedouin Arabs and grammarians in the earlier stages of development of the codified Arabic language. Bedouin Arabs were naturally proper speakers of the language because they were born to it, while grammarians, who were mostly non-Arab Muslim converts, wanted to know the reasons behind any form of speech that appeared to deviate from approved sources. The two groups became archenemies: the Bedouins considered grammarians to be self-selected jurors preoccupied with how something should be said, and not what was actually said. Scholars of Arabic who approach the writings of enslaved Africans should not act like the new grammarian and guardian class; they should keep these historical and circumstantial circumstances in mind when deciphering these texts without audience.

Therefore, we should think more creatively about the nature and environment of the Arabic writings of American slavery. Imposing our modern definition of historical Arabic—classical, Qur'anic or Modern Standard—is not the right starting point in deciphering these manuscripts. The obsessive attention some people have paid to the idiosyncrasies of these documents is misplaced, resulting too often in dismissing a text as bad Arabic. Observers who engage in this regime of grammar correctness tend to miss the clues buried in these soliloquies.

Comparisons of different kinds of writing by enslaved authors will clarify their distinct social and cultural aims. Abdulrahman ibn Ibrahima was a man in a hurry in 1828, making a whirlwind lecture tour with the American Colonization Society after his manumission. He would hastily scribble short documents in Arabic for his audience, from whom he sought donations to purchase the freedom of his enslaved children. These documents, which have never been systematically analyzed, rarely corresponded to the way he described them to his listeners. Their contents mattered far less than their exotic appearance. Such performance pieces of Arabic, prepared as spectacle for an audience of white Christians, contrast with the writings of Shaykh Sana See in Panama in the 1860s. These short texts were addressed "to all the Muslim men and women" as teachings of religious practice, quoting a text from Iran about a weekly schedule of prayers believed to have the power to release captives from prison; the relevance of this practice to members of an enslaved community is obvious.[8]

Returning to the question of Omar's voice, we are still faced with its paradoxical qualities. Nominally addressed to white enslavers, his documents are written with materials that could only have been read by fellow scholars trained in Islamic seminaries. Knowing he had no audience, he declared, "I cannot write my life." When commanded to do so, he provided an account in which every section was rewritten. He wrote sermons to his enslavers, filled with harsh condemnations of the arrogance of the rich and powerful. He dabbled in his Arabic Bible, but he did not read it closely. He evidently did not self-censor, since no one could read what he wrote. More than anything else, his writings resemble messages in bottles, cast out to sea in the hope of reaching unknown readers capable of reading and understanding him. His appeal to return to Africa went unheard.

But we can hear that appeal today, if we take Omar's writing seriously, and stop listening to the distorted tales of enslavers and missionaries. This means adding the Arabic literature of Africa to the shelves of world literature that Goethe imagined. Then we might think of Omar ibn Said back in Africa, by the two rivers. Can his messages in bottles be read? Can Omar's voice be heard? It depends on how well we can listen.

APPENDIX

Omar's *'Ajamī* English: American Words and Names in Arabic Script

The table below provides a summary of the Arabic transcription used by Omar ibn Said to write English words and names (see table 4.1 for his Arabic transcriptions of English titles of biblical books). In the table, the first column has the standard English term or name, the second shows the Arabic transcription (transliterated in Latin letters), and the third has the document number followed by a period and the page number of the original manuscript (e.g., 4.22 = Document 4, page 22). It should be understood that Omar could not read English, so whenever he wrote down English words and names in Arabic letters, he was not technically transliterating a written text; he was transcribing what he heard in ways that sometimes echo the southern accent of the Carolinas. In this respect the English words and names that he wrote in Arabic letters (often including short vowels) are another form of *'ajamī*, the writing of local languages in Arabic script, a widespread feature of Muslim societies.

ENGLISH	ARABIC TRANSCRIPTION	LOCATION IN ORIGINAL MANUSCRIPT
WORDS AND PHRASES		
August	*aksat; 'ūkas; a'qāst*	6.1, 18.1
church	*shahrā'*	4.15, 4.15, 4.22
end	*'ind*	18.1
general	*dhinal*	1.1, 4.16, 4.20, 4.22, 12.1
governor	*kamunah*	4.22

I write this	*ā rayt dis*	1.1
jail	*jīl*	4.15
major	*maydha*	1.1
master	*mastah*	4.19, 6.2, 6.3, 9.1, 12.1
Monday	*mandī*	7.1, 18.1
November 4, 1819	*nuwibah fuwwā ātīn ḥadad an nātīn*	1.1
November	*nuwibah*	7.1
October	*uktūbarah*	6.1
town	*tūn*	1.1

NAMES AND PLACES

Africa	*āfirkā*	1.2
America	*markā*	4.17, 4.18, 4.19
Bladen County	*balaydan kawtin*	4.16, 4.22
Charleston	*dhālstan*	4.15, 4.16 (twice), 4.22
Fayetteville	*faydil*	4.15 (twice)
Foard	*fuwwad*	7.1
Handa	*handah*	4.15
Hunter	*ḥuntuh*	4.5, 4.14
John	*dhūn*	4.19, 9.1
Johnny	*dhūnī*	6.3
Johnson	*dhānsan*	4.15 (twice)
Liza	*laysah*	4.19, 9.1, 12.1
Lucy	*lūsah*	4.19
Margaret	*mākit*	4.19, 9.1, 12.1

Martha Jayne	*māsā jayn*	4.18, 4.19, 9.1
Melissa	*muwlisah*	4.19
Miriam/Mary	*mīryam, mayra*	4.19, 9.1, 12.1
Mrs. Francis Bowen	*mis firasiṣ būmwā*	11.1
Mitchell	*midhal*	4.16
Mumford, Betsy	*mamfaddah, bitsih*	4.16, 4.19, 9.1
Mumford, Bob	*mamfaddah, bāb*	4.16
New Hanover	*nū ḥanūfah*	6.3
North Carolina	*nūf dhālayn*	4.17, 4.18, 4.19, 6.3
Owen, Jim	*ʿūʾan, dhīm*	1.1, 4.16 (3 times), 4.17, 4.19 (twice), 4.20, 4.22, 9.1, 12.1, 18.1
Owen, John	*ʿūʾan, dhūn*	1.1, 4.17, 4.19
Owen, Nell	*ʿūʾan, nal*	4.19
Owen, Tom	*ʿūʾan, tuwm*	4.19
Raleigh	*rūlī*	1.1
Sophia	*sufāyah*	4.19, 9.1, 12.1
South Carolina	*sūf dhālayn*	4.17, 4.18
Taylor	*taylah*	6.1 (4 times), 6.2, 6.3
Taylor, Harriette	*taylah, hāriyata*	6.1, 6.2
Taylor, John	*taylah, dhūn*	6.1, 6.2, 6.3
Taylor, Kitty	*taylah, kitih*	6.1, 6.2
Thomas	*tāmas*	4.18, 4.19, 9.1, 12.1
Wilmington City	*wilmitun sitih*	6.3

NOTES

INTRODUCTION

1. Cooper, "Omar ibn Said Day."
2. Moore, *Stories Old and New of the Cape Fear Region*, 139.
3. "Extract from the Letter in the *Journal*."
4. Grier, "Uncle Moreau."
5. Bedell, "African Prince Moro"; Freeman, *A Plea for Africa*, 36–39.
6. "Extract from the Letter in the *Journal*."
7. Bedell, "African Prince Moro"; Freeman, *A Plea for Africa*, 36–39.
8. Gurley, "Secretary's Report."
9. Grier, "Uncle Moreau."
10. Bedell, "African Prince Moro"; Freeman, *A Plea for Africa*, 36–39.
11. Bedell, "African Prince Moro"; Freeman, *A Plea for Africa*, 36–39.
12. "From the Wilmington *Herald*."
13. Hunwick, "'I Wish to Be Seen in Our Land Called Afrika.'"

CHAPTER 1

1. Diouf, "God Does Not Allow Kings to Enslave Their People"; Sylviane Diouf, email to Mbaye Lo, February 1, 2020.
2. Robinson, *Chiefs and Clerics*, 5.
3. Barry, *Senegambia and the Atlantic Slave Trade*, 5.
4. Ibn Ḥazm, *Rasā'il ibn Ḥazm al-Andulusī*, 133.
5. Fage, "Upper and Lower Guinea," 484.
6. Palmer, "M. Delafosse's Account of the Fulani."
7. Niane, *Histoire des Mandingues de l'ouest*, 47.
8. Ware, *The Walking Qur'an*.
9. Gomez et al., *Pragmatism in the Age of Jihād*, 29.
10. Gomez et al., *Pragmatism in the Age of Jihād*, 27.
11. Park, *The Travels of Mungo Park*, 73.

12. Niane, *Histoire des Mandingues de l'ouest*, 49.

13. Quoted in Ka, "L'enseignement arabe au Sénégal."

14. Translation 2.1, Document 4.

15. Kamara, Shukrī, and Imbākī, *Akthar al-rāghibīn fī al-jihād*, 38.

16. Email correspondence with Professor Cherif Keita, May 11, 2021.

17. Diouf, "God Does Not Allow Kings to Enslave Their People."

18. Translation 3.1, Document 1.

19. Gnkane, "Omar ibn Said."

20. Diaz, *Europe and the People without History*.

21. Bâ, *Aspects de la civilisation africaine*, 21.

22. Hegel, *The Philosophy of History*, 99.

23. Atkins, *Voyage to Guinea, Brazil and the West Indies in HMS Swallow and Weymouth*, 61.

24. Bell, "Thomas Jefferson Reviews Phillis Wheatley."

25. Mason, *The Poems of Phillis Wheatley*, 7.

26. Lawrence, *Islamicate Cosmopolitan Spirit*.

27. Bâ, *Aspects de la civilisation africaine*, 22.

28. Also cited as "The eldest are the wisest in the community," this saying is the subject of a popular song by the contemporary Senegalese singer Youssou N'Dour; see Cathcart, *Notes from Africa*.

29. Quoted in Abaka, "Ancestor Veneration," 72.

30. Niane, *Sundiata*, 1.

31. Niane, *Sundiata*, 2.

32. Ware, *The Walking Qur'an*.

33. Ka, "L'enseignement arabe au Sénégal," 58.

34. Kamara, Shukrī, and Imbākī, *Akthar al-rāghibīn fī al-jihād*, 27.

35. Fage, "Slavery and the Slave Trade in the Context of West African History."

36. Diouf, "God Does Not Allow Kings to Enslave Their People."

37. Ka, "L'enseignement arabe au Sénégal," 114.

38. Ware, *The Walking Qur'an*, chaps. 1 and 3.

39. Lovejoy and Hogendorn, *Slow Death for Slavery*.

40. Searing, *West African Slavery and Atlantic Commerce*.

41. Niane, *Histoire des Mandingues de l'ouest*, 48.

42. Quoted in Kane, *Beyond Timbuktu*, 7.

43. al-Qayrawānī, *Risāla*, 215.

44. Hall and Stewart, "The Historic 'Core Curriculum.'"

45. Kane, *Beyond Timbuktu*, 76.

46. Launay, *Islamic Education in Africa*.

47. Ngom, "Ajami Literacies of West Africa," 143.

48. Abū Madyan Shuʿayb al-Ghawth, *Dīwān*, 23.

49. Hunwick, *Timbuktu and the Songhay Empire*.

50. Hunwick, *Timbuktu and the Songhay Empire*, 54.

51. Boyd, *The Caliph's Sister*.

52. Asmaʾu, *Collected Works*, 73.

53. Diouf, *Servants of Allah*.

54. Samb, *Al-Adab al-Sinighālī al-ʿArabī*, 36.
55. Babou, "Généalogie, éducation et baraka."
56. Babou, *Fighting the Greater Jihad*.
57. Quoted in Babou, *Yā Jumlatan*.
58. Lo and Nadhiri, "Contextualizing 'Muridiyyah,'" 231–40.
59. Brenner, *Réflexions sur le savoir islamique en Afrique de l'ouest*, 9.
60. Samb, *Al-Adab al-Sinighālī al-ʿArabī*, 149.
61. Schmitz, "L'historiographie des Peuls musulmans," 862.
62. Samb, *Al-Adab al-Sinighālī al-ʿArabī*, 156–56.
63. Robinson, "Un historien et anthropologue sénégalais," 89–116.
64. Kamara, *Tabshīr al-khāʾif al-ḥayrān*, 15–22.
65. Hilliard, "Al-Majmūʿ al-nafīs," 175–86.
66. Khan, *Ṣaḥīḥ al-Bukhārī*.
67. Robertson, *Denmark Vesey*.
68. Lo and Ernst, "The 1850's Photographic Portrait of Omar ibn Said," 447.

CHAPTER 2

1. Bedell, "African Prince Moro."
2. Pascal, *Design and Truth in Autobiography*, 10.
3. Nance, *How the Arabian Nights Inspired the American Dream*.
4. Cotheal, "The Life of Omar-Ben-Saeed"; excerpts also published in Dwight, "Condition and Character of Negroes in Africa," 88–90.
5. Cotheal omitted nearly all of page 15 of the manuscript by carelessly jumping from one instance of the word translated as "purchased" to the next.
6. Cotheal, "The Life of Omar-Ben-Saeed."
7. Jameson, "Autobiography of Omar ibn Said," 789.
8. Bird, "Translation of the Life of Omar ibn Said."
9. Bird, "Isaac Bird to Theodore Dwight," April 8, 1863.
10. Jameson, "Autobiography of Omar ibn Said."
11. Osman and Forbes, "Representing the West in the Arabic Language," 332.
12. Curiel, "The Life of Omar ibn Said," 34.
13. Black, "The Second Persona."
14. Ong, *The Presence of the Word*.
15. Ong, *Orality and Literacy*.
16. Kahera, "'God's Dominion.'"
17. Ware, *The Walking Qurʾan*.
18. Hall, "How Slaves Used Islam."
19. Khalīl ibn Isḥāq al-Jundī, *Al-Mukhtaṣar fī al-fiqh ʿalá madhhab al-Imām Mālik ibn Anas*, 5.
20. The phrase "a gift rather than as a constraint" (*faḍlan lā wujūban*) is found in the Qurʾan commentary of al-Qurṭubī, and in the writings of ʿAbd al-Qādir al-Jīlānī, among others.
21. Chapman, "Black Freedom and the University of North Carolina."
22. Calo, "The Yeoman Myth," 15.
23. Crow and Escott, *A History of African Americans in North Carolina*, 53.

24. Cecelski, *The Waterman's Song.*

25. Owen, "John Owen Papers," folder OP-572/1.

26. Powell, "Owen, Thomas."

27. Parramore, "Owen, James."

28. Grier, "Uncle Moreau."

29. Grier, "Uncle Moreau."

30. Morris, "The Completion of the Western North Carolina Railroad."

31. Battle, *History of the University of North Carolina*, 1:200–218.

32. Owen, "Owen, John."

33. Gatewood, "'To Be Truly Free.'"

34. *Catalogue of the Members of the Dialectic Society*, 7, 23.

35. Parker, *Running for Freedom*, 3–28.

36. Johnson, *Ante-bellum North Carolina*, 56.

37. Johnson, *Ante-bellum North Carolina*, 469.

38. Horton, "George Moses Horton," 7.

39. Sherman, *The Black Bard of North Carolina*, 3.

40. Barrett, *To Fight Aloud Is Very Brave*, 227.

41. Inscoe, "Walker, David."

42. Inscoe, "Walker, David."

43. Inscoe, "Walker, David."

44. Quoted in Bleser, *Secret and Sacred*, viii.

45. Morphis, *The Autobiography of a Negro.*

46. Morgan, *Laboring Women.*

47. Campbell and Elbourne, *Sex, Power, and Slavery.*

48. Chapman, "Black Freedom and the University of North Carolina," 30.

49. Leloudis et al., "Grimes Residence Hall."

50. "List of Slaves with Birth Dates."

51. UNC Graduate School, "Hinton James."

52. Chapman, "Black Freedom and the University of North Carolina," 16.

53. "Extract from the Letter in the *Journal.*"

54. Hodgson, "The Gospels."

55. "Prince Omeroh."

56. "Prince Omeroh."

57. This is a modified quotation from a major textbook on Islamic law and theology, Khalīl ibn Ishāq al-Mālikī, *Al-Mukhtaṣar fī al-fiqh ʿalá madhhab al-Imām Mālik ibn Anas*, 8. Omar has added the phrase "with the good."

58. Pages 6–13 of the notebook are blank. That gap of eight pages makes it appear as if he started over on page 14 with A.2 as a formal invocation. Several other sections seem to start at the top of a page: C.1 on page 17, D.2 on page 20, E.2 on page 21, and B.2 on page 22.

59. The word Omar uses here is *al-shahrā'*, which is a transliteration of "church." It has been untranslated in all previous translations, or it has been mistranslated as a form of the Arabic word *shahr*, "month." It is used four times in the document. First Omar runs to it (the church) from Johnson's place; fugitives were often directed to and hosted in churches; and the church was the most important station along the line of the Underground Railroad.

So in this journey of 215 miles (70 hours walking) between Charleston (South Carolina) and Fayetteville (North Carolina), Omar was most likely instructed to only take shelter in church buildings, which is what he also did upon arrival in Fayetteville.

60. The same word is used here, *al-shahrā'*.

61. The same word is repeated here, *al-shahrā'*.

62. Omar uses the phrase *where is* your name rather than *what is* your name. The sense is, "What is your name? Omar or Sayyid?"

63. Omar describes incomprehension of a foreign language with the phrase, "I do not hear." This is cross-linguistic interference; in Senegalese languages, including Wolof and Halpulaar, people ask, "Do you hear a language?" rather than "Do you speak . . ." or "Do you know a language?"

64. Written as *bāb mamfaddah*.

65. Omar would be considered a "runaway slave." The Federal Fugitive Slave Act of 1793 required the return of fugitives to their owners. Since no one claimed Omar during this fourteen-day stay in the jailhouse, Bob Mumford, the sheriff of Cumberland County, took him home as county property. In a normal situation, an unclaimed "runaway slave" would have been auctioned at the Fayetteville Market House to cover the jail's costs. But it was Omar's luck that Mumford happened to be related to the Owens, a prominent family in Bladen County, who paid his bond and offered to take in Omar while the process ran its course.

66. Omar does not recognize Mitchell, which means Mitchell was not sent by Omar's Charleston owner, Johnson. Mitchell may well have been a slave catcher and might have bid on Omar in Charleston.

67. According to stories and popular writing, Omar was attached to Jim Owen, who then decided to purchase him from Mitchell. Knowing the mutual affection between Omar and his hosts, Mitchell overcharged the Owen family on the price of Omar.

68. Previous translations have read this as "with my brothers" (*ma'a ikhwatī*), which makes no sense, but the script is not entirely clear; it should be read as "with his brother" (*ma'a ikhwatihi*), using the plural of respect to refer to John Owen, as a parallel with D.2, "with his wife." Also, the verb should be read in the fourth form as "he has me read" the Gospel (*yuqri'unī*), since "he reads to me" would normally be in the first form with an additional preposition (*yaqra'u 'alayya*). This correction also applies to the revised section B.4, below.

69. This theological fragment, the doctrine that God's generosity is free and not imposed as a necessity, is expressed in the typical language of Islamic theology. It is repeated below in the revision of this section, and it also occurs in Document 6, as a sequel to or comment on the creed of al-Qayrawānī. Yet Omar uses it here to describe reading the New Testament. Previous translations have mistranslated the phrase *ḥālan wa ma'ālan*, meaning "now and at the end," by mistakenly reading the last word as *mālan*, "in wealth."

70. This is the language used in the Qur'an to describe the Bible: "We revealed the Torah, in which there is guidance and light . . . and we gave him [Jesus] the Gospel, in which there is guidance and light" (Qur'an 5:44, 5:46). Previous translators rendered this passage in both its iterations (D.1, D.2) as a prayer in the imperative mood: "Open my heart . . ." While this reading is grammatically possible (*aftaḥ*), there is nothing in the style of the "Autobiography" to suggest that Omar was bursting into Christian prayer, tempting though this assumption

may have been to their missionary goal. His dry and laconic description of his shift from a Muslim to a Christian environment, and his protest of the impossibility of writing his life, lead us to read the verb as indicative (*aftaḥa*), "he opened."

71. Omar uses an unconventional way of numbering the year, which reflects his training background in Arabic.

72. General James Owen (d. 1865) and his wife had seven children: Sophia, Martha, Mary, Margaret, John, Eliza, and Thomas.

73. This expression is similar in form and meaning to the expression in the Qur'an 11:78, where it has the overtone of blame: "Now fear God, and cover me not with shame about my guests! Is there not among you a single right-minded man?"

74. On top and to the right margin of the page Omar inserts the word *al-awwal*, "the first," which should be treated as an adverb (*awwalan*), "at first." We translate this word here as "previously."

75. As in D.1 above, the theological fragment on the creed of al-Qayrawāni is quoted again to comment on the Gospel.

76. Now Omar adds to his description of the Gospel al-Khalīl's praise of God's generosity.

77. Here too the words *al-awwal* and *Muḥammad* are inserted above the third line, which when corrected reads as *innī awwalan uṣallī [mā] qāla Muḥammad*, "Previously I would pray [what] Muhammad said."

78. The word "harm" (*ḍarar*) is used twice in this section, first to describe Omar's capture and enslavement as "great harm," and second to specifically exempt Jim Owen from any charge of cruelty or bad treatment.

79. The same word is repeated here, *al-shahrāʾ*.

CHAPTER 3

1. Bencheneb, "Al-Sanūsī, Abū ʿAbd Allāh Maḥammad b. Yūsuf b. ʿUmar b. Shuʿayb"; Hall and Stewart, "The Historic 'Core Curriculum.'"

2. al-Sanūsī al-Ḥasanī, *Sharḥ wāsiṭat al-sulūk*.

3. Dalen, "Method and Message," 109. The Hill Manuscript Museum and Library (https://www.vhmml.org/) has digitized twelve manuscripts of this text from libraries in Tombouctou.

4. al-Hawḍī al-Tilimsānī, *Wāsiṭat al-sulūk*.

5. Gril, "Abū Madyan Shuʿayb."

6. Abū Madyan Shuʿayb al-Ghawth, *Dīwān*, 86–91.

7. Dobronravin, "Não só mandingas," 223. That manuscript is in the collection of Professor Paolo Farah of the University of São Paulo.

8. Shafik, "Poema de exhortación piadosa," 96–102. In reference to this poem, we follow the verse numbering of Ahmed Shafik, who discovered a manuscript in Libya containing fourteen additional lines not found in the 2011 edition of the *Dīwān*.

9. Sahih Muslim, Book 6, Hadith 305.

10. Omar ibn Said, Translation 3.1, Document 1.

11. This formula, found in five of Omar's other documents, is presented here in a longer form; the final clause ("their condition in this world") only occurs here.

12. al-Ḥawḍī al-Tilimsānī, *Wāsiṭat al-sulūk*. Omar's version adds the conjunction "and" (*wa*) at the beginning of the verse, and it changes the final vowel of each half verse from a short *a* to a long *a*.

13. Abū al-Qāsim ibn ʿAlī al-Ḥarīrī al-Baṣrī, *Mulḥat al-iʿrāb*, 2. There are several divergent spellings in the quotation.

14. Muḥammad ibn ʿAbd Allāh ibn Mālik, *Alfiyyat ibn Mālik fil-naḥw wal-taṣrīf*, verse 24, p. 73.

15. This is another verse from al-Ḥarīrī's poem on Arabic grammar (*Mulḥat al-iʿrāb*, 28), listing five particles that introduce the vocative case; that is, direct address of someone as "you." The English equivalents are approximate. With the name of Jim Owen following closely after, this verse signals that he also is addressed as "you" in the letter.

16. This formula is repeated in several of the documents.

17. Abū Madyan Shuʿayb al-Ghawth, *Dīwān*, 86–91.

18. The second page begins by repeating the opening verse from al-Ḥarīrī already quoted.

19. It is striking that Omar introduces both the Qurʾan and hadith sayings of Muḥammad as the word of God.

20. Allison, *The Crescent Obscured*, 206.

21. Taylor, "Letter: John Louis Taylor to Francis Scott Key."

22. Stuart, "Arabic Grammar."

23. Post, "Arabic-Speaking Negro Mohammedans in Africa."

24. Austin, *African Muslims in Antebellum America*, 513–16n29.

25. O'Reilly, "Manuscript Inquiry, Heartman Collection." It was formerly believed that this document contained Christian prayers, but that turns out to have been the speculation of an early cataloger.

26. Barr, "Arabic Verse with an Unusual History."

27. H. O. R, *The Governing Race*, 20.

28. Douglass, *Narrative of the Life of Frederick Douglass, an American Slave*, 118.

29. Idris, "Ibn Abī Zayd al-Ḳayrawānī."

30. Conley, "Spartanburg Museum Documents West African Nobleman Turned Slave"; Einboden, "Spartanburg Manuscript."

31. The word October (*uktūbarah*) is crossed out and replaced by August, in two different Arabic spellings, on the margin. The names are written in Arabic script as *kitih taylah, dhūn taylah, hāriyat taylah*.

32. al-Qayrawānī, *Risāla*, 9. The words "and the bitter" were omitted from the quotation.

33. This unidentified theological fragment, which reads like a continuation or commentary on the preceding quotation from al-Qayrawānī, is written in standard Islamic theological language. It is quoted twice in the "Autobiography."

34. The names are written in Arabic script as *mastah taylah, kitih taylah, dhūn taylah, hāriyat taylah*.

35. Written in Arabic script as *mastah . . . dhūnī taylah wilmiṭan sitih nū ḥanūbah nūf dhālayna*.

36. Jones, *The Religious Instruction of the Negroes in the United States*.

37. Rahhahman, "Copy of the Lord's Prayer, in Arabic."

38. Here Omar is blending two very similar but not identical passages from the Qurʾan.

39. This is one of several places where Omar uses a common scribal way of closing a document, using the expression "it is finished [*tammat*]," equivalent to "the end" in English.

40. The word *aʿmār* (literally, "lifetimes") is not normally a name in Arabic. Omar may be using one of the nicknames given to him, Moro, Moreau, Omeroh, and the like, addressing himself.

41. Vimercati Sanseverino, "Al-Dimyāṭī."

42. Zarrūq, *Kitāb sharḥ al-asmāʾ allāh al-ḥusnā*, fol. 12; Kugle, *Rebel between Spirit and Law*.

43. The second line of the theological ode *wāsitat al-sulūk* (The pearl necklace of the path) by a North African scholar known as al-Ḥawḍī al-Tilimsānī (d. 1505), also quoted in Translation 3.1, Document 1.

44. al-Dimyāṭī, "Al-Qaṣīda al-Dimyāṭiyya."

45. "Martyrdom of Crispus Attucks!,'" 3. The identification of the manuscript as Sumner's copy is clear from the nearly identical description of both documents as consisting of "Arabic sentences" and the obvious reference to Omar and James Owen.

46. O'Connor, "Popular and Talismanic Uses of the Qurʾān."

47. Brockett, "Aspects of the Physical Transmission of the Qurʾan in 19th-Century Sudan."

48. Prisse d'Avennes, *L'art arabe d'après les monuments du Kaire*, plate 61.

49. Simpson, "Expanding Boundaries: A Manuscript of the Qurʾan from Sub-Saharan Africa." This illustration is on the inside of the upper cover of the second volume of this Qurʾan.

50. Prussin, *Hatumere*, 89–90, fig. 4.12b; 93, fig. 4.12i.

51. "Charm."

52. Epelboin et al., *Un art secret*.

53. Prussin, *Hatumere*, 73–77.

54. This tunic is catalog no. 71.1900.44.14 at the Quai Branly Museum in Paris.

55. Prussin, *Hatumere*, 92, fig. 4.12e.

56. Prussin, *Hatumere*, 87.

CHAPTER 4

1. Rankin, *History of First Presbyterian Church*, 119–20.

2. "Presbyterian Church Sessional Records."

3. Gerbner, "Crossing and Conversion."

4. Bedell, "African Prince Moro"; Freeman, *A Plea for Africa*, 36–39.

5. Gurley, "Secretary's Report."

6. Grier, "Uncle Moreau."

7. Grier, "Uncle Moreau."

8. Bedell, "African Prince Moro"; Freeman, *A Plea for Africa*, 36–39.

9. Gurley, "Secretary's Report."

10. Taylor, "Letter: John Louis Taylor to Francis Scott Key."

11. Bedell, "African Prince Moro."

12. Grier, "Uncle Moreau."

13. Cowper, *The Complete Poetical Works*, 73.

14. Freeman, *A Plea for Africa*, 39.

15. Gurley, "Secretary's Report."

16. Turner, "Cowper, Slave Narratives," citing Marcus Wood.

17. Stewart, "Dissimulation in Sunni Islam and Morisco Taqiyya."

18. Mirrlees, "John Hill and the Early Attempt to Study a West African Language," 108.

19. "The Mohamedan Negro."

20. Grier, "Uncle Moreau," 1859 version.

21. A Wayfaring Man, "Meroh."

22. Kidd, *American Christians and Islam*, chap. 3.

23. Coon, *North Carolina Schools and Academies*, 66, 397, 566; Huske, *A History of the Parish of St. John's*, 16.

24. Huske, *A History of the Parish of St. John's*, 16.

25. From the *Mukhtaṣar* of al-Khalīl, a popular legal work quoted twice in the "Autobiography."

26. "Temptations" or "tests" (*tajārib*), like the phrase "he tests" (*jarraba*), both come from the same Arabic root, J-R-B.

27. The formulas "In the name of God the Merciful, the Compassionate" (known as the *basmala* or Qurʾanic blessing) and "may God bless our master Muhammad" (the *taṣliya* or Prophetic blessing), either simply as stated or in more elaborate constructions, are typically invoked by Muslim authors at the beginning of any document. The *basmala* is also found at the beginning of nearly every sura of the Qurʾan.

28. This formula uses the masculine preposition for "her" grave, underlining the fixed character of the formula.

29. Foard, *North America and Africa*, 64.

30. The book dealer's prospectus for this manuscript proposed to read the initials of the document's first recipient on the reverse as "E. M. P.," but no one having those initials can be connected to the document. An additional note on a separate piece of paper mentions the name "Gen. McClellan." This can only be George B. McClellan, who would become a famous Union general in the Civil War; at the time this document was written, McClellan was occupied with the railroad industry. Comparison of the initials on this paper with known examples of McClellan's signature indicates that the initials should be read as "G. McC.," so he was the first owner of the document.

31. As in Document 6, Omar appears to struggle with writing the English word "August" in the Arabic script, spelling it in two different ways. The Arabic word for Monday is *ithnān*. Although McClellan gave the date 1857 for General Owen's gift of the document, this is contradicted by Omar's date of Monday, August 4, 1856, which must be correct, since August 4 fell on a Monday that year.

32. Omar uses the Arabic word for psalm (*al-mazmūr*), and the number fifty, followed by his spelling of the English word "psalm" as it sounds, in Arabic script (*sām*). The numbering of the Psalms in Arabic follows the Vulgate Bible, so this is Psalm 50 in Arabic, and Psalm 51 in English Bibles, as indicated by a handwritten addition in English at this point in the document.

33. Here the Arabic version follows the Coptic text, from which it was evidently translated, using the indicative "you wash me . . . you cleanse me" instead of the imperative "wash me . . .

cleanse me," which is used in the Hebrew and Greek versions. See Saydon, "The Origin of the 'Polyglot' Arabic Psalms," 228.

34. Several miscopied words are as follows: 51:4, *ṣanaʿtu* is written as *sanaʿtu*; 51:5, *ḥabala* as *jabala*; 51:10, *jaddidhu* as *ḥaddidhu*; 51:15, *shifatī* as *sifatī*; 51:16, *shiwāʾ* as *siwāʾ*.

35. The signature is written inside a rectangle with scrolled corners.

36. These words (the Arabic *tammat*, "it has ended," and the English word "end" written in Arabic letters as ʿ*ind*) are inside a six-pointed star.

37. Brown, "Conversion," 22.

38. Medhurst, "Filled with the Spirit," 561.

CHAPTER 5

1. Quoted in Damrosch, *What Is World Literature?*, 1.

2. Goethe, *Essays on Art and Literature*, 225.

3. Post, "Arabic-Speaking Negro Mohammedans in Africa"; See, "Translation of Sheikh Sana See 1850's Manuscript."

4. "Members" (*Journal of the American Oriental Society*), xi; "Members" (*Transactions of the American Ethnological Society*), v.

5. Marr, *The Cultural Roots of American Islamicism*.

6. Pickering, "Address."

7. Gomez, "Muslims in Early America"; Diouf, *Servants of Allah*.

8. Ernst, *Following Muhammad*, chap. 2.

9. "Sermon on Religion," n.d., Rev. Henry Bosworth Covington papers, personal library of Carl W. Ernst, Chapel Hill, NC.

10. Spellberg, "Could a Muslim Be President?," 485.

11. English, *A Narrative of the Expedition to Dongola and Sennaar*, 3.

12. English, *A Narrative of the Expedition to Dongola and Sennaar*, 62.

13. Alford, *Prince among Slaves*, 128.

14. Einboden, *Jefferson's Muslim Fugitives*, 2.

15. Thompson, "Study of the Arabic Language."

16. Dwight, "Condition and Character of Negroes in Africa," 90.

17. Thompson, "Study of the Arabic Language."

18. Dwight, "Condition and Character of Negroes in Africa," 80.

19. Haines, *Jonas King*, 196.

20. Haines, *Jonas King*, 72.

21. Yohannon, "Emerson, Ralph Waldo."

22. Lewis, "The Koran, African Mohammedanism," 35, 40.

23. Mathews, *Slavery and Methodism*, 81.

24. Jones, *The Religious Instruction of the Negroes in the United States*, 125.

25. Myers, *The Children of Pride*, 347.

26. Wilson, *Western Africa*, iii.

27. Wilson, *Western Africa*, 81.

28. Foard, *North America and Africa*, 62.

29. Foard, *North America and Africa*, 63.

30. Foard, *North America and Africa*, 63.

31. Moore, *Stories Old and New of the Cape Fear Region*, 149.

32. Moore, *Stories Old and New of the Cape Fear Region*, 149.

33. There are more than fifteen letters concerning Arabic manuscripts in the Library of Congress collection in which Dwight played a role.

34. Dwight, "Condition and Character of Negroes in Africa," 83.

35. Dwight, "On the Sereculeh Nation," 452.

36. Benson, "Stephen Benson to Theodore Dwight."

37. Lo and Ernst, "The 1850's Photographic Portrait of Omar ibn Said."

38. Rogers and Barbash, *To Make Their Own Way in the World*, 11.

39. "Prince Omeroh."

40. Cecelski and Tyson, *Democracy Betrayed*.

41. Brundage, *The Southern Past*, 105.

42. Quoted in Davis and Gates, *The Slave's Narrative*.

43. McCarus, "The History of Arabic Studies in the United States," 207.

44. Lo, "Taking the Arabic Classroom Beyond the American Experience," 14.

45. Foster, *Yale and the Study of Near Eastern Languages in America*, 21.

46. du Ponceau, "Notebooks on Philology."

47. "Moses Stuart."

48. de Sacy, *Grammaire arabe*.

49. Stuart, *A Grammar of the Hebrew Language*, iv.

50. Bryson, *An American Consular Officer in the Middle East in the Jacksonian Era*; Mackall, "William Brown Hodgson."

51. "William Brown Hodgson."

52. Hodgson, *A Catalogue of Arabic, Turkish and Persian Manuscripts*.

53. Hodgson, *Extrait d'une traduction MS. en langue berbère*.

54. Bleek, *The Library of His Excellency Sir George Grey: Philology*, 252; Hodgson, "Letter to Josiah Quincy."

55. Operstein, "The French Connection," 83–84.

56. Hammond, "James Henry Hammond Papers."

57. Rahhahman, "Copy of the Lord's Prayer, Written in Arabic."

58. Hodgson, "William Brown Hodgson to Theodore Dwight."

59. Hodgson, *The Foulahs of Central Africa and the Slave Trade*.

60. "Study of Ancient Crania."

61. "The Morton Crania Collection."

62. Hodgson, *The Science of Language*, iii.

63. Hodgson, *The Science of Language*, iii.

64. "Procès-verbal de la séance du 29 septembre 1843," xliii.

65. d'Avezac, "Notice sur le pays et le peuple des Yébous," 7.

66. Hodgson, "The Gospels," 269.

67. Hodgson, "The Gospels," 269.

68. Diouf, *Dreams of Africa in Alabama*, 186–87.

69. Portrait of William Brown Hodgson by Carl Brandt, A-1361–084, Georgia Historical Society, Savannah.

70. Taylor, "Letter: John Louis Taylor to Francis Scott Key."

71. Bedell, "African Prince Moro."

72. Bedell, "Prince Moro," 153.

73. d'Avezac, "Notice sur le pays et le peuple des Yébous," 7; Hodgson, "The Gospels," 269.

74. Cotheal, "The Life of Omar Ben Saeed."

75. "Letter from the North State."

76. Grier, "Uncle Moreau."

77. A Wayfaring Man, "Meroh."

78. Post, "Arabic-Speaking Negro Mohammedans in Africa."

79. "A Remarkable Negro."

80. "Proceedings in New Haven," xlix.

81. C. A. H., "Omeroh."

CONCLUSION

1. "Prince Omeroh."

2. Moore, "Prince of Arabia."

3. Hodgson's 1830 catalog of his personal library includes "Scheick Khalil, on civil and ecclesiastical law," undoubtedly the *Mukhtaṣar* of Khalīl (Hodgson, *A Catalogue of Arabic, Turkish and Persian Manuscripts*, 8).

4. Dwight, "Condition and Character of Negroes in Africa."

5. Brockelmann, *Geschichte der arabischen Litteratur*, 3:436–79.

6. Mencken, *The American Language*, 689–90.

7. Hunwick and O'Fahey, *Arabic Literature of Africa*.

8. Bayoumi, "Moving Beliefs."

BIBLIOGRAPHY

MANUSCRIPTS

Benson, Stephen A. "Stephen A. Benson to Theodore Dwight (Letter)." July 19, 1860. Omar ibn Said Collection, E445.N8 O43, no. 2. Washington, DC: Library of Congress.

Bird, Isaac. "Isaac Bird to Theodore Dwight." April 8, 1863. Omar ibn Said Collection, E445. N8 O43, no. 6. Washington, DC: Library of Congress.

———. "Translation of the Life of Omar ibn Said." Ca. 1860–64. E445.N8 O43, no. 27. Washington, DC: Library of Congress.

"Charm." Philadelphia, ca. 1772. Du Simitière Collection, B10.F4. Library Company.

Cotheal, Alexander, trans. "The Life of Omar Ben Saeed, a Foulah Slave." 1848. E445.N8 O43, no. 28. Washington, DC: Library of Congress.

al-Dimyāṭī, Muḥammad ibn Aḥmad. "Al-Qaṣīda al-Dimyāṭiyya." N.d. 5078. Tokyo University, Institute for the Study of Oriental Culture.

du Ponceau, Peter Stephen. "Notebooks on Philology." 1815–34. Mss. 410.D92. Philadelphia: American Philosophical Society.

Hammond, James Henry. "James Henry Hammond Papers." 1773–1893. Durham, NC: Duke University Libraries.

al-Ḥawḍī al-Tilimsānī. Wāsiṭat al-sulūk. Paris, n.d. Département des manuscrits, Arabe 5671, fols. 133a–37a. Paris: Bibliothèque nationale de France.

Hodgson, William Brown. "Letter to Josiah Quincy." May 9, 1836. 564.2 Berber (folded into the endpapers of Hodgson's Extrait d'une traduction MS. en Langue Berbère de quelques parties de L'Écriture Sainte). Cambridge, MA: Harvard Divinity School Library.

———. "William Brown Hodgson to Theodore Dwight (Letter)," March 11, 1861. Omar ibn Said LOC Collection, E445.N8 O43, no. 1. Library of Congress.

Hodgson, William Brown, Condy Roguet, and Abduhl Arrahhahman. "William Brown Hodgson to John Vaughan, December 24, 1828; September 21, 1837, APS Digital Library." John Vaughan Papers, Mss. B.V462. Philadelphia: American Philosophical Society.

"List of Slaves with Birth Dates." 1806–56. John Owen Papers, PC.812. Raleigh: North Carolina State Archives.

"Martyrdom of Crispus Attucks! March 5th, 1770, 'The Day Which History Selects as the Dawn of the American Revolution!'" 1858. Broadside. BDSDS. Boston: American Antiquarian Society.

Omar ibn Said. "Document 1, Letter to John and James Owen." November 4, 1819. JWJ MSS 185x. New Haven, CT: Yale University Library.

———. "Document 2, The Lord's Prayer, No. 1." N.d. DC0211s-1. Davidson, NC: Davidson College Library.

———. "Document 3, The Lord's Prayer, No. 2." N.d. DC0211s-2. Davidson, NC: Davidson College Library.

———. "Document 4, Autobiography." 1831. Omar ibn Said Collection, E445.N8 O43, no. 24. Washington, DC: Library of Congress.

———. "Document 5, Qur'an Verses, No. 1." 1845. Charles F. Heartman Collection, MS 293. New York: New-York Historical Society.

———. "Document 6, The Taylor Verses." 1853. Spartanburg, SC: Spartanburg County Historical Association.

———. "Document 7, Psalm 23, No. 1." 1855. Rare Book Collection, VCB F649f suppl. Chapel Hill: University of North Carolina.

———. "Document 8, The Chapter of Help." 1857. Rare Book Collection, VCpB M837k. Chapel Hill, NC: University of North Carolina.

———. "Document 9, Owen Talisman, No. 1." N.d. John Owen (1787–1841) Papers, 1786–1970, PC.812. Raleigh: North Carolina Archives.

———. "Document 10, The Lord's Prayer, No. 3." N.d. John Owen (1787–1841) Papers, 1786–1970, PC.812. Raleigh: North Carolina Archives.

———. "Document 11, Notations to the Bible." N.d. 220.59 B58ar 1811. Davidson, NC: Davidson College Library.

———. "Document 12, Owen Talisman, No. 2." N.d. Owen and Barry Family Papers, 1820–1978, Sp. Coll. # 1247, folders 6 and 11, OBC003. Wilmington, NC: New Hanover County Library.

———. "Document 13, Psalm 23, No. 2." N.d. Owen and Barry Family Papers, 1820–1978, Sp. Coll. # 1247, folders 6 and 11, OBC002. Wilmington, NC: New Hanover County Library.

———. "Document 14, Romans." N.d. Owen and Barry Family Papers, 1820–1978, Sp. Coll. # 1247, folders 6 and 11, OBC001. Wilmington, NC: New Hanover County Library.

———. "Document 15, Qur'an Verses, No. 2." N.d. Owen and Barry Family Papers, 1820–1978, Sp. Coll. # 1247, folders 6 and 11, OBC001. Wilmington, NC: New Hanover County Library.

———. "Document 16, Qur'an Verses, No. 3." N.d. Charles Sumner scrapbook, MS Am 1.68, page 47. Cambridge, MA: Houghton Library, Harvard University.

———. "Document 17, Signature." N.d. "Arabian," Simon Gratz Collection, Alphabetical Series. Philadelphia: Philadelphia Historical Society.

———. "Document 18, The Billheimer Verses." 1856. North Carolina Collection, VCp X S132L. Chapel Hill: Wilson Library, University of North Carolina.

Owen, John. "John Owen Papers." n.d. Southern Historical Collection, 572-z. Wilson Library, University of North Carolina.

"Presbyterian Church Sessional Records." N.d. Wilmington, NC: Lower Cape Fear Historical Society Archives.

Rahhahman, Prince Abduhl. "Copy of the Lord's Prayer, in Arabic." September 21, 1837. Translated by William Brown Hodgson. John Vaughan Papers, Mss. B.V462. Philadelphia: American Philosophical Society.

See, Shaykh Sana. "Translation of Sheikh Sana See 1850's Manuscript." 1863. Translated by William Hanna Thomson. E445.N8 O43, no. 30. Washington, DC: Omar ibn Said LOC Collection, Library of Congress.

Stuart, Moses. "Arabic Grammar." N.d. Special Collections, Moses Stuart Papers (RG 294), New Haven, CT: Yale Divinity School Library.

Taylor, John Louis. "Letter: John Louis Taylor to Francis Scott Key," December 10, 1819. Beinecke Rare Book and Manuscript Library, JWJ MSS 185. New Haven, CT: Yale University Library.

Zarrūq, Aḥmad. *Kitāb sharḥ al-asmā' allāh al-ḥusnā*. May 15, 1774. Cod. Arab. 082-01. Leipzig, Germany: Universitätsbibliothek Leipzig.

BOOKS AND ARTICLES

Abaka, Edmund. "Ancestor Veneration." In *The Oxford Encyclopedia of African Thought*, edited by Abiola Irele and Biodun Jeyifo, 71–73. New York: Oxford University Press, 2010.

Abū Madyan Shuʿayb al-Ghawth. *Dīwān*. Edited by ʿAbd al-Qādir Suʿūd and Sulaymān al-Qurashī. Beirut: Kitāb-Nāshirūn, 1432/2010.

al-Ḥarīrī al-Baṣrī, Abū Muḥammad al-Qāsim ibn ʿAlī. *Mulḥat al-iʿrāb*. Riyad: Markaz al-Turāth lil-Barmajīyāt, 2013.

Alford, Terry. *Prince among Slaves*. New York: Oxford University Press, 2007.

Allison, Robert. *The Crescent Obscured: The United States and the Muslim World, 1776–1815*. Chicago: University of Chicago Press, 2000.

Alryyes, Ala A. *A Muslim American Slave: The Life of Omar ibn Said*. Madison: University of Wisconsin Press, 2011.

American Ethnological Society. "History." 2022. https://americanethnologist.org/about/history.

"A Remarkable Negro." *North Carolina Presbyterian*, August 9, 1863.

Asma'u, Nana. *Collected Works of Nana Asma'u, Daughter of Usman Dan Fodiyo (1793–1864)*. Edited by Jean Boyd and Beverly B. Mack. African Historical Sources Series, no. 9. East Lansing: Michigan State University Press, 1997.

Atkins, John. *A Voyage to Guinea, Brazil, and the West-Indies; in His Majesty's Ships the Swallow and Weymouth*. London: Ward and Chandler, 1737.

Austin, Allan D. *African Muslims in Antebellum America: A Sourcebook*. New York: Garland, 1984.

Bâ, A. Hampaté. *Aspects de la civilisation africaine: Personne, culture, religion*. Paris: Présence Africaine, 1993.

Babou, Cheikh Anta. *Fighting the Greater Jihad: Amadu Bamba and the Founding of the Muridiyya of Senegal, 1853–1913*. Athens: Ohio University Press, 2007.

———. "Généalogie, éducation et baraka (grâce divine) dans la famille Mbakke: Une exploration de quelques sources de l'autorité spirituelle d'Amadu Bamba." *Afrique & histoire* 7, no. 1 (2009): 199–234.

Bamba, Ahmadou. *Yā Jumlatan*. Touba, Senegal: Hizbut Tarqiyyah Darū Khoudūss, 2011.

Barr, Alison. "Arabic Verse with an Unusual History." *New-York Historical Society Museum & Library: From the Stacks* (blog), March 9, 2016. https://blog.nyhistory.org/arabic-verse -with-an-unusual-history/.

Barrett, Faith. *To Fight Aloud Is Very Brave: American Poetry and the Civil War*. Amherst: University of Massachusetts Press, 2012.

Barry, Boubacar. *Senegambia and the Atlantic Slave Trade*. Cambridge: Cambridge University Press, 1997.

Battle, Kemp P. *History of the University of North Carolina from Its Beginning to the Death of President Swain, 1789–1868*. 2 vols. Raleigh, NC: Edwards & Broughton, 1907–12.

Bayoumi, Moustafa. "Moving Beliefs." *Interventions: International Journal of Postcolonial Studies* 5 (2003): 58–81.

Bedell, Gregory Townsend. "African Prince Moro." *Philadelphia Recorder* 3, no. 20 (August 13, 1825): 79.

———. "Prince Moro." *African Repository* 1, no. 5 (July 1825): 152–54.

Bell, J. L. "Thomas Jefferson Reviews Phillis Wheatley." *Boston 1775* (blog), December 31, 2012. https://boston1775.blogspot.com/2012/12/thomas-jefferson-reviews-phillis.html.

Bencheneb, H. "Al-Sanūsī, Abū ʿAbd Allāh Maḥammad b. Yūsuf b. ʿUmar b. Shuʿayb." In *Encyclopaedia of Islam*, 2nd ed., edited by P. Bearman. Leiden, the Netherlands: Brill, 2012. dx.doi.org.libproxy.lib.unc.edu/10.1163/1573-3912_islam_COM_1001.

Black, Edwin. "The Second Persona." *Quarterly Journal of Speech* 56, no. 2 (1970): 109–19.

Bleek, W. H. I. *The Library of His Excellency Sir George Grey: Philology*. London: Trübner, 1858.

Bleser, Carol, ed. *Secret and Sacred: The Diaries of James Henry Hammond, a Southern Slaveholder*. New York: Oxford University Press, 1988.

Boyd, Jean. *The Caliph's Sister: Nana Asmaʾu, 1793–1865, Teacher, Poet, and Islamic Leader*. Totowa, NJ: F. Cass, 1989.

Brenner, Louis, and R. Otayek. *Réflexions sur le savoir islamique en Afrique de l'ouest*. Digital edition. Bordeaux: Centre d'Étude d'Afrique Noire, 1985.

Brockelmann, Carl. *Geschichte der arabischen Litteratur*, vol. 3. Leiden, the Netherlands: E. J. Brill, 1943.

Brockett, Adrian. "Aspects of the Physical Transmission of the Qurʾan in 19th-Century Sudan: Script, Declaration, Binding and Paper." *Manuscripts of the Middle East* 2 (1987): 45–67.

Brown, D. A. "Conversion." *Churchman* 65 (n.d.): 21–27.

Brundage, W. Fitzhugh. *The Southern Past: A Clash of Race and Memory*. Cambridge, MA: Belknap Press of Harvard University Press, 2005.

Bryson, Thomas A. *An American Consular Officer in the Middle East in the Jacksonian Era: A Biography of William Brown Hodgson, 1801–1871*. Atlanta: Resurgens, 1979.

C. A. H. "Omeroh." *Farmer and Mechanic*, September 23, 1880.

Calo, Adam. "The Yeoman Myth: A Troubling Foundation of the Beginning Farmer Movement." *Gastronomica: The Journal for Food Studies* 20, no. 2 (2020): 12–29.

Campbell, Gwyn, and Elizabeth Elbourne, eds. *Sex, Power, and Slavery*. Athens: Ohio University Press, 2014.

Catalogue of the Members of the Dialectic Society, Instituted in the University of North Carolina, June 3rd, 1795. Raleigh, NC: Weekly Post, 1852.

Cathcart, Jenny. *Notes from Africa: A Musical Journey with Youssou N'Dour*. London: Unbound, 2019.

Cecelski, David S. *The Waterman's Song: Slavery and Freedom in Maritime North Carolina*. Chapel Hill: University of North Carolina Press, 2012.

Cecelski, David, and Timothy Tyson, eds. *Democracy Betrayed: The Wilmington Race Riot of 1898 and Its Legacy*. Chapel Hill: University of North Carolina Press, 1998.

Chapman, John K. "Black Freedom and the University of North Carolina, 1793–1960." PhD diss., University of North Carolina at Chapel Hill, 2006.

Conley, Linda. "Spartanburg Museum Documents West African Nobleman Turned Slave." *GoUpstate*, November 24, 2012. www.goupstate.com/article/20121124/News/605146430.

Coon, Charles L. *North Carolina Schools and Academies, 1790–1840: A Documentary History*. Raleigh, NC: Edwards & Broughton, 1915.

Cooper, Roy. "Omar ibn Said Day: A Proclamation." May 23, 2019. https://governor.nc.gov /documents/governor-cooper-proclaims-omar-ibn-said-day-2019.

Cotheal, Alexander, trans. "The Life of Omar-Ben-Saeed, a Foulah Slave." *General Baptist Repository and Missionary Observer*, n.s., 12 (1850): 556–58.

Cowper, William. *The Complete Poetical Works of William Cowper: With Life, and Critical Notice of His Writings*. Boston: Gould & Lincoln, 1853.

Crow, Jeffrey J., and Paul D. Escott. *A History of African Americans in North Carolina*. Raleigh: North Carolina Department of Cultural Resources, Division of Archives and History, 1992.

Curiel, Jonathan. "The Life of Omar ibn Said." *Saudi Aramco World* 61, no. 2 (2010): 34–39.

Dalen, Dorrit van. "Method and Message." In "Doubt, Scholarship and Society in Seventeenth-Century Central Sudanic Africa," special issue, *Islam in Africa* 20 (2016): 107–53.

Damrosch, David. *What Is World Literature?* Princeton, NJ: Princeton University Press, 2003.

d'Avezac, [Armand]. "Notice sur le pays et le peuple des Yébous en Afrique." *Mémoires de la Société Ethnologique* 2, no. 2 (1845): 1–267.

Davis, Charles T., and Henry Louis Gates Jr., eds. *The Slave's Narrative*. New York: Oxford University Press, 1985.

de Luna, Kathryn M., and Ericka A. Albaugh, eds. *Tracing Language Movement in Africa*. New York: Oxford University Press, 2018.

de Sacy, Silvestre. *Grammaire arabe à l'usage des élèves de l'école spéciale des langues orientales vivantes*. Paris: Imprimerie Imperiale, 1810.

Diaz, Eric R. *Europe and the People without History*. Berkeley: University of California Press, 1982.

Diouf, Sylviane A. *Dreams of Africa in Alabama: The Slave Ship "Clotilda" and the Story of the Last Africans Brought to America*. New York: Oxford University Press, 2007.

———. "God Does Not Allow Kings to Enslave Their People." In Ala A. Alryyes, *A Muslim American Slave: The Life of Omar ibn Said*, 162–81. Madison: University of Wisconsin Press, 2011.

———. *Servants of Allah: African Muslims Enslaved in the Americas*. New York: New York University Press, 2013.

Dobronravin, Nikolay. "Não só mandingas: Qasīdat al-Burda, poesia ascética (*zuhdiyyāt*) e as *Maqāmāt de al-Ḥarīrī* nos escritos dos negros muçulmanos no Brasil oitocentista." *Afro-Ásia*, no. 53 (2016): 185–226.

Douglass, Frederick. *Narrative of the Life of Frederick Douglass, an American Slave.* New York: Oxford University Press, 2000.

Dwight, Theodore, Jr. "Condition and Character of Negroes in Africa." *Methodist Review* 46 (January 1864): 77–90.

———. "On the Sereculeh Nation, in Nigritia: Remarks on the Sereculehs, an African Nation, Accompanied by a Vocabulary of Their Language." *American Annals of Education and Instruction* 5, no. 10 (1835): 451–56.

Einboden, Jeffrey. *Jefferson's Muslim Fugitives: The Lost Story of Enslaved Africans, Their Arabic Letters, and an American President.* New York: Oxford University Press, 2020.

———. "Spartanburg Manuscript." *Arabic Slave Writings and the American Canon.* 2011. www.niu.edu/arabicslavewritings/spartanburg_ms/index.shtml.

English, George Bethune. *A Narrative of the Expedition to Dongola and Sennaar: Under the Command of His Excellence Ismael.* Boston: Wells and Lilly, 1823.

Epelboin, Alain, Constant Hames, Johana Larco Laurent, and Jean Louis Durand. *Un art secret: Les écritures talismaniques de l'Afrique de l'Ouest.* Paris: Institut du monde arabe, 2013.

Ernst, Carl W. *Following Muhammad: Rethinking Islam in the Contemporary World.* Islamic Civilization and Muslim Networks. Chapel Hill: University of North Carolina Press, 2003.

———. "The Global Significance of Arabic Language and Literature." *Religion Compass* 7, no. 6 (2013): 191–200.

"Extract from the Letter in the *Journal.*" *Wilmington Chronicle* 8, no. 38 (January 27, 1847): 2.

Fage, J. D. "Slavery and the Slave Trade in the Context of West African History." *Journal of African History* 10, no. 3 (July 1969): 393–404.

———. "Upper and Lower Guinea." In *The Cambridge History of Africa,* vol. 3, *From c. 1050 to c. 1600,* edited by Roland Oliver, 3:463–518. Cambridge History of Africa. Cambridge: Cambridge University Press, 1977.

Foard, John. *North America and Africa: Their Past, Present and Future, and Key to the Negro Problem.* Statesville, NC: Brady, 1904.

Foster, Benjamin R. *Yale and the Study of Near Eastern Languages in America, 1770–1930.* Council on Middle East Studies Working Papers. New Haven, CT: Yale Macmillan Center, n.d.

Freeman, Frederick. *A Plea for Africa: Being Familiar Conversations on the Subject of Slavery and Colonization.* Philadelphia: William Stavely, 1838.

"From the Wilmington *Herald:* An African Scholar." *Daily Register,* February 5, 1853.

Gatewood, Willard B. "'To Be Truly Free': Louis Sheridan and the Colonization of Liberia." *Civil War History* 29 (1983): 332–48.

Gerbner, Katherine. "Crossing and Conversion: Conversion and Race in Colonial Slavery." *SSRC: The Immanent Frame* (blog), June 26, 2018. https://tif.ssrc.org/2018/06/26/conversion -and-race-in-colonial-slavery/.

Gnkane, Adam. "Omar ibn Said: Un natif du Fuuta Tooro, esclave aux États-Unis (1806–1863)." *Bulletin de l'Institut Fondamental d'Afrique Noire* 60, no. 1–2 (2021): 11–53.

Goethe, Johann Wolfgang von. *Essays on Art and Literature,* vol. 3. Edited by John Gearey; translated by Ellen von Nardroff and Ernest H. von Nardroff. New York: Suhrkamp, 1986.

Gomez, Michael A. "Muslims in Early America." *Journal of Southern History* 60, no. 4 (1994): 671–710.

Gomez, Michael A., David Anderson, Carolyn Brown, Christopher Clapham, and Patrick Manning. *Pragmatism in the Age of Jihād*. Cambridge: Cambridge University Press, 2009.

Grier, Mathew Blackburne. "Uncle Moreau." *North Carolina Presbyterian*, July 23, 1859.

———. "Uncle Moreau." *North Carolina University Magazine* 3, no. 7 (September 1854): 307–9.

Gril, Denis. "Abū Madyan Shuʿayb." In *Encyclopaedia of Islam, THREE*, edited by Kate Fleet, Gudrun Krämer, Denis Matringe, John Nawas, Devin J. Stewart, and Everett K. Rowson. Leiden, the Netherlands: Brill, 2016. dx.doi.org.libproxy.lib.unc.edu/10.1163/1573-3912 _ei3_COM_24740.

Gurley, R. R. "Secretary's Report: Ralph Randolph Gurley." *African Repository and Colonial Journal*, 13, no. 7 (July 1837): 201–6.

Haines, F. E. H. *Jonas King, Missionary to Syria and Greece*. New York: American Tract Society, 1879.

Hall, Bruce S. "How Slaves Used Islam: The Letters of Enslaved Muslim Commercial Agents in the Nineteenth-Century Niger Bend and Central Sahara." *Journal of African History* 52 (2011): 279–97.

Hall, Bruce S., and Charles C. Stewart. "The Historic 'Core Curriculum' and the Book Market in Islamic West Africa." In *The Trans-Saharan Book Trade*, edited by Krätli Graziano and Ghislaine Lydo, 8:109–74. Leiden, the Netherlands: Brill, 2010.

Hegel, Georg Wilhelm Friedrich. *The Philosophy of History*. Translated by J. Sibree. New York: Willey, 1944.

Hilliard, Constance B. "*Al-Majmūʿ al-nafīs*: Perspectives on the Origins of the Muslim Torodbe of Senegal from the Writings of Shaykh Musa Kamara." *Islam et sociétés au sud du Sahara* 11 (1997): 175–86.

Hodgson, William Brown. *A Catalogue of Arabic, Turkish and Persian Manuscripts: The Private Collection of W. B. Hodgson*. Washington, DC: Duff Green, 1830.

———. *Extrait d'une traduction MS. en langue berbère de quelques parties de l'écriture sainte: contenant XII chapitres de S. Luc*. London: Aux frais de la Société Biblique Britannique et Étrangère, 1833.

———. *The Foulahs of Central Africa, and the African Slave Trade*. Washington, DC: National Institute for the Promotion of Science, 1843.

———. "The Gospels: Written in the Negro Patois of English, with Arabic Characters, by a Mandingo Slave in Georgia." *African Repository (1850-1892)* 36, no. 9 (September 1860): 268–71.

———. *The Science of Language: A Lecture: Sanscrit and Hebrew, the Two Written, Primitive, Languages Compared*. Newport, RI: F. A. Pratt, 1868.

H. O. R. *The Governing Race: A Book for the Time, and for All Times*. Washington, DC: Thomas McGill, 1860.

Horton, George Moses. "George Moses Horton, 1798–1880: The Hope of Liberty. Containing a Number of Poetical Pieces." Documenting the American South. 2004. https://docsouth .unc.edu/southlit/horton/horton.html.

Hunwick, John. "'I Wish to Be Seen in Our Land Called Afrika': 'Umar b. Sayyid's Appeal to Be Released from Slavery (1819)." *Journal of Arabic and Islamic Studies* 5 (2003): 62–77.

————. *Timbuktu and the Songhay Empire: Al-Saʿdi's Taʾrīkh al-Sūdān down to 1613, and Other Contemporary Documents*. Leiden, the Netherlands: Brill, 1999.

Hunwick, J. O., and R. S. O'Fahey, eds. *Arabic Literature of Africa*. Handbook of Oriental Studies: The Near and Middle East. Leiden, the Netherlands: E. J. Brill, 1994.

Huske, Joseph C. *A History of the Parish of St. John's, Fayetteville, N.C., from 1817 to 1831*. Fayetteville, NC: Fayetteville Office Supply, 1976.

Ibn Ḥazm, Abū Muḥammad ʿAlī ibn Aḥmad ibn Saʿīd al-Andalusī. 2013. *Rasāʾil ibn Ḥazm al-Andalusī*. Riyad: Markaz al-Turāth lil-Barmajīyāt, 2013.

Ibn Mālik, Muḥammad ibn ʿAbd Allāh. *Alfiyyat ibn Mālik fil-naḥw wal-taṣrīf*. Edited by Sulayman ibn ʿAbd al-ʿAzīz al-ʿUyūnī. Riyad: Maktabat Dār al-Minhaj, 2010.

Idris, H. R. "Ibn Abī Zayd al-Ḳayrawānī." In *Encyclopaedia of Islam*, 2nd ed. Leiden, the Netherlands: Brill, 2007. dx.doi.org.libproxy.lib.unc.edu/10.1163/1573-3912_islam_SIM_3061.

Inscoe, John C. "Walker, David." In *Dictionary of North Carolina Biography*, edited by William S. Powell, 6:110–11. Chapel Hill: University of North Carolina Press, 1994.

Jameson, John Franklin. "Autobiography of Omar ibn Said, Slave in North Carolina, 1831." *American Historical Review* 30, no. 4 (1925): 787–95.

Johnson, Guion Griffis. *Ante-bellum North Carolina: A Social History*. Chapel Hill: Academic Affairs Library, University of North Carolina at Chapel Hill, 2002.

Jones, Charles Colcock. *The Religious Instruction of the Negroes in the United States*. Savannah, GA: Thomas Purse, 1842.

Ka, Thierno. "L'enseignement arabe au Sénégal: L'école de Pir-Saniokhor: Son histoire et son rôle dans la culture arabo-islamique au Sénégal du XVIe au XXe siècle." PhD diss., Université de Paris-Sorbonne, 1982.

Kahera, Akel Ismail. "'God's Dominion': Omar ibn Said's Arabic Literacy and Anti-slavery Disposition." *South Carolina Review* 46, no. 2 (2014): 126.

Kamara, Musa. *Tabshīr al-khāʾif al-ḥayrān wa tadhkīruhu bisāṭ raḥmat Allāh al-Karīm al-Mannān* [*The Spreading of Good News for the Fearful and Confused and His Reminder of the Broadness of the Mercy of God, the Generous, the Bestower*]. Dakar: Islamic Institute of Dakar, 2014.

Kamara, Musa, Aḥmad Shukrī, and Khādim Imbākī. *Akthar al-rāghibīn fī al-jihād baʿd al-nabīʾīn man yakhtāru al-ẓuhūr wa-malaka al-bilād wa-lā yubālī bi-man halaka fī jihādihi min al-ʿibād* [*Most of the Would-Be Post-prophetic Jihadists Choose to Appear and Take Over the Country with No Concern for Those Believers Destroyed by Their Attack*]. Rabat: Maʿhad al-Dirāsāt al-Ifrīqīyah, 2003.

Kane, Ousmane Oumar. *Beyond Timbuktu: An Intellectual History of Muslim West Africa*. Cambridge, MA: Harvard University Press, 2016.

Khalīl ibn Isḥāq al-Jundī. *Al-Mukhtaṣar fī al-fiqh ʿalá madhhab al-Imām Mālik ibn Anas*. Edited by Gustave Richebé. Paris: Al-Maṭbaʿ al-Sulṭānī al-Muʿammar, 1855.

Khan, Muḥammad Muhsin, ed. and trans. *Ṣaḥīḥ al-Bukhārī: The Translation of the Meanings of Sahih al-Bukhari: Arabic-English*. Riyadh: Darussalam, 1997.

Kidd, Thomas S. *American Christians and Islam: Evangelical Culture and Muslims from the Colonial Period to the Age of Terrorism*. Princeton, NJ: Princeton University Press, 2013.

Kugle, Scott. *Rebel between Spirit and Law: Ahmad Zarruq, Sainthood, and Authority in Islam*. Bloomington: Indiana University Press, 2006.

Launay, Robert, ed. *Islamic Education in Africa: Writing Boards and Blackboards*. Bloomington: Indiana University Press, 2016.

Leloudis, James, et al. "Grimes Residence Hall." https://historyandrace.unc.edu/wp-content/uploads/sites/1091/2021/06/Grimes-final.pdf.

"Letter from the North State." *Providence Daily Journal*, December 22, 1846.

Lewis, Tayler. "The Koran, African Mohammedanism." In *The People of Africa*, edited by William Henry Schieffelin, 35–43. New York: Anson D. F. Randolph, 1871.

Lawrence, Bruce B. *Islamicate Cosmopolitan Spirit*. Hoboken, NJ: Wiley-Blackwell, 2021.

Lo, Mbaye. "Taking the Arabic Classroom Beyond the American Experience: Navigating Contexts, Texts and Students." In *The Arabic Classroom: Context, Text and Learners*, by Mbaye Lo, 13–26. Abingdon, UK: Routledge, 2019.

Lo, Mbaye, and Carl W. Ernst. "The 1850's Photographic Portrait of Omar ibn Said: The Eloquence of Resilience." *Muslim World* 110, no. 3 (2020): 428–50.

Lo, Mbaye, and Aman Nadhiri. "Contextualizing 'Muridiyyah' within the American Muslim Community." *African Journal of Political Science and International Relations* 4, no. 6 (June 2010): 231–40.

Lovejoy, Paul E., and Jan S. Hogendorn. *Slow Death for Slavery: The Course of Abolition in Northern Nigeria, 1897–1936*. Cambridge: Cambridge University Press, 1993.

Mackall, Leonard L. "William Brown Hodgson." *Georgia Historical Quarterly* 15, no. 4 (1931): 324–45.

Marr, Timothy. *The Cultural Roots of American Islamicism*. Cambridge: Cambridge University Press, 2006.

Mason, Julian D., ed. *The Poems of Phillis Wheatley*. Chapel Hill: University of North Carolina Press, 1966 [1989].

Mathews, Donald G. *Slavery and Methodism: A Chapter in American Morality, 1780–1845*. Princeton, NJ: Princeton University Press, 1965.

McCarus, Ernest. "The History of Arabic Studies in the United States." In *The Arabic Language in America*, edited by Aleya Rouchdy, 207–21. Detroit: Wayne State University Press, 1992.

Medhurst, Martin J. "Filled with the Spirit: Rhetorical Invention and the Pentecostal Tradition." *Rhetoric & Public Affairs* 7, no. 4 (2004): 555–72.

"Members." *Journal of the American Oriental Society* 1 (1847): xi.

"Members." *Transactions of the American Ethnological Society* 1 (1845): v.

Mencken, H. L. *The American Language*. New York: Knopf, 1949.

Mirrlees, Patricia. "John Hill and the Early Attempt to Study a West African Language." In *Sowing the Word: The Cultural Impact of the British and Foreign Bible Society, 1804–2004*, ed. Stephen K. Batalden, Kathleen Cann, and John Dean, 98–120. Sheffield, UK: Sheffield Phoenix, 2004.

"The Mohamedan Negro." *North Carolinian* 13, no. 729 (February 12, 1853): 3.

Moore, Louis T. "Prince of Arabia." *Greensboro Daily News*, February 13, 1927.

———. *Stories Old and New of the Cape Fear Region*. Wilmington, NC: Friends of Louis T. Moore and the Louis T. Moore Memorial Fund, 1968.

Morgan, Jennifer L. *Laboring Women: Reproduction and Gender in New World Slavery*. Early American Studies. Philadelphia: University of Pennsylvania Press, 2004.

Morphis, Sam. *The Autobiography of a Negro*. Orange County: North Carolina Historic Information, 2011.

Morris, Margaret W. "The Completion of the Western North Carolina Railroad: Politics of Concealment." *North Carolina Historical Review* 52, no. 3 (1975): 256–82.

"The Morton Crania Collection." Penn Museum. December 2021. www.penn.museum/sites/morton/.

"Moses Stuart." *Yale, Slavery & Abolition: Who Yale Honors* (blog), January 21, 2022. www.yaleslavery.org/WhoYaleHonors/stuart.html.

Myers, Robert Manson, ed. *The Children of Pride: A True Story of Georgia and the Civil War.* New Haven, CT: Yale University Press, 1972.

Nance, Susan. *How the Arabian Nights Inspired the American Dream, 1790-1935.* Chapel Hill: University of North Carolina Press, 2009.

Ngom, Fallou. "Ajami Literacies of West Africa." In *Tracing Language Movement in Africa,* edited by Kathryn M. de Luna and Ericka A. Albaugh, 143-64. New York: Oxford University Press, 2018.

Niane, Djibril Tamsir. *Histoire des Mandingues de l'ouest: Le royaume du Gabou.* Paris: Association ARSAN, 1989.

———. *Sundiata: An Epic of Old Mali.* Translated by G. D. Pickett. Harlow, UK: Pearson, 2006.

O'Connor, Kathleen Malone. "Popular and Talismanic Uses of the Qurʾān." In *Encyclopaedia of the Qurʾān,* edited by Jane Dammen McAuliffe. Leiden, the Netherlands: Brill, 2008. dx.doi.org.libproxy.lib.unc.edu/10.1163/1875-3922_q3_EQCOM_00152.

Ong, Walter J. *Orality and Literacy: The Technologizing of the Word.* London: Routledge, 1982.

———. *The Presence of the Word: Some Prolegomena for Cultural and Religious History.* New York: Simon & Schuster, 1967.

Operstein, Natalie. "The French Connection: William Brown Hodgson's Mission in Algiers and the *Dictionnaire de la langue franque.*" *Mediterranean Language Review* 26 (2019): 67-90.

O'Reilly, Edward. "Manuscript Inquiry, Heartman Collection, New-York Historical Society." Email message to Carl Ernst, June 25, 2021.

Osman, Ghada, and Camille F. Forbes. "Representing the West in the Arabic Language: The Slave Narrative of Omar ibn Said." *Journal of Islamic Studies* 15, no. 3 (2004): 331-43.

Owen, Guy. "Owen, John." In *Dictionary of North Carolina Biography,* edited by William S. Powell, 4:412-13. Chapel Hill: University of North Carolina Press, 1991.

Palmer, H. R. "M. Delafosse's Account of the Fulani." *Journal of the Royal African Society* 13, no. 50 (1914): 195-203.

Park, Mungo. *The Travels of Mungo Park.* London: J. M. Dent, 1932.

Parker, Freddie L. *Running for Freedom: Slave Runaways in North Carolina, 1775-1840.* New York: Routledge, 1993.

Parramore, T. C. "Owen, James." In *Dictionary of North Carolina Biography,* edited by William S. Powell, 4:412. Chapel Hill: University of North Carolina Press, 1991.

Pascal, Roy. *Design and Truth in Autobiography.* Abingdon, UK: Routledge, 2016.

Pickering, John. "Address." *Journal of the American Oriental Society* 1, no. 1 (1843): 1-60.

Post, George. "Arabic-Speaking Negro Mohammedans in Africa." *African Repository* 45, no. 5 (May 1869): 129-33.

Powell, William S. "Owen, Thomas." In *Dictionary of North Carolina Biography,* edited by William S. Powell, 4:413-14. Chapel Hill: University of North Carolina Press, 1991.

"Prince Omeroh: Romantic Experience of a Princely Slave—A Strange Story of the Old Plantation Days." *Farmer and Mechanic,* June 25, 1884.

Prisse d'Avennes, Émile. *L'art arabe d'après les monuments du Kaire depuis le VIIe siècle jusqu' à la fin du XVIIIe.* Paris: A. Morel, 1877.

"Proceedings in New Haven, October 1868." *Journal of the American Oriental Society* 9 (1868): xli–l.

"Procès-verbal de la séance du 29 septembre 1843." *Mémoires de la Société Ethnologique* 2, no. 1 (1845): xxxvii–xl.

Prussin, Labelle. *Hatumere: Islamic Design in West Africa*. Berkeley: University of California Press, 1986.

al-Qayrawānī, Ibn Abī Zayd. *Risāla*. Edited by Aḥmad Muṣṭafá Qāsim al-Ṭahṭāwī. Cairo: Dār al-Faḍīla, n.d.

Rankin, Harriot Sutton. *History of First Presbyterian Church, Fayetteville, North Carolina*. Fayetteville, NC: n.p., 1928.

Robertson, David. *Denmark Vesey: The Buried Story of America's Largest Slave Rebellion and the Man Who Led It*. New York: Knopf Doubleday, 2009.

Robinson, David. *Chiefs and Clerics: Abdul Bokar Kan and Futa Toro, 1853–1891*. Oxford Studies in African Affairs. Oxford, UK: Clarendon, 1975.

———. "Un historien et anthropologue sénégalais: Shaikh Musa Kamara." *Cahiers d'études africaines* 28, no. 109 (1988): 89–116.

Rogers, Molly, and Ilisa Barbash, eds. *To Make Their Own Way in the World: The Enduring Legacy of the Zealy Daguerreotypes*. New York: Peabody Museum Press, 2020.

Samb, Amar. *Al-Adab al-Sinighālī al-ʿArabī: Al-hadiyya al-Sinighāliyya min al-murjān fī al-ʿuqūd al-adabīyah lil-ʿUrbān* [Senegalese Arabic Literature: The Senegalese Gift of a Literary Coral Necklace to the Literati]. Algiers: Al-Sharika al-Waṭaniyya lil-Nashr wa-al-Tawzīʿ, 1978.

al-Sanūsī al-Ḥasanī, Abū ʿAbd Allāh Muḥammad ibn Yūsuf. *Sharḥ wāsiṭat al-sulūk*. Edited by Nizār Ḥammādī. Damascus: Dār al-Taqwā, 1440/2018.

Saydon, P. P. "The Origin of the 'Polyglot' Arabic Psalms." *Biblica* 31, no. 2 (1950): 226–36.

Schmitz, Jean. "L'historiographie des Peuls musulmans d'Afrique de l'ouest: Shaykh Muusa Kamara (1864–1945), saint et savant." In *AOF: Réalités et héritages, sociétés ouest-africaines et ordre colonial, 1895–1960*, edited by Charles Becker, S. M'baye, and I. Thioub, 862–72. Dakar: Direction des Archives nationales du Sénégal, 1997.

Searing, James F. *West African Slavery and Atlantic Commerce: The Senegal River Valley, 1700–1860*. Cambridge: Cambridge University Press, 1998.

Shafik, Ahmed. "Poema de exhortación piadosa: *Maqṣūrat al-ŷawhara* de Abū Madyan: traducción y notas." *Al-Andalus Magreb: Estudios árabes e islámicos* 23 (2016): 93–126.

Sherman, Joan R. *The Black Bard of North Carolina: George Moses Horton and His Poetry*. Chapel Hill: University of North Carolina Press, 1997.

Simpson, Marianna Shreve. "Expanding Boundaries: A Manuscript of the Qur'an from Sub-Saharan Africa, W.853." *Journal of the Walters Art Museum* 62 (2004): 237–39.

Spellberg, Denise A. "Could a Muslim Be President? An Eighteenth-Century Constitutional Debate." *Eighteenth-Century Studies* 39, no. 4 (2006): 485–506.

Stewart, Devin. "Dissimulation in Sunni Islam and Morisco Taqiyya." *Al-Qantara* 24, no. 2 (2013): 439–90.

Stuart, Moses. *A Grammar of the Hebrew Language*. Andover, MA: Gould & Newman, 1835.

"Study of Ancient Crania." *Boston Medical and Surgical Journal* 31, no. 21 (December 25, 1844): 422–23.

Thompson, Thomas Perronet. "Study of the Arabic Language." *African Repository and Colonial Journal* 5, no. 4 (1829): 94–111.

Turner, Katherine. "Cowper, Slave Narratives, and the Antebellum American Reading Public." *Cowper & Newton Journal* 6 (2012). https://cowperandnewtonmuseum.org.uk /journal/j6-article-turner/.

UNC Graduate School. "Hinton James." 2004. https://gradschool.unc.edu/funding/grad school/weiss/interesting_place/history/hinton.html.

Vimercati Sanseverino, Ruggero. "Al-Dimyāṭī, Nūr al-Dīn." In *Encyclopaedia of Islam, THREE*, edited by Kate Fleet, Gudrun Krämer, Denis Matringe, John Nawas, Devin J. Stewart, and Everett K. Rowson. Leiden, the Netherlands: Brill, 2015. dx.doi.org .libproxy.lib.unc.edu/10.1163/1573-3912_ei3_COM_26037.

Ware, Rudolph T. *The Walking Qur'an: Islamic Education, Embodied Knowledge, and History in West Africa*. Islamic Civilization and Muslim Networks. Chapel Hill: University of North Carolina Press, 2014.

A Wayfaring Man [William S. Plumer, pseud.]. "Meroh, a Native African." *New York Observer* 41, no. 2 (January 8, 1863).

"William Brown Hodgson." In *Prabook*. World Biographical Encyclopedia, 2021. https:// prabook.com/web/william.hodgson/3759856.

Wilson, J. Leighton. *Western Africa: Its History, Condition, and Prospects*. New York: Harper & Brothers, 1856.

Yohannon, John D. "Emerson, Ralph Waldo." In *Encyclopaedia Iranica*, 8:414–15. New York: Encyclopædia Iranica Foundation, 1998.

GENERAL INDEX

INDEX OF SCRIPTURAL CITATIONS
AND OMAR'S DOCUMENTS

OMAR IBN SAID DOCUMENTS